THE HOLLYWOOD

The Hidden History of Hollywood in the C

Paddy Calistro and Fred E. Basten
An Angel City Press Book

Universe

THE HOLLYWOOD ARCHIVE

The Hidden History of Hollywood in the Golden Age

Paddy Calistro and Fred E. Basten
An Angel City Press Book

Universe

First published in
the United States of America in 2000
by UNIVERSE PUBLISHING
A Division of Rizzoli International
Publications, Inc.
300 Park Avenue South
New York, NY 10010

2000 2001 2002 2003 2004 2005 / 10 9 8 7 6 5 4 3 2 1

Design: Mirko Ilić Corp., New York

Printed in Singapore

To

Ronald D. Haver
1939–1993

in memory
of his love of
the movies
and
of a life well spent
preserving films
and
their history

CONTENTS

Hollywood Archive. The very name takes us back, way back. It conjures up images of cobwebbed rooms filled with shelves of old-fashioned film reels in dusty metal cans. Of warehouses packed to the brim with drooping feathers and half-torn lace attached to over-used costumes. Of file cabinets crammed with dingy folders, in turn stuffed with dog-eared photographs and faded press clippings. Of finding that one special image that makes the grimy search worthwhile.

Many of the photographs in this book came from exactly those kinds of sources, places where the rare, unpublished photographs still lay in wait of discovery. Others came from the more carefully catalogued files owned by people and institutions that truly honor Hollywood, places where authors and editors can dig deep to find that wonderful rare picture that adds a thousand unwritten words to an otherwise incomplete story. Still others were carefully preserved in family albums and vaults, photos cherished by loved ones and shared only now.

The Hollywood Archive looks at Hollywood from its earliest days through its Golden Age (from 1896 through the 1960s) in the most subjective way—with love. We examined the various aspects that comprise the culture of the place and picked favorite topics, some serious, some not: the beginnings of important things (like Hollywood's first famous film, sex on film, color on film, voices on film and the first great director), everything that's fake that we love to believe (from hairstyles and body shapes to apes who stand on skyscrapers), the way stars lived in the real world (really lived and mythically lived, that is), the way they lived only in the cinematic world (the life of a First Lady when she was "just" an actress, movie kisses and those animals who saved lives), how real life and reel life converged (a Kennedy came to Hollywood and fell in love, the scientist of the millennium met the art form of the century, and Bette Davis gave advice to her lovelorn fans), what stars did when they were acting like "real" folks (frolicking with their kids, playing ping pong or just simply taking a day off), the people who made us break into a smile or laugh 'til our sides hurt (by simply seeing the dimples in their cheeks or by being a mule that talked or men that didn't), the glamour and mystery of Hollywood nights (the evening gowns actresses wore and the nightclubs celebs frequented, and the vampires that only emerged as the sky went dark), and finally the ways that Hollywood celebrates endings and preserves itself (from the last lines of famed films, to great rear ends to the graves fans visit decades after stars' passings). We also asked a critic who comes into people's homes via television to give his unedited comments about Hollywood—all the things he never had a chance to say on air.

Next we've turned to a select group of people who experienced Hollywood from one very up-close and personal perspective or another. They've written their unique views. No one else can tell their story their way.

The complete book of Hollywood? No, never, not even close. There is no such book, and any that claim to be complete are part of a lie. The Hollywood story is made up of films too plentiful to count (not to mention, view), and an almost infinite number of actors, actresses, producers, directors, and other artists who have contributed to the world of movie making. So a Hollywood bible would demand millions of pages and still be lacking detail. Any authors, editors, or publishers who promise readers a complete history of Hollywood had best stop publishing other books, devote themselves to a life of total research and expect an unsalable final work that must be bound in more volumes than an old-fashioned encyclopedia, a tome that's still incomplete. So be it; Hollywood life is complex—and ever-changing.

That said, *The Hollywood Archive* is three hundred and fifty-two pages celebrating the old Hollywood scene: the scenes left in, the scenes cut out, the scene stealers, and what went on behind those scenes. It is subjective, imbued with a love of the movies and movie stars. It stops just about the time Hollywood got even bigger than its own life. We love old Hollywood. Don't you?

Paddy Calistro,
Scott McAuley, and
Fred E. Basten
for Angel City Press
By the sea in Santa Monica
2000

INTRODUCTION

1

Movies have been entertaining us since 1895 thanks to the likes of Thomas Edison, but Hollywood . . . when did it become "Tinseltown"? A woman whose father made it happen tells the story. When did "director" get a capital "D"? A man whose father earned it recalls. And when did movies grab us in the first few minutes, and how do sets define a film? In Hollywood it's all about the Beginnings. . . .

In the beginning, filmmakers censored themselves, but films became too risqué for the public to tolerate. The blindfolded, seminude musicians strumming on a bearskin rug are just a touch of writer-director Erich von Stroheim's genius in his classic *The Merry Widow* (1925).

THE ROOTS OF HOLLYWOOD

BY BETTY LASKY

I n 1913, my father, Jesse L. Lasky, sent his best friend, Cecil B. DeMille, from New York City to a sleepy village named Hollywood to make *The Squaw Man* (1914), never dreaming that their first movie venture would lay the foundation stone of a great industry.

For my father, unlike other movie pioneers, California was a homecoming. He was proud of being a native son of a native son. My grandfather was born in Sacramento, where his father had settled in 1848, after a covered-wagon crossing on the Oregon Trail.

My father's early years were characterized by failure. Growing up in rural San Jose, he had learned to play the cornet and imagined he would be discovered by John Philip Sousa, "the March King," but Sousa never heard him play. My father followed his hero Jack London to Alaska after the gold rush of 1889, but gold eluded him. He sailed to Hawaii, where he became one of the few non-natives to play in the Royal Hawaiian Band. Returning to San Francisco, he set his sights on vaudeville, performing a duo cornet act with his sister Blanche, and then he started to produce high-class musical vaudeville acts in New York. These were the lush days of vaudeville, and the money rolled in. Success in vaudeville, however, led to the loss of my father's first fortune in the Folies Bergére, a lavish Broadway theater-restaurant he built with Henry B. Harris in 1911 that failed after four months. It was a lucky failure; a year later, Adolph Zukor, a former penny-arcade operator, introduced the feature film to America. My

father wisely followed his lead.

My father's attention now turned to Hollywood and a weather-beaten barn in an orange grove on Selma Avenue and Vine Street—the new West Coast offices for his film studio, where *The Squaw Man* would be filmed—that had until then accommodated owner Jacob Stern's horses and carriage. Much of the filming took place on an outdoor stage beside the barn. In addition, many scenes were filmed at various nearby locations including Los Angeles, Hemet, Palomar, and Sun Valley in the San Fernando Valley.

The Squaw Man, based on playwright Edwin Milton Royle's "thrilling Western drama," was Hollywood's and the Jesse L. Lasky Feature Play Company's first feature-length film. It succeeded beyond my father's wildest dreams—cost, as documented in my father's papers, $21,600.51; net producer's profit, as also documented, $244,700. The success was no small thanks to the company's intrepid first-time director-general Cecil B. DeMille, his mentor and experienced co-director Oscar Apfel, and the wily salesmanship of the company's general manager (and my father's brother-in-law) Samuel Goldfish (later known as Sam Goldwyn).

For *The Squaw Man's* leading players, Dustin Farnum, the two-fisted stage hero of *The Virginian,* and the diminutive British-born actress Winifred Kingston, the screen production represented the beginning of new careers in the "fast expanding New Art." At one point during the filming, Farnum wrote to a friend in the East, "this dude is having a rumbustious good time. I've enjoyed some royal rough-riding on a cow pony that developed stage fright. Had a thrilling experience in my auto when it ran away with me while DeMille got a few hundred feet of sensational film."

In late 1914, following five weeks in what my father described as "God's country and man's paradise," he announced plans to accelerate the company's output from a modest twelve pictures a year to an extravagant thirty, and he name dropped long-forgotten players and film titles. He neglected to mention that he and Mr. DeMille had just stolen Blanche Sweet from

Previous pages: A historic landmark of Hollywood's earliest days, the original "Lasky Barn" had a porch added to it in the 1950s when it was still on the Paramount lot and used as a set for a long-running television series. A miniature of the Lasky Company studio-barn—exactly as it looked in 1914, including the laboratory and stage—can be viewed and studied at the Hollywood History Museum located in the historic art deco Max Factor building on Highland Avenue just south of Hollywood Boulevard. A marvel of ingenuity created by Eugene L. Hilchey, a modelmaker and dedicated archivist of silent-era movie studios, it even includes miniatures of the founding fathers and their leading players, along with the long-gone pepper trees and telephone poles on Vine Street. How fitting that a replica of the old barn that marked the birth of Hollywood, Movie Capital of the World, is enshrined in a place for visitors to learn about the history of the film industry.

Below: In 1916, the most important men in Hollywood gathered to form Hollywood's most important motion-picture studio, Famous Players–Lasky Company. From left, Jesse L. Lasky, Adolph Zukor, Samuel Goldfish (who would later be known as Sam Goldwyn), Cecil B. DeMille, and Al Kaufman (the studio operations manager for Zukor's company who became the West Coast studio manager when the companies merged).

Above: In 1914, in the offices of the Lasky Feature Play Company, Jesse L. Lasky, seated, is joined by, from left, directors Cecil B. DeMille, Oscar Apfel, and actors Dustin Farnum (from *The Squaw Man*), Edward Abeles, and Robert Edeson.

Following pages: Circa 1915, one of Hollywood's earliest entrepreneurs, Jesse L. Lasky, surveys the barn on Selma and Vine Streets, while standing on the original stage where *The Squaw Man* was filmed beginning in 1913. Much later he called the years he ruled Paramount with Zukor (1916–32) the "best years of my life." And he wrote, "We took the original barn along with us as a reminder of the modest way we started." Many of the more than one thousand films he supervised bore the personal stamp of his life of adventure, his sense of the romantic, and his intense pride in the American heritage—none more so than the great silent epics *The Covered Wagon* (1923), *The Vanishing American* (1925), *Beau Geste* (1926), and *Wings* (1927), which won the first Academy Award.

under the nose of D. W. Griffith to play the feminine lead in DeMille's *The Warrens of Virginia* (1915), resulting in Griffith's top leading lady stepping into the same top spot at Lasky's.

Meanwhile, the studio-barn, with adjoining film lab and outdoor stage (a rental studio that Mr. DeMille had sublet from its tenants, entrepreneur Louis Burns and his partner, filmmaker Harry Revier, for $250 a month, for four months, upon his arrival in Los Angeles in late December 1913), had been upstaged by a huge glass studio. "The best in California," my father bragged, and he went on to describe "a plant of machinery for the making of all our properties, a new wardrobe department," and numerous other additions. Years later, Mr. DeMille would recall with a chuckle that there was no need to put Lasky's "prize jewel," world-renowned opera diva Geraldine Farrar, in a horse stall in the barn when she came to Hollywood in 1915 to make *Carmen* and *Maria Rosa* (1916).

By 1917, after the Lasky Company merged with its friendly rival, Adolph Zukor's Famous Players Film Company, the enlarged studio ran all the way down Vine Street to Sunset Boulevard, with its vast back lot stretching east to Argyle Avenue. Landlord Jacob Stern let the property go for $37,500. In 1926, Famous Players–Lasky razed most of it and spent $1 million for the twenty-six-acre United Studios on Marathon Street, where Paramount Pictures has been located since the company's reorganization in 1935.

During the years my father worked with Zukor, the old barn remained on the Marathon Street lot. I never visited it there; I wonder if Valentino, Marlene Dietrich, and Pola Negri ever strolled through its shadow. My brother Jesse, a longtime DeMille writer, told me he fenced there with Cary Grant when it was used as a gym. In the 1950s a porch was added, railroad tracks were built outside, and the barn became part of the set for the *Bonanza* television Western series. A California historical landmark since 1956, it now sits across from the Hollywood Bowl, serving as a small museum.

DE MILLE ON DEMILLE

BY RICHARD DE MILLE

T he first time I saw Jesus I was four years old. He was standing in our garden under an olive tree. It was 1926, and Father was making *The King of Kings* (1927). Our house was at the top of a hill in what had been an olive grove. While Jesus stood for a close-up, grips and prop men rushed about. Off scene, under the trees, beggars and disciples were sitting on the grass, talking or playing cards, waiting to be called. Bertha and I walked among them on the Mount of Olives. (Bertha was my nurse. Father didn't put either of us in the movie.)

One birthday I received a set of toy boats, which I sailed around Father as he sat in the bathtub. Father took his wash-cloth, captured a big bubble of air, and let it go under the boats, which almost knocked them over. I got very excited, and he did it again. None of my boats sank, but a few years later Father sank the Egyptian fleet at the Battle of Actium, which caused

DeMille directs Fredric March and Elissa Landi on the set of *Sign of the Cross* (1932). As Richard de Mille notes, "When Father made *The Sign of the Cross,* the Paramount sound truck was filled with marvelous gadgets. One of them was a microphone through which you could speak to all the people on the set. Lions were bounding up the stairs into the arena, to tear and rend the Christians, which would make the Romans shudder, cheer, or laugh. When I saw the lions, I thought it would be fun to roar at them through the sound department microphone. I got in a lot of trouble for that."

Cleopatra (Claudette Colbert) to hold a poisonous snake to her breast. It was sad to see such a beautiful woman dying, even in a movie.

Father made *The Squaw Man* three different times. The first two, in 1914 and 1918, were silent, but the third had sound. That was at MGM in 1931, when I was nine. Lupe Velez was playing the unlucky Indian wife, who commits suicide. When I saw her putting the pistol to her heart, I braced myself for the bang, but there was only a click. The bang got put in later—a technical lesson that came in handy when I worked on training films in the Army Air Force Motion Picture Unit at Hal Roach studio, which we called "Fort Roach."

When I was nineteen, Father hired me to work on the set of *Reap the Wild Wind* (1942). My job was to keep an eye on the telephone light and creep around the silent set whispering my line: "Telephone for you." Victor Varconi was playing a sailor taking soundings over the side to see if the ship was getting too close to the reef. Victor's line was: "No bottom, sir." As the rehearsal went on and on, some of us in the studio crew worried that we might lose a day and get no bonus for saving time. Our line was: "No bonus, sir." We thought it was funny. Father didn't think it was funny. His line was: "QUIET ON THE SET!" Everybody shut up. I don't remember getting a bonus.

Fifteen years before, Varconi had played prominent parts, like Prince Dimitri in *The Volga Boatman* (1926) and Pontius Pilate in *The King of Kings* (1927), but like many silent actors he and his Hungarian accent had been brushed aside by the coming of sound. Father didn't forget about his former silent players, and they kept showing up in his later movies. A minor role in *The Ten Commandments* (1956), Father's final picture, was played by H. B. Warner. Thirty years earlier, I had seen H. B. Warner standing in our garden, playing Jesus.

Above: The DeMille family, from left, son Richard, Mrs. DeMille, Cecil B., and daughters Katherine and Cecilia
Opposite: After *The Squaw Man* was released in 1914, DeMille posed for a publicity shot in his office.

SEX BEFORE CENSORSHIP

Harry Cohn, head of Columbia Pictures and one of the most hated men in Hollywood because of his tyrannical control of his studio and stars, stood up at a closed-door session of industry moguls, made a proclamation, and his colleagues praised him. They even applauded him.

He had just suggested that Will Hays "go f&*# himself." Cohn's direct approach was worth celebrating in the early 1930s, or at least the other studio heads thought so. After all, it was Hays, a former chairman of the Republican National Committee and postmaster general under President Warren G. Harding, who in 1922 had accepted the job as president of the Motion Picture

Right: In the romantic comedy *Hula* (1927), Clara Bow as Hula Calhoun, appears to be totally nude, but is actually clothed in a sheer, skin-toned swimsuit.
Below: In *A Daughter of the Gods* (1916), swimming champion Annette Kellermann bares it all for director Herbert Brenon as she sits among waterfalls, in one of early Hollywood's most risqué scenes.

Producers and Distributors of America and became the film industry's moral arbiter of good taste. The industry hired him, hoping that he could help convince critics that the industry was policing itself. The plan back-fired. Dedicated to turning films into right-eous examples of decency, Hays took his job seriously, and developed the official Production Code to protect audiences from anything that Hays or the Catholic Church—or any church—might find objectionable. The goal of the code, which was enforced begin-ning in 1934, was to establish "correct stan-dards of life," protecting the public from scenes—or even underlying themes—that would "lower the moral standards." Thus anything that shouted—or whispered—sex, crime, or brutality was at the top of the censor's snip list. Cruelty to animals, slurs against racial groups or the government, swearing or other "dirty" words (including "pansy"), and anything to do with drugs were censored. As of July 15, 1934, Hays's Office bestowed the "Purity Seal" on films that abided the rules, and the industry agreed not to distribute or screen films without it. They agreed under protest, but history has shown that more people started going to the movies once films became "more respectable."

Although the rules were stringent and filmmakers were seething, the code was merely a response to an industry gone wild, argued public interest groups outraged by torrid scandals in Hollywood and films with titles as blatant as *Sex* (1920). Prior to the code, films repeatedly crossed the bounds

Above: Scantily clad musicians perform in a silent operetta, *The Merry Widow* (1925), with Von Stroheim bringing debauchery and sadism to the world of the Hapsburgs.
Right: Choreographer Busby Berkeley encour-aged costume designer Milo Anderson to show more than decency dictates in *Footlight Parade* (1933).
Opposite: Disguised as a devil woman in one of the most alluring gowns ever designed by Adrian, actress Kay Johnson stars in *Madam Satan* (1930), one of DeMille's challenges to the Hays Office and its censors.

of acceptability. As early as 1896, Edison's Kinetoscope film *The Kiss* showed a Victorian couple (May Irwin and John C. Rice) stealing a smooch (an act many decried as pornographic), and in 1902, another Edison film featured a naked woman displaying herself to a man. In 1922, F. Scott Fitzgerald's *Beautiful and the Damned* showcased petting parties, wild dancing, and liquor carried in hip flasks—all signs of times that left ministers and moralists chagrined. In *Prodigal Daughters* (1923), Gloria Swanson as Swifty Forbes, a member of the modern generation, "went too far," challenged the sexual mores of society, and had to be saved by her daddy—a story with a moral, yes, but its sexual theme was more than the rigid could abide. Cecil B. DeMille directed *Madam Satan* (1930), with its bare, devil costume and an unmarried couple sleeping in the same bed, and *The Sign of the Cross* (1932), with its overtones of lesbianism and sadism as well as a blatant orgy. An industry that had worked under the guise of self-censorship had stepped way out of bounds. And Hays and the Production Code stepped in to clean up the acts.

The photographs on these pages are publicity stills for films made prior to the 1934 enforcement of the Production Code.

Right: DeMille's *The Sign of the Cross* (1932) tested the will of the Hays Office, pushing not only the limits of nudity (notice the flower on the nipple), but the symbols of sadism and perversion, as he softened chains with gentle blossoms.
Opposite: Only costume designer Gilbert Adrian had the nerve and the talent to create a loincloth that would cover the endowments of Johnny Weissmuller as Tarzan, while allowing the Ape Man the freedom of movement to swing wistfully through the trees.

HOLLYWOOD'S FIRST BAD GIRL
BY PHILLIP DYE

I n 1917, Theda Bara was regarded with awed fascination for her roles as a man-devouring femme fatale who ruined lives for the sheer pleasure of the havoc she wrought. She was also the first movie sex goddess. Certainly *Cleopatra* (1917) was the highwater mark of her career.

William Fox, immigrant theater owner turned movie mogul, had hired the unknown actress to star as "the Vampire" in the film *A Fool There Was* (1915), in which respectable men were led astray by a seductive femme fatale. It was a sensation when released, and "vamp" became both verb and noun in the English language.

Fox Film Corporation created a bizarre publicity campaign around its new discovery. Press statements claimed that Theda Bara was the daughter of a French artist and an Arab princess, "born in the shadow of the sphinx" and "weaned on serpent's blood." Bara contributed to the hoopla in staged interviews, playing up her impossibly exotic background while haughtily turning aside questions about her real origins, even after most people knew she was really Theodosia Goodman from Cincinnati, Ohio, born in 1890, into a respectable, average, middle-class family.

While few actually believed the nonsense about her being "the wickedest woman in the world," fans adored Bara as a glamorous fantasy figure of the movies. Fox provided other vehicles worthy of his biggest star, mostly variations on what were called "vampire" roles, bearing suggestive

Above: A beautiful portrait of Theda Bara as Cleopatra. The buxom, full-figured Bara was considered the first movie sex goddess.

Opposite: "The Serpent of the Nile" putting the moves on Julius Caesar (Fritz Leiber) in *Cleopatra*. The movie provoked the wrath of the Kansas state censors, who demanded that the studio cut offensive scenes, such as "suggestive advances of Cleopatra on Caesar" and "closeups of Cleopatra and Antony in the embracing scene on the couch, where Cleopatra's body is exposed." The tough Chicago censor simply banned the movie because of the overt sexuality and near nudity of the vamping Cleopatra.

titles such as *Sin* (1915), *The Devil's Daughter* (1915), and *The Tiger Woman* (1917). Bara spent these films wreaking devastation on unsuspecting males, chewing up the scenery while wearing gorgeous gowns that flaunted the agitated heaving of her bosom. As one of her costars put it, "She doesn't steal the show; she is the show."

After she had made twenty-three movies at the Fox studios in New Jersey, *Cleopatra* was the first film Bara would make in Hollywood, which was becoming the major center of film production. Huge sets were built at the new Fox studio and other locations around Los Angeles to provide the "magnificent settings of desert, palace, and sea," but the movie was all about Theda Bara, cinematic love goddess.

Cleopatra premiered in New York on October 14, 1917, and was an immediate smash hit, despite the fact that at two hours, it was nearly double the length of most feature films of the period. The *New York Tribune* was "completely overwhelmed," saying the spectacle "simply beggars description and Theda Bara has never before looked so beautiful."

The *Dramatic Mirror* gushingly observed, "Those who like to see Theda Bara should not fail to take advantage of the opportunity afforded in *Cleopatra,* for, certainly, they will never see more of her, nor—on the other hand—will they ever find their adored one running truer to form."

"Many may say that it's awful, but the chances are that they will go back a second time so that they will be able to detail fully to their friends why the aforesaid friends should not go," commented *Moving Picture World.*

Although not a landmark film, the 1917 *Cleopatra* signifies Hollywood becoming the movie center of the world, with the star system and the studio system setting the standard to dominate how movies were henceforth to be made, and it firmly established the glamour and romance of the Hollywood dream machine.

Above: Poster for *Cleopatra.* As the *New York Times* observed, "Thus does the ill-starred Queen of Egypt become the well-starred queen of the movies." Another reviewer commented, "The fact that it is a story about Cleopatra dignifies it sufficiently to pull in many who would turn up their noses at an ordinary Bara production." *Moving Picture News* posed the question: "Do the people flock to see *Cleopatra* because of Cleopatra or because of Theda Bara? With due deference to Egypt's queen it must be confessed that Theda Bara wins. Mr. Fox realizes this. In his billing he presents Theda Bara as Cleopatra, and not even *Cleopatra* featuring Theda Bara." A tremendous success in its time, stills, lobby cards, and posters are all that remain of this lost film.
Opposite: Theda Bara claimed to have consulted Egyptologists for the creation of her costumes for her role in *Cleopatra* (1917), although the resulting costumes were more fanciful than historically accurate, being more focused on a "frank display of her physical charms."

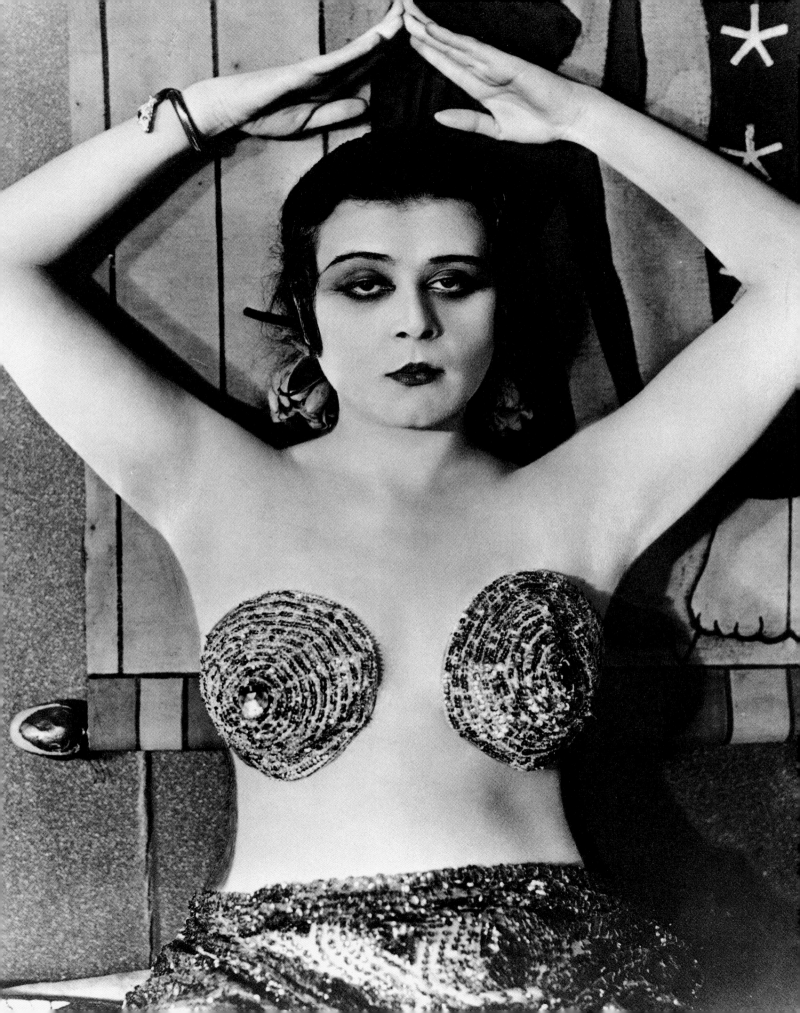

THE FIRST TALKIES

BY MARC WANAMAKER

Because Warner Bros. debuted *Don Juan* starring John Barrymore in 1926 with a synchronized musical soundtrack, and the following year released *The Jazz Singer* starring Al Jolson in a part-synchronized musical soundtrack with talking sequences, these films have been characterized as the first sound films ever produced.

It is true that Warner Bros. films were the first commercial sound films produced by a major company to invest in sound-equipped studios and theaters, and that Warner Bros. took an unprecedented risk, betting everything on an unproven novelty. However, *Don Juan* and the Warner brothers were not the first to the sound party. Before Harry, Albert, Sam, and Jack L. Warner (who owned nickelodeon theaters before incorporating their film studio in 1923) took a chance, it was Alice Blache of the Gaumont Company of France who by 1906 had produced more than a hundred short films using the Gaumont Chronophone. Before that, Edison had linked his own cylinder recording machine with his camera in early 1891, creating the same effect. But Edison did not think this idea was a commercial enterprise and eventually scrapped the idea.

By 1913, Edison developed the Kinetophone for installation in nickelodeon parlors. About 260 of these films were made before Edison again retired the sound film in 1915. Twice burned, Edison was quoted in 1926 saying that "Americans require a restful quiet in the moving picture theater and for them talking from the lips of the figures on the screen destroys the illusion . . . the idea is not practical. The stage is the place for the spoken word." Thus, Edison ceded sound films to other entrepreneurs—and to a new technology that was louder and clearer than his mechanical phonograph. Western Electric licensed and improved on Dr. Lee De Forest's Audion tube, developing electric amplifiers capable of boosting signals a hundredfold for use in the emerging long-distance telephone network. De Forest then used the amplifiers to build a sound projector for motion pictures. By 1922, he opened sound studios in New York City, and within a year he was experimenting with short films for release to sound-equipped theaters around the country under the De Forest Phonofilm name.

This novelty needed theaters and films. William Fox of the Fox Film Corporation was willing to put money into sound development. He purchased the Theodore Case and Earl Sponable sound system, which was superior to that of De Forest. In 1925 Fox acquired West Coast Theaters, a large theater chain. He also purchased a German sound-film system known as Tri-Ergon, incorporating it with the Case and Sponable system and then naming the result Fox-Case while continuing research to perfect it for installation in his new theater chain. But deployment was delayed due to the continuing experimentation Fox demanded.

Around the same time, Warner Bros. acquired the Vitagraph Film Company of New York, which included story materials as well as studios on both coasts and a film-distribution system. With this expansion the time was ripe for the Warners to finance sound technology. The other major studios watched and waited. By 1925 Warner Bros. was first to equip its studios and theaters with new sound equipment. The sound system they chose was

Long remembered as the first talkie, Al Jolson's *The Jazz Singer* (1927) was not the first sound motion picture, but the first with talking sequences.

the Vitaphone, developed by the Bell Laboratories. This system synchronized a record with a projector, unlike the competing Fox System that incorporated a soundtrack on the film itself. The "record" system was cumbersome and would eventually be replaced by the more practical sound-on-film system.

By August 1925, the Warner brothers announced that all of the Western Electric equipment was installed at the old Vitagraph studios in Brooklyn and ready for sound film production. They started with musical short films and shortly thereafter embarked on making a feature film with sound-synchronized musical accompaniment. *Don Juan* opened on August 6, 1926, in New York to rave reviews. William Fox premiered the Movietone sound-on-film system on January 5, 1927. The first public showing of Fox's first sound feature film was *What Price Glory* and a Movietone newsreel showing the Lindbergh flight, which was news around the world at the time. Within a month, Paramount, MGM, First National, Universal, and others signed an agreement to take a year to study the competing sound systems and then jointly select a single system to avoid the costs and consequences of incompatibility.

The Warners wanted another sound feature, but this time with talking sequences. After choosing the Broadway musical *The Jazz Singer* and casting the great singer-entertainer Al Jolson in the lead role, work began for the first time on a Vitaphone production made entirely on the West Coast. After its premiere on October 6, 1927, the Warner brothers—after investing their millions in theaters, studios, new technology, and foreign distribution—were not sure that it would be a success and were prepared for the collapse of the Warners' studio. But just as *Don Juan* proved successful, so did *The Jazz Singer*. By 1928, all the major and minor studios in the country were gearing up for sound. By 1930, most of the studios were using the sound-on-film system because of its superior sound. Additionally, it was cheaper and more practical to use than the record system, which was prone to synchronization mistakes and order mix-ups of the discs.

Talking pictures created a whole new set of obstacles for cast and crew. The microphones could not be moved. The actors had to position themselves near a hidden microphone, which might be in a bouquet of flowers, in a lamp, or under a table—just about anywhere. In addition, actors were cautioned not to move away from a hidden mike before they had finished a speech and not to start talking again until they were directly in front of another mike. Airplanes flying over studios often ruined scenes being shot. The studios sometimes had to fly "silence" balloons to warn aircraft, place red flags, and paint large warnings on the studio roofs. Technicians learned how to dampen sounds and to muffle the whir of camera motors—at first with camera booths, then camera blimps.

After the success of many early sound feature films, by 1930, the studios began major construction programs, almost totally rebuilding their studios into sound-film factories. New sound stages were built and sound departments formed, and by 1934 most U.S. studios had sound facilities. Along with the sound revolution at the studios came human drama. Many silent-film actors found their careers at an abrupt end, and those with good voices, especially those from the stage, saw their careers take off.

The silent film is an art form that is fascinating to watch. But the marriage of sound and picture led to great commercial success for the motion-picture industry and, perhaps more important, established a new and lasting art form. Because of the sound revolution, the motion picture became an intrinsic part of the world's culture.

Right: Sid Grauman and Jack Warner, left, stand in front of the Vitaphone truck, which brought the first sound equipment to Hollywood's Egyptian Theatre in 1926.
Middle: In 1928, MGM first recorded Leo the Lion roaring for its official opening logo. In a New Jersey recording studio, MGM added synchronized sound effects and music to its completed silent picture *White Shadows in the South Seas* in time for its New York premiere. That night, the public also heard Leo roar for the first time.
Bottom: Warner Bros.' first sound film, *Don Juan,* opened at New York's Warners' Theatre.
Opposite: Joan Crawford was one of the few actresses who successfully made the transition from silent films to talkies. Seen here she's recording dialogue for *Our Blushing Brides* (1930).

OPENING LINES

Just as the opening lines of a successful book set the tone and mood for what is to come, so must the opening lines in a motion picture. They are the first words an audience hears, the very beginning of an unforgettable experience. Or so hopes the writer.

Screenwriters labor over opening lines—crafting, recrafting, whittling, expanding—until the beginning is perfect, the tone and mood exactly as they want it to be. But unlike any other artist involved in the filmmaking process, the writer then gives over his or her work and the changes begin. The director takes that writer's baby and adopts it as his or her own. Often rewrite specialists come in to polish it. Even actors and actresses manipulate the words. The script changes, sometimes so much that experienced writers, such as Julius Epstein of *Casablanca* (1943) fame, express their

Right: Natalie Wood and Warren Beatty in *Splendor in the Grass*
Below: Paul Newman in *Cool Hand Luke*

disillusion with the process this way: "What amuses me is that they pay a million dollars for a script, then put another writer on to rewrite it."

The following beginnings of remarkable films are from various decades; some were selected because they were Academy Award nominees and winners in the screenplay category, but all were chosen because this team of editors couldn't forget them.

Rosalind Russell in *Auntie Mame*

SPLENDOR IN THE GRASS (1961)

(Southwest Kansas, 1928. Two teenagers, Bud [Warren Beatty] and Wilma Dean [Natalie Wood] are parked near a waterfall in Bud's car. It is early evening and they are making out.)

Deani: Bud . . .
Bud: Deani, please.
Deani: I'm afraid. No, Bud. Don't, Bud.
Bud: Deani . . .
Deani: We mustn't, Bud. No. No . . . Bud, don't be mad.
Bud: I'd better take you home.

Screenplay: William Inge. Academy Award. (Warner Bros.)

AUNTIE MAME (1958)

(After making out his Last Will and Testament in September 1928, Edwin Dennis drops dead in a Chicago health club. "In the event of my demise," reads the Will, "I direct my faithful servant, Norah Muldoon, to deliver [my only son] Patrick, to my sister and next of kin, Mame Dennis, at 3 Beekman Place, New York City." Norah and Patrick are seen riding in a cab to Beekman Place, holding a Chicago newspaper headlining Edwin Dennis's death.)

Patrick: You've been reading this for a week, Norah. Why'd you bring it to New York?
Norah: It's the only way I can make myself believe it. Besides, I thought your Auntie Mame would like it as a remembrance of your poor sainted father. (Turning to cabbie.) Don't you be going by way of the North Pole, driver. We're not greenhorns, you know!

Screenplay: Betty Comden and Adolph Green from the play by Jerome Lawrence and Robert E. Lee. Based on the novel by Patrick Dennis. (Warner Bros.)

CASABLANCA (1942)

(With the coming of World War II, refugees began streaming into the port city of Casablanca in French Morocco. Above the crowded street in a small office, a shortwave radio operator reads an incoming announcement.)

To all officers . . . two German couriers carrying important officials' documents murdered on train from Oran. Murderer and possibly accomplices heading for Casablanca. Round up all suspicious characters and search them for stolen documents. Important.

Screenplay: Julius J. Epstein, Philip G. Epstein, and Howard Koch. Academy Award. (Warner Bros.)

THE BIG SLEEP (1946)

(Standing at the door to the Sternwood estate, Philip Marlow [Humphrey Bogart] rings the bell and is let in by the butler. As he waits in the foyer, a young woman, Carmen Sternwood [Martha Vickers], enters.)

Marlow: My name's Marlow. General Sternwood wanted to see me.
Butler: Yes, Mr. Marlow. Come in, please, sir.
Marlow: Thank you. (As Carmen enters.) Morning.
Carmen: You're not very tall, are you?
Marlow: Well, I try to be.
Carmen: Not bad looking, but you probably know it. What's your name?
Marlow: Reilly. Doghouse Reilly.
Carmen: That's a funny kind of name.
Marlow: Think so?
Carmen: Uh huh. What are you, a prizefighter?
Marlow: No, I'm a shamus.
Carmen: What's a shamus?
Marlow: A private detective.

Screenplay: William Faulkner, Leigh Brackett, and Jules Furthman from the novel by Raymond Chandler. (Warner Bros.)

COOL HAND LUKE (1967)

(On a quiet night in a darkened public parking lot, a lone man, Luke [Paul Newman], is quietly cutting parking meters from their poles when a police car pulls up, catching Luke in the headlights.)

Police: What are you doing there, fella?
Luke: I'm just cutting . . . uh . . . not doing anything.
Police: You'd better come along with us.
Luke: (Grins smugly, then laughs. Next stop: a Southern prison and two years on a chain gang.)

Screenplay: Donn Pearce and Frank R. Pierson from the novel by Donn Pearce. Academy Award nomination. (Warner Bros.)

SUMMERTIME (1955)

(As a train nears Venice, a spinster American tourist, Jane Hudson [Katharine Hepburn], hands a folder of Venice to a gentleman passenger so she can photograph it.)

Jane: I beg your pardon. Hold onto this a sec, will you, please?
Passenger: Yes, certainly.
Jane: In a little closer, if you don't mind. Up a little higher. Now, still! (She takes the picture.) This is Venice we're coming into now, isn't it?

Passenger: Yes, we'll be there in about two minutes now. This is the lagoon.
Jane: Oh, boy, got to get a shot of this. (She runs out of film and reloads.) Oh, golly, fifth one of these I've used already. Haven't even gotten there yet!

Screenplay: David Lean and H. E. Bates. Based on the play *The Time of the Cuckoo*, by Arthur Laurents. (United Artists/Lopert)

FUNNY GIRL (1968)

(Comedienne-singer Fanny Brice [by Barbra Streisand in her Academy Award–winning screen debut] pauses outside the Ziegfeld Theater to see her name in lights above the marquee, then walks to the artist's entrance and backstage where she stops before a full-length mirror. Posing momentarily, she speaks to her reflected image.)

"Hello, gorgeous."

Screenplay: Isobel Lennart from her stage play. (Columbia/Rastar)

STARS IN THEIR EYES

S tarlets. Hollywood is crawling with them. Always was. The earliest starlets represented the future of the film industry, and these days, few appreciate that fact, laying money on proven talent rather than exploring the new. But when the first film moguls were shaping a new and creative world of entertainment, starlets were an integral part of the business. Moguls took chances on them based on instincts. Photographers glamorized the girls. And an organization of studio publicists spent years hyping them. The first thirteen Wampas (the acronym for Western Association of Motion Picture Advertisers) Baby Stars were "born" in 1922, a group of young actresses, hand-picked by Wampas members, "who have shown the most talent and promise for eventual stardom." The girls were presented, like debutantes, at a ball or "frolic" as it was called, and they became a promotional tool of the industry, like a baker's dozen of smiling Miss Hollywoods.

Of the first group, Bessie Love and Colleen Moore were the names that stood the test of time, but others such as Patsy Ruth Miller (who played Esmerelda to Lon Chaney's Quasimodo in *The Hunchback of Notre Dame* [1923] and eventually ran a Hollywood hair salon) and Mary Philbin (who starred opposite Chaney in *The Phantom of the Opera* [1925] and other Universal films) had notable careers in silent pictures. Lois Wilson, a favorite of Cecil B. DeMille, went from screen to stage and then to television.

From subsequent groups of Wampas Baby Stars came some of Hollywood's

Above: In the mid-1940s, Metro-Goldwyn-Mayer's publicity team was at work to promote starlets Frances Rafferty, Dorothy Morris, and Vicki Lane, so why not put them on the backs of three baby elephants from the Tarzan pictures? Frances Rafferty's career outlasted the others; she made her last film in 1961 and spent five years on the television show *December Bride* in the 1950s.
Opposite: 1926 was a big year for the Wampas Baby Stars: Joan Crawford (bottom left), Dolores Costello and Mary Astor (fourth and fifth from bottom left), Janet Gaynor (top right), Dolores Del Rio and Fay Wray (third and fourth from top right). Silent star Marceline Day is at the peak of the ladder.

biggest names: Laura La Plante (1923), Clara Bow (1924), Mary Astor (1926), Dolores Costello (1926), Joan Crawford (1926), Dolores Del Rio (1926), Janet Gaynor (1926; she copped the first Academy Award two years later for her acting), Fay Wray (1926), Sally Rand (1927), Lupe Velez (1928), Loretta Young (1929), Anita Louise (1931), and Ginger Rogers (1932) were among them. Careers were launched from Wampas exposure, but by 1934, the last group of stars had been selected and Wampas itself dissolved.

For the next dozen years, studios put money and time behind their starlets, but by the late 1940s, promoting established stars became every studio's focus. Starlet power came from the young women them-selves: perhaps they could get interest from a mogul (they took a lesson from Jane Russell, whose bosom's famous appeal caused Howard Hughes to give her the lead in *The Outlaw* [1940], her first film, strictly based on his appreciation of her voluptuous thirty-eight-inch chest). Or catch the eye of a photographer (Tom Kelley's nude photo-graph of Monroe set her apart from hun-dreds of other young starlets who were perhaps more talented). Or just be a damned good actress noticed by the right person in the right place at the proverbial right time (Katharine Hepburn got her first Hollywood contract from RKO after a Hollywood scout saw her on the Broadway stage, and Audrey Hepburn was discovered by the novelist Colette while the young actress was filming a British film, *Monte Carlo Baby* [1951], on the French Riviera).

Starlets are to be celebrated for their talents, for their beauty, for their tenacity, and always for their audacity. They have always made Hollywood interesting. Howard Hughes definitely thought so.

Opposite: In 1935, after the demise of Wampas and its Baby Stars, the film studios started marketing their own starlets in the Wampas manner. Here, the Paramount Proteges: (from top to bottom) Katherine DeMille, Gail Patrick, Wendie Barrie, Gertrude Michael, Ann Sheridan, and Grace Brady.
Above: The 1928 Wampas Baby Stars included young actresses whose names would be big on marquees, but the girls went through the rigors of starletdom to get them there.

HOW DISNEY FOUND HIS VOICES

When Walt Disney began his company in 1923 with his brother Roy, he really had no thought of putting voices to his cartoon characters. The movies were "voiceless" then and the artwork was his primary interest. By 1928 sound had come to the movies and Disney experimented with his first sound cartoon, *Steamboat Willie,* and subsequently used his own voice in a high, squeaky pitch for the voice of Mickey Mouse, a character he had just created.

With each cartoon, new animated characters were introduced, even talking animals, flowers, and trees. Finding the right voices to fit these earliest creations was not easy. And while it is no secret that Walt Disney had a great eye for art, he also had a great ear for voices.

In 1933, before Donald Duck had even hit the drawing board, Clarence Nash worked in the promotional department of a big milk company in Southern California. As a special stunt, Nash drove a little cart and pony team around to Los Angeles grade schools, where he put on programs of bird and animal imitations.

During his stint with the milk company, Nash heard that a young fellow who made cartoons for the movies—Disney by name—was in the market for a bird and animal imitator to do some recording, so he made his way to the fledgling Disney Studio for an audition. Nash went through all his tricks: bird calls, cat meows, dog barks, horse whinnies, and then, just as Disney wandered onto the sound stage, he finished with his imitation of a frightened little girl reciting "Mary Had a Little Lamb."

"Gee, that fellow sounds like a duck talking, you know that?" Disney remarked to one of his fellow workers. "Let's keep him in mind in case we ever want to do a duck character."

The following year, Disney and his staff decided that Mickey Mouse needed a contrasting character, one who could do mischievous foolery, such as slip on banana peels and get the worst of things in general. In short, he could become involved in situations that Mickey, the hero, never would.

Even when work started on a "Silly Symphony" cartoon short called *The Little Wise Hen,* nobody thought that the duck character in the picture was the "missing link" they were looking for, especially Walt Disney, who was a stickler for perfection and technical quality. Then someone remembered the man who could talk like a duck, and Nash was hired to do the duck's voice.

After *The Wise Little Hen* (1934) was finished, the newly introduced Donald Duck stood out to such an extent that he was given a starring role with Mickey in a subsequent picture called *Orphan's Benefit* (1934). From then on, the talking duck became a hero in countries all over the world. Even Clarence Nash became a star in his own right. He was soon nicknamed "Ducky," and found himself appearing as himself in *The Reluctant Dragon* (1941), an animated and live-action feature film about the Disney Studio, in which Nash is seen during a typical recording session.

Walt Disney's first large-scale studio, on Hyperion Avenue, just south of Griffith Park in the Silverlake district of Los Angeles, was Disney headquarters for fourteen years, beginning in 1926.

Scouts at Disney were continually testing voices, which were logged into the vast studio voice index, in an effort to find the perfect voice for each part. So many voices were tested that there was a standing gag that "a voice could be found for anything, even an oyster."

Pinto Colvig was one of the voice discoveries. The son of an Oregon judge, Colvig started out as a newspaperman and cartoonist, but switched to traveling with a circus band, where he learned the various sounds made by different animals. He created the voices of Goofy (originally called Dippy Dawg). He also spoke for Grumpy in *Snow White and the Seven Dwarfs* (1937), and Practical Pig in *Three Little Pigs* (1933).

One of Disney's most memorable voices belonged to Sterling Holloway, a former stage comic and singer, who had a long movie career, during which he appeared in more than one hundred films, as every manner of dufus. He used his molasses voice for a number of Disney's animal characters, including Mr. Stork in *Dumbo* (1941), the adult Flower in *Bambi* (1942), the Cheshire Cat in *Alice in Wonderland* (1951), and the much beloved Winnie the Pooh in films from 1966 through 1977. Holloway was a Disney favorite because of his distinctive voice and personality, which aided the animators in their approach to the art.

As for Walt Disney himself, he continued to be the squeaky, falsetto voice of Mickey Mouse for more than twenty years. It was one of his pet jobs—in more ways than one.

BRINGING COLOR TO THE MOVIES

"Color on the motion picture screen? Never!" scoffed filmmakers in the first decade of the twentieth century. Performers, too, laughed at the idea, and for good reason. Why risk their careers on a gimmick that could jeopardize the success of their films?

Movies in color had long been the dream of international film pioneers: Louis Jacques Daguerre, James Clerk Maxwell, H. W. Vogel, Emile Reynaud, Georges Méliès, and the brothers Lumière. But their efforts had been costly and time consuming since each frame had to be individually hand-tinted. Even Thomas Edison, who produced a color film of a stage success, *Annabell's Butterfly Dance,* hand-tinted the entire thirty-five-foot length, frame by frame.

In 1915 a new enterprise named Technicolor made color movies a possibility on a commercial basis. But the going wasn't easy at first, even for Technicolor, headed by Dr. Herbert T. Kalmus, a graduate of the Massachusetts Institute of Technology (the name Technicolor was in honor of his alma mater) and a former chemistry and physics professor. Instead of forging ahead in giant leaps, Dr. Kalmus and his partners—two fellow M.I.T. graduates, Daniel Comstock and Burton Westcott—moved in a smaller steps to maintain quality control, conserve time and money, develop a natural-looking color

Janet Leigh, as a Russian jet pilot on a spy mission, charms American airman John Wayne in Howard Hughes's Technicolor production, *Jet Pilot* (filmed in 1950, released in 1957)

process, and ultimately to project the image with standardized equipment.

Using the same two-color components—red and green—devised in 1910 by Kinemacolor, Kalmus's team produced a ten-minute one-reel film. A refurbished railroad car, Technicolor's first laboratory, made its way from Boston to Jacksonville, Florida, where the filming of *The Gulf Between* (1918) took place.

Between 1917 and 1926, Technicolor released its first two-color feature film, *The Toll of the Sea*. The first film with artificially lit interiors, *Cytherea* (1924), came out, along with several star vehicles, including *Stage Struck* (1925), with Gloria Swanson, and Douglas Fairbanks's *The Black Pirate* (1926).

The first surge of real enthusiasm for Technicolor came between 1928 and 1930, as more and more producers rushed to add color to the new sound movies. The result was a series of subpar productions with garishly tinted pictures—still in the two-color process—that did Technicolor more harm than good. Dr. Kalmus, who had opened a facility in Hollywood, decided to embark on one last push to overcome Technicolor's basic shortcoming, the lack of a three-color—or full-color—image. In 1932, Technicolor introduced a new camera that finally could successfully record all three colors: red, green, and blue.

Producers were still skeptical. However, Walt Disney, who had never used the two-color process in his cartoons, was so impressed with the new full-color image that in 1932 he released *Flowers and Trees* (1932), the first full-color Technicolor film. The following year came Disney's animated *Three Little Pigs*. In 1934, the first live-action short in three-color was released, *La Cucaracha*.

The door opened slowly, but studios gradually began adding Technicolor sequences to their releases. By the end of the 1930s, Technicolor had become a star in its own right. And by 1939, *Gone with the Wind* and *The Wizard of Oz* proved that there was no limit to the impact of color on the big screen.

Above: The new Technicolor plant in Hollywood, mid-1920s
Opposite: Trade ad for *Dancing Pirate* (1936), the first musical in the new full-color Technicolor
Below: Henry Fonda takes a break during the production of *The Trail of the Lonesome Pine* (1936), the first outdoor drama filmed in full color, to pose with the new three-color Technicolor camera.

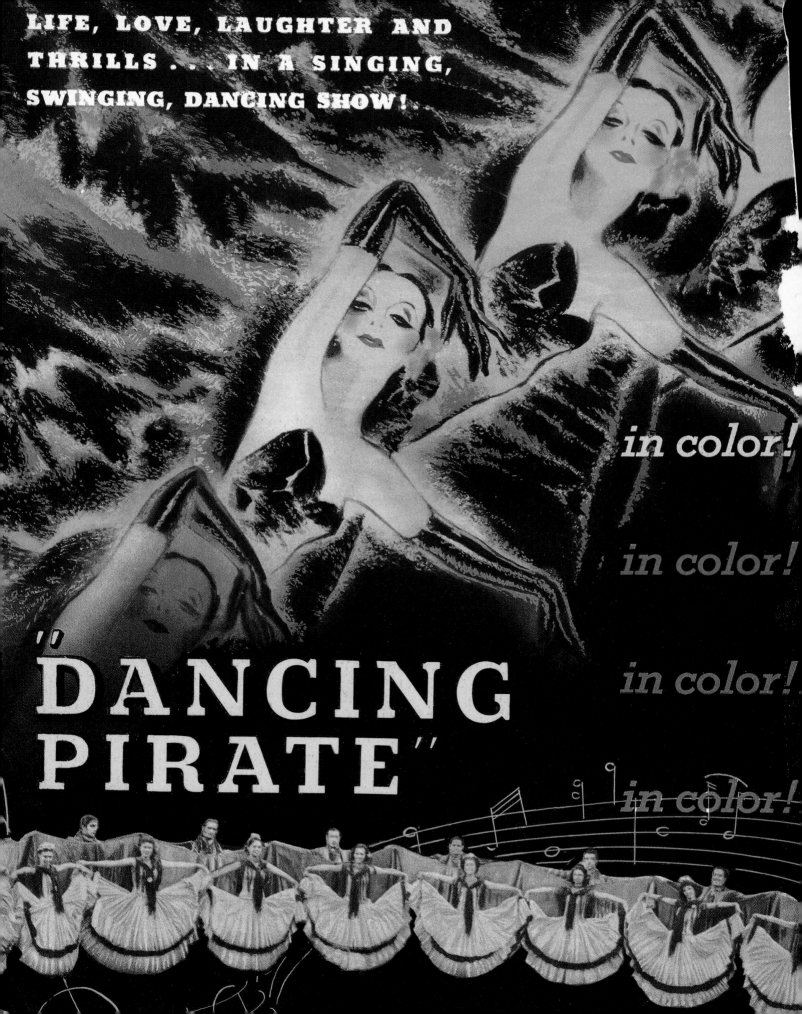

THE ART OF PRODUCTION DESIGN

BY HAROLD MICHELSON

Once the script is accepted by the director, art direction marks the beginning of every production—the art director oversees the look of the movie, specifically the sets. No set means no film. Since the 1950s, directors have asked Harold Michelson to be their films' art director: to commence the production, to set the mood for a film, to create its visual nuances, to influence the tone of the actors, to inspire the cinematographer, to tell the audience what time and place they have traveled to. For jobs done so very, very well, Michelson has been rewarded with two Academy Award nominations: for Star Trek: The Motion Picture *(1979) and* Terms of Endearment *(1983). And who can ever forget the sets he designed for Warren Beatty's* Dick Tracy *(1990)?*

—The Editors

It was different in the beginning. There were no giant sound stages. No banks of floodlights. No special effects or wondrous technology. No warehouses filled with every period of furnishings and props imaginable. Film stock and cameras were primitive. The pioneer movie designers and stylists had very little to work with, yet created settings that audiences believed.

Then sets were designed by master carpenters. As knowledgeable as many of them were, however, their work was limited as far as historically accurate details were concerned. So set design was turned over to an "artistic executive"—the art director.

Harold Michelson's first big assignment for Paramount was as a storyboard artist, or illustrator, for Cecil B. DeMille's *The Ten Commandments* (1956). His storyboard panel, right, shown with a corresponding still from the epic film, below, demonstrates the tremendous initial contribution of an art director to the finished film. Art direction by Hal Pereira, Walter H. Tyler, and Albert Nozaki

Throughout the 1930s and 1940s, each of the studios had a primary art director: Cedric Gibbons (MGM), Richard Day (United Artists), Hans Dreier (Paramount), Van Nest Polglase and Albert S. D'Agostino (RKO Radio), Anton Grot (Warner Bros.), Lionel Banks (Columbia), Lyle Wheeler and John DeCuir (Twentieth Century-Fox), and Alexander Golitzen (Universal)—they controlled their studio's visual image. Today, art directors and production designers are independent, so each film looks different.

Art director and production designer are interchangeable terms. I've been nominated for Academy Awards in both jobs, but, in each, my work is much the same—I do the drawings that determine the look of the film. The title "production designer" was originated by David O. Selznick during the making of *Gone with the Wind* (1939). There were three art directors on that film, but it was William Cameron Menzies who did the storyboards. Creating thousands of small sketches, Menzies laid out the picture, scene by scene, showing the camera angles. He even included lighting effects.

I remember seeing Menzies's sketches of Atlanta burning. A scene was drawn in silhouette showing Rhett and Scarlett in the wagon against the fire, and that was exactly the way the scene was filmed. Menzies's storyboard sketches created the mood, not only for that scene, but for the entire film. So Selznick rewarded him with the new title, production designer.

In creating a look and a style for a motion picture, we are one minute researchers and artists, the next architects and lighting experts. When we pull it together, we hope we have made something memorable.

Richard Burton, left, Jay Robinson, and Jean Simmons, in the first CinemaScope production, *The Robe* (1953), demonstrate the historically correct spectacle created by art directors Lyle R. Wheeler and George W. Davis. Their work won the art directors an Academy Award.

2

Making believe makes us go to the movies. Fantasy creates our dreams, gives us something to work for, to aspire to, to take refuge in, to be glad about. That we can see gorgeous women looking just too perfect, gorillas who are bigger than life, men who pretend to be women, and tales more horrible than we'd ever want to live, is because movies allow us to indulge in make-believe. Herewith the pictures and stories of what can't be real.

MAKE-BELIEVE

Diana Lynn smirks as she watches Ronald Reagan play "daddy" to a chimp in *Bedtime for Bonzo* (1951).

MAKING UP

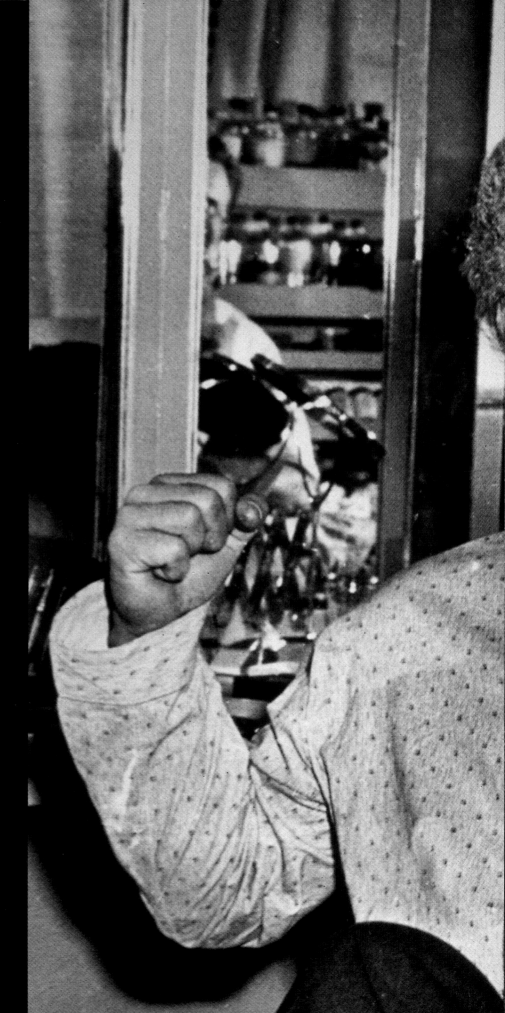

Hooray for Hollywood.
You may be homely in your neighborhood,
But if you think you can be an actor,
See Mr. Factor.
He'd make a monkey look good.
Within a half an hour
You'll look like Tyrone Power.
Hooray for Hollywood.

—"Hooray for Hollywood"
from *Hollywood Hotel* (1937)
by Richard A. Whiting and Johnny Mercer

Hollywood makeup changed the face of the world. It took the world of make-believe into the homes of American girls who wanted to be as beautiful as their screen idols. Wigmaker and barber Max Factor first perfected a face paint that worked under the hot lights of the movie set in 1914 for the likes of Charlie Chaplin and Tom Mix; two years later, he introduced a variation on that makeup for females and put it in drugstores across the country. With it, American women could have the flawless faces of their favorite stars. Suddenly, nice girls wore makeup, not just floozies. Before the 1920s dawned, Factor had introduced false eyelashes, and by the time flappers started flapping, American women were batting faux lashes

Jack P. Pierce, head of makeup at Universal from 1936 to 1946, transforms Lon Chaney, Jr., into 1941's most horrible monster, the Wolf Man.

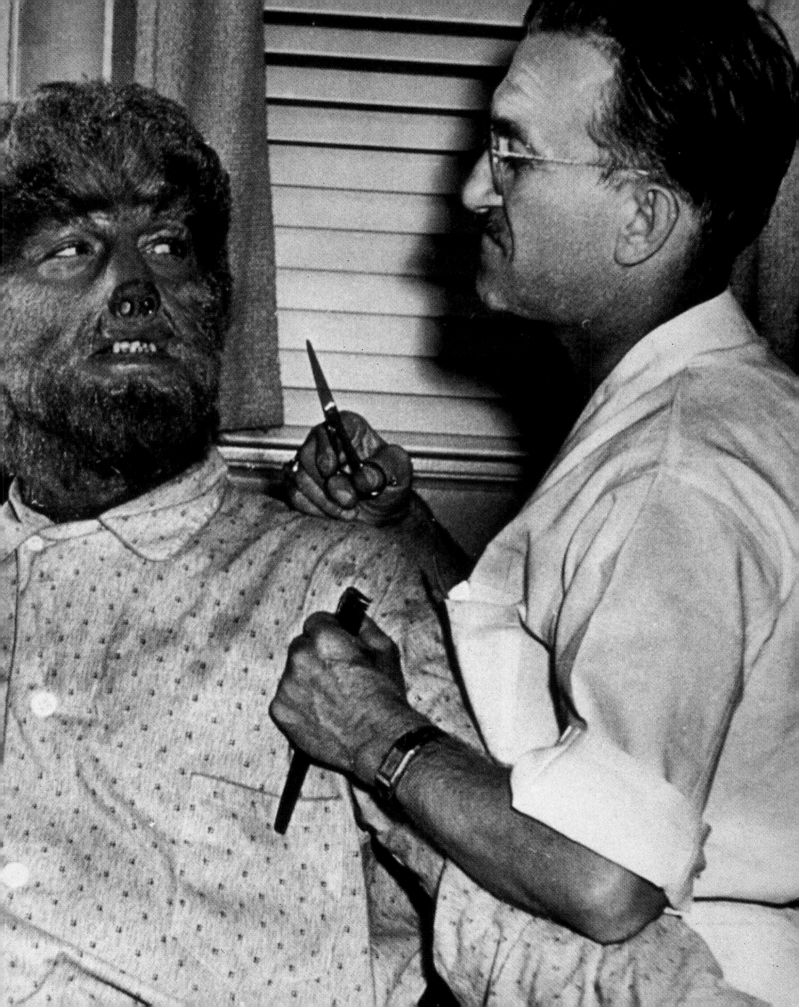

right along with Clara Bow and Greta Garbo.

Factor's contemporaries, George Westmore and his sons, Mont, Perc, Ern, Wally, Bud, and Frank (the first of a four-generation family dynasty of Hollywood makeup artists who set the standards for film makeup throughout the twentieth century), dominated both the beauty scene and the monster scene in Hollywood, with George painting the face of Mary Pickford in *The Black Pirate* (1926), Mont doing the makeup for *Gone with the Wind,* Perc giving Joan Crawford her dramatic lips and brows in *Mildred Pierce* (1945), Wally creating the faces of the 1931 version of *Dr. Jekyll and Mr. Hyde,* Bud putting a happy face on Doris Day in *Pillow Talk* (1959) and Sandra Dee in *Tammy Tell Me True* (1961). Jack P. Pierce developed a reputation for turning normal-looking guys like Boris Karloff into the legendary monster of Dr. Frankenstein, so he was named head of makeup at Universal in 1936, where he became the master of horrific faces such as Dracula, the Wolf Man, and the Phantom of the Opera.

That the same artists who shaped the horrors of the screen taught its beauties to be more beautiful is another one of the ironies of Hollywood. More power, they would say, to make-believe.

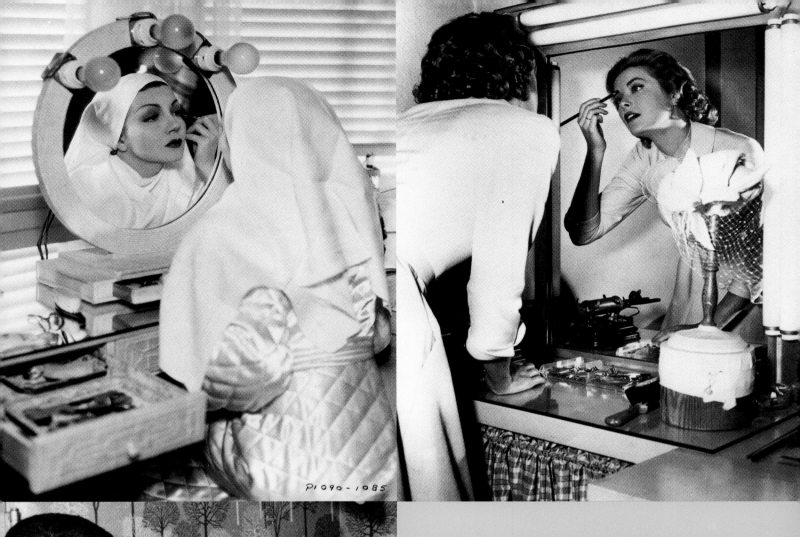

P1090-1085

Opposite top: Jean Harlow became a spokesperson for Max Factor consumer cosmetics, endorsing the products in print advertisements that plugged her newest films.

Above left: Claudette Colbert insisted on applying her own makeup for her films, but beginning in the late 1920s, she did photography sessions with Max Factor himself to promote his newest products.

Above right: When Grace Kelly filmed *The Country Girl* (1954), makeup artist Wally Westmore taught her the makeup techniques of transforming from downtrodden housewife to society lady.

Opposite bottom: Between takes on the set, makeup artists and hairstylists help actors and actresses to maintain a consistent look throughout a scene. Here Paulette Goddard is primped by makeup man Otis Malcolm and hairdresser Hedy Mjorud.

Left: Robert Schiffer was Rita Hayworth's makeup man for years. "She had one eye a little smaller than the other, so I used to take a false eyelash and place it at an angle, then glue her own eyelash to it, just to even her eyes out."

ON THE SAME WAVELENGTH

Historical films suffer from hairstylists who can't escape the present. And most films set in the future look undeniably contemporary because hair designers can't deliver. That's why Princess Leia Organa's hairdo in the first *Star Wars* (1977) film was so memorable: its ram's-horn coils over each of Carrie Fisher's ears were an imaginative, if ugly, stretch. How predictable it would have been to see her wearing the winged Farrah Fawcett style that had swept the nation by 1976. Had it been so, viewers wouldn't have complained, being used to such vagaries. But they never would have remembered the fair Leia.

Princess Leia's notwithstanding, film styles can set trends. Consider Louise Brooks's bob with bangs. Besides becoming the *de rigueur* do of its flapper day, Coco Chanel and Edith Head copied Brooks's style and wore it to their graves. A similar geometric cut transformed the 1960s as Vidal Sassoon's biggest hairstyle, and the bob has remained the hairdo of choice for stylish Anna Wintour, who was editor of *Vogue* magazine even as the twentieth century turned to the twenty-first.

Though auburn and golden blond had been the most popular shades of the war years, by the end of the 1940s, a starlet named Monroe brought platinum to the fore, in the shade popularized by Jean Harlow. Sure, Elizabeth Taylor and Audrey Hepburn would wow audiences with their dark-haired, dark-eyed beauty, but Monroe's bleached locks caused the need for hair

Above: During the war years, long hair was essential for movie stars. The sexy short hairdos of the 1920s and modest styles of the Depression years gave way to voluminous curls and hair as long as it would grow—like Lana Turner's.
Opposite: Not every Hollywood style was meant to be copied, but rather to be marveled at. In *Marie Antoinette* (1938), Sydney Guilaroff styled the remarkable wigs (created by Max Factor) for Norma Shearer, and frequently decorated them with real gems from renowned French jeweler Van Cleef and Arpels.

conditioner in every bathroom and allowed Clairol to claim that blondes indeed have more fun. Sydney Guilaroff, the studio hairstylist who took credit for Marilyn's color and cut in her films as early as *Asphalt Jungle* (1950), described her look as "beautiful but troubled." He continually lightened her hair until 1952, when he found the perfect platinum for *Gentlemen Prefer Blondes* (1953), the shade she maintained with little deviation.

The film industry has paid little attention to its hairstylists, never acknowledging their contributions with a dedicated Academy Award (hairstyles are considered part of the makeup category that was introduced in 1981, but have yet to be specifically honored). Had there been awards, names such as Guilaroff and Nellie Manley would have surfaced in the early years. Guilaroff was MGM's head stylist for dozens of years, tending to the tresses of Joan Crawford, Lana Turner, Marlene Dietrich, Judy Garland, and, of course, Monroe. As he told the story, he was also lover to Greta Garbo and Ava Gardner. (Never mind that the curly perm with diamond-studded gewgaws he gave Garbo in *Two-Faced Woman* [1941] is partially credited with ending her career.) Manley, who was for years Guilaroff's counterpart at Paramount, created styles for the likes of Sophia Loren, Shirley MacLaine, Natalie Wood, and Mia Farrow (though it was Sassoon who cropped Farrow's hair short, á la Jean Seberg, to help her escape her "Alice in Wonderland" image).

The industry may have snubbed the hair contingent, but the public doesn't. In the early 1990s, longtime Hollywood colorist Lori Davis, whose work has appeared on the heads of hundreds of stars including Meryl Streep, Arnold Schwarzenegger, and Cher, introduced hair-care products that were sold on television. Within minutes of airing, the advertisement had generated thousands of sales. No matter that Davis's products were among the most expensive around. To have hair like a star, no price is too high.

Above: The ultimate symbol of women's liberation in the 1920s, Louise Brooks's vampy bob caused women around the world to shorten their hair to match their shortened skirts. Sydney Guilaroff took credit for cutting the do in his New York salon, where he worked before coming to Hollywood.

Opposite: Howard Hughes demanded that cameramen focus on Jane Russell's bosom in *The Outlaw* (1943), but he also made certain that her hair was as sensual as possible. He brought in a private stylist whose name has been lost. In this publicity shot, her hair gets more attention than her breasts.

Below: Veronica Lake's peek-a-boo blond hair made her a Hollywood legend, not her meager films. So popular was the style among the Rosie the Riveter contingent that it was banned in wartime factories because of workplace accidents. The government requested that she wear her hair pulled back in the film *So Proudly We Hail* (1943), in hopes of putting an end to the trend. No luck. Obviously derived from Lake's look, Lauren Bacall's flowing pageboy in *To Have and Have Not* (1944), often secured on its waved right side with a barrette, became an overnight sensation.

HOLLYWOOD A LA MODE

With designers such as Adrian, Travis Banton, Edith Head, Irene, and Helen Rose vying to create stars' on-screen and offscreen wardrobes, Golden Age actresses lived in a world of fashion that was too glamorous to believe. Studios demanded that their stable of actresses wear lavish gowns and furs to match their equally lavish lifestyles—all staged to create an image. No wardrobe budgets were spared. Stories of Marlene Dietrich's and Joan Crawford's affairs with clothes became legendary. Crawford

Below: Carole Lombard, circa 1940, was a screwball comedienne on screen, but a sophisticated fashion model in studio-sponsored promotional images, this time in a gown by Irene (née Lentz), who also designed her costumes for *Mr. and Mrs. Smith* (1941).

Right: Marie Prevost starred as a model in the 1928 film *Blonde for a Night*, an early look at fashion on film.
Below: In *Lucy Gallant* (1955), Jane Wyman, seated, plays a hard-nosed retailer, and the fashion business is central to the plot. Edith Head appears in the film and designed all the costumes.

changed clothes ten times a day, even hourly, and owned at least sixteen fur coats at a time, including ermines, minks, beavers, and broadtail lambs. Dietrich traveled with eight sizes of the same boot, so that if her legs swelled, she always had the right size available. Paramount spent hundreds of dollars to meet Dietrich's demand for lace-encrusted nylon stockings—anything to enhance her famed legs.

But other stars were indulged as well. Lucille Ball became the clotheshorse for RKO, posing for photographers in hundreds of fashion shoots and taking the clothes home to her personal closet to wear whenever she was in public. Many top actresses flew to Paris to attend pricey fashion shows. Others, even as early as Mary Pickford and Mae West in the 1920s, simply ordered their gowns from sketches sent to them by French designers. Elsa Schiaparelli was a favorite of Mae West and vice versa, the designer having shaped the bottle for her famed fragrance, Shocking, after the

Right: Hollywood fashion has always been a world of make-believe, as best exemplified by this fantasy scene from director William Dieterle's *Fashions of 1934* (1934).
Below: The ultimate clotheshorse of 1930s Hollywood, Marlene Dietrich did no fashion photography unless it was dramatic, alluring, and consistent with her mysterious image. Here, the gown is by her longtime designer and friend, Travis Banton.

actress's curvaceous body.

The fashion show became a recurring theme on-screen, with films in every decade taking audiences to glitzy runways. In *Lucy Gallant* (1955), Paramount's Edith Head made a cameo appearance, commentating one of the most extravagant fashion show scenes of the mid-1950s. She had become a star in her own right, due to movie magazine and newspaper how-to columns that bore her signature.

Fashions worn in films and movie magazine spreads were the only means that fans had to pick up trends. Although the Academy Awards shows of the late twentieth century came to be known each year as "the biggest fashion show on earth," early awards ceremonies weren't typically viewed by the public, and only in the late 1980s and 1990s did fashion become an integral part of the event.

Trendies who think that high fashion is unique to films of the late twentieth century that starred Gwyneth Paltrow, Julia Roberts, or Cameron Diaz need only look back to decades past to see what stars were wearing, long before the midcentury onset of fashionable types like Audrey Hepburn or Grace Kelly.

Below: Gilbert Adrian, MGM designer for stars such as Joan Crawford, Jean Harlow, and Katharine Hepburn. Here, with his muse, Garbo

Left: Lauren Bacall plays a fashion designer in *Designing Woman* (1957), but it's costume designer Helen Rose who took offscreen kudos for this elegantly styled film.

Below: What a fashion show: Bacall, Monroe, and Grable take center stage. Note Monroe's clear plastic platforms, one of her personal trademarks, worked into one of her best-loved films, *How to Marry a Millionaire* (1953). Charles LeMaire and William Travilla teamed to design the clothes.

HAIRY HEROES
BY FAY WRAY

T hey swung through the trees, right into our hearts. Chimps were the hairy heroes of jungle pictures throughout the 1930s and 1940s, cute little guys with exotic names like Cheetah, Gaga, and Bonzo. Johnny Weissmuller had his faithful pet chimpanzee—a substitute son until Boy came along?—throughout his long reign as Tarzan, and chimps were common pals for Dorothy Lamour in her island romps. Ronald Reagan even "adopted" a chimp in Bedtime for Bonzo (1951) that forever will be associated with him. But it was the biggest hairy creature of all whose name is imprinted in our minds. Kong. KING KONG. This was no man in an ape suit. No, in his way Kong was very real, as Fay Wray, the woman who wriggled and screamed in his loving grasp, explains seven decades later. . . .
— The Editors

Although I made perhaps a hundred pictures, *King Kong* (1933) is certainly the one most remembered. I no longer make any effort to escape the questions about it. I am intrigued to read that there are those who find sociological, even religious, symbolism in the film and some who consider Kong representative of mankind. I am not dismayed when I observe an attractive young man

Lee J. Cobb, Raymond Burr, Anne Bancroft, and Warren Stevens stand guard over the imprisoned title character in *Gorilla at Large* (1954), filmed in 3-D.

wearing a lapel button with the words: "King Kong Died for Our Sins."

When Merian C. Cooper first called me into his new offices at RKO, he showed me pictures of the giant ape climbing up the side of the newly completed Empire State Building, and he saw my dismay. "He won't be a real ape. He'll be a small figure but we're going to make him look fifty feet high. All in animation," he said to comfort me. He told me they were considering another actress who was to be at RKO, Katharine Hepburn. "She's good, but not as good as you." I got the part and donned a blond wig.

Though Kong was only an eighteen-inch-high doll, the arm that held me was about eight feet long and inside that furry arm there was a steel bar and the whole contraption (with me in the hand) could be raised and lowered like a crane. The fingers would be pressed around my waist while I was in a standing position. I would then be raised about ten feet. As I kicked and squirmed and struggled in the ape's hand, his fingers would gradually loosen and begin to open. My fear was real as I grabbed onto his wrist, his thumb, wherever I could to keep from slipping out of that paw!

Kong opened at Radio City Music Hall (and two weeks later in Hollywood at Grauman's Chinese). I was very uncomfortable watching the film that night, mostly because of my screaming—too much, too much, I thought. I didn't realize that the little Kong doll had to be given life by means of the sounds I made. I didn't believe my eyes when I read in the *Hollywood Reporter:* "Fay Wray brilliant in *King Kong.*" Brilliant? I didn't realize for many years that *King Kong* had made an enduring impact. Now, when I'm in New York, I look at the Empire State Building and feel as though it belongs to me.

Cheetah the chimp gets in trouble as Boy, played by Rickie Sorensen, watches in *Tarzan's Fight for Life* (1958).

SWITCHING ROLES

T he last two decades of the twentieth century featured several stars who played the he/she switch: Dustin Hoffman as that flirtatious female, *Tootsie* (1982); Robin Wiliams as the audacious *Mrs. Doubtfire* (1993); Julie Andrews as the debatable Victor or Victoria in *Victor/Victoria* (1982); even voluptuous Barbra Streisand getting by as a little boy in *Yentl* (1983). Some films featured sophisticated themes such as *The Crying Game* (1992), in which Jaye Davidson played the loving if deceitful "female" Dil, or *Boys Don't Cry* (1999), for which Hilary Swank won the best actress Academy Award for her portrayal of Teena Brandon, alias Brandon Teena, the girl who was finally killed for adopting the guise of a boy.

The roots of cross-acting and cross-dressing surfaced in comedies frequently throughout the first half of the century, when the likes of Laurel and Hardy, Charlie Chaplin, and the Marx Brothers found their way into women's clothes to make believe and make us laugh. Though she was famous

Top: Bob Hope sets a trend in grandmotherly dressing in *The Lemon Drop Kid* (1951).
Opposite: Even the wizardry makeup of Ben Nye couldn't turn leading man Cary Grant into a pretty woman in *I Was a Male War Bride* (1949).
Right: Wearing costumes designed by Orry-Kelly, Tony Curtis, left, and Jack Lemmon flank an embarrassed Maurice Chevalier when the Frenchman visited the set of *Some Like It Hot* (1959).

for her tuxedoes in the 1920s, Dietrich wore pants to assert her freedom as a woman, not to assume a man's identity. In the early years of Hollywood, it was generally laughable for a man to don woman's garb. Cary Grant made a pretty funny woman with a wig and WAC uniform in *I Was a Male War Bride* (1949), but the year before, Ingrid Bergman had to be a serious *Joan of Arc* (1948) to dress like a man on-screen.

Some of America's favorite male stars became prototypes of future he/shes. As years passed Williams's *Mrs. Doubtfire* assumed a style quite close to a much earlier Bob Hope's granny in *The Lemon Drop Kid* (1951). And when, in Columbia's comic Western *Shut My Big Mouth* (1942), Joe E. Brown, the funnyman renowned for his big mouth, colored it red and donned a wig, he looked surprisingly like a prototype for Tony Curtis as one of the gal musicians in Billy Wilder's wild *Some Like It Hot* (1959).

Switching roles has been a recurring theme in Hollywood, one that hopefully will never go away, to make viewers laugh, to make viewers think, and in the case of stories like Teena Brandon's, to make them cry.

Top: Ray Bolger (with actress Allyn McLerie), who played Scarecrow in *The Wizard of Oz*, plays an equally comical rich aunt in *Where's Charley?* (1952).
Opposite: Jack Lemmon clowns in the makeup room on the set of *Some Like It Hot* (1959), after his makeup was applied for the cross-dressing scenes. He wore wigs in the film, so he never really had to sit under the hair dryer.
Right: Joe E. Brown laughs with starlet Lyn Swann, with the comedian posing as a female in *Shut My Big Mouth* (1942).

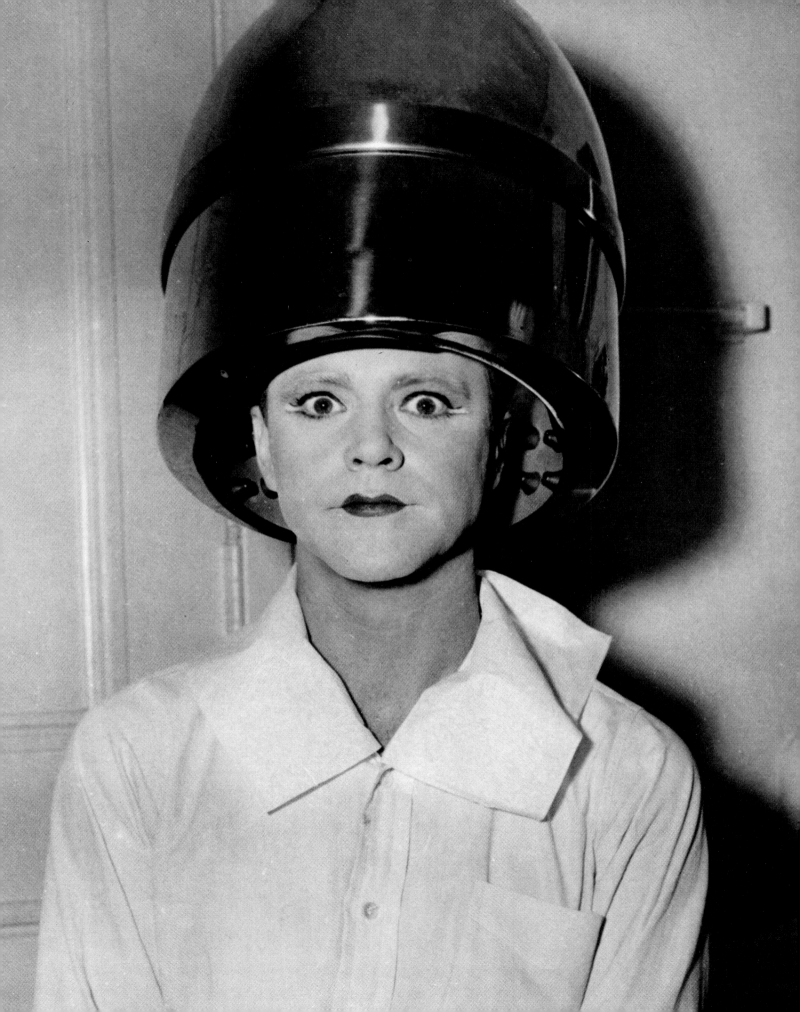

STAR BODIES
BY SHEILA PERKINS

Pity the poor moviegoer. There's no comparing normal bodies with the cinematic ones. The camera adds pounds, costumes subtract pounds; lighting adds shape, defines curves, and straightens lines. What isn't perfect has teams of people to correct it; what is gets amplified. If the Hollywood body isn't exactly make-believe, the premise that its shape is readily achievable borders on fantasy. Indeed, in movie magazines of the Golden Age, articles bearing star bylines suggested ways to trim down by exercising. In the late 1920s Joan Crawford advocated dancing: "I just dance whenever I have a chance," she said. "On the weekends I spend time practicing the newest steps." The next decade, Betty Grable suggested an hour a day of tap dancing to keep a body in shape, as did Eleanor Powell, who offered special steps that would help keep readers' legs trim. —The Editors

The 1920s brought the emaciated look to the screen with Marlene Dietrich and Carole Lombard flaunting their willowy images (despite the fact that neither was tall). Stars were starving themselves to look more like men, curves being an absolute taboo. A five-foot-one-inch Gloria Swanson was sleek and sophisticated at 110 pounds, always dressing to make her short stature look six feet tall. Cheek bones were hollow, and boyish figures were the fashion. Not until the 1930s, when Adrian gave Joan Crawford broad shoulders and a bustline,

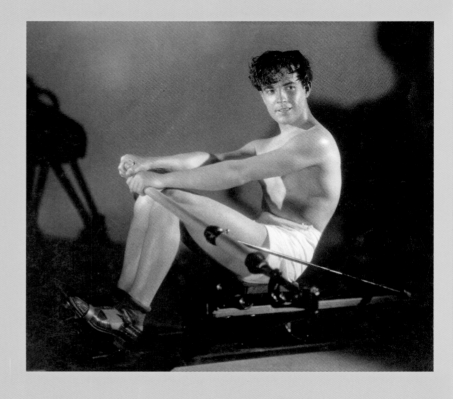

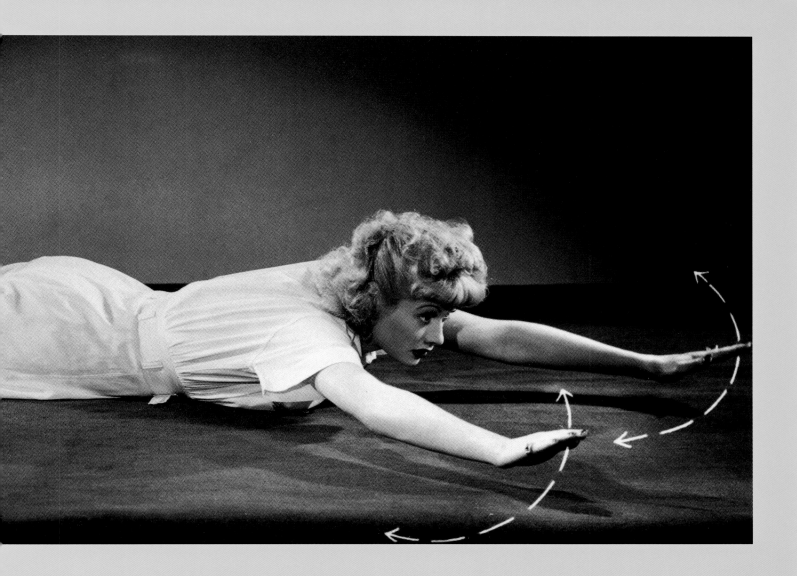

Above: What we love about Lucy is the way she makes us laugh, even when she's trying to show us how to exercise. Here the beloved Miss Ball keeps her back straight while doing simultaneous arm and leg lifts for an RKO promotional shot that appeared in *Photoplay-Movie Mirror* magazine in the late 1940s.
Left: Jayne Mansfield and her muscleman husband Mickey Hargitay had a home gym as early as 1963.
Opposite: A rowing machine never looked better than when Ramon Novarro broke a simulated sweat in 1924. Novarro had exercise equipment in his home, an unusual accoutrement in the 1920s. Most stars worked out at the studios or at local gyms.

did stars—Mae West notwithstanding—look anything but tiny, boyish, and flat. Trim bodies with gentle curves were stylish throughout most of the 1940s until Johnny came marching home.

But the constant pressure to fight flab led stars to turn their bodies over to Louise Long, a pricey masseuse hidden in the Hollywood environs, whose two-to-four-hour treatments eliminated the ripples and dimples now called cellulite. She pounded the fat away, often leaving her clients not just temporarily black and blue, but leaner and firmer. Then she insisted they exercise to aid the treatment. Long's long and very private list of stars included client names such as Marlene Dietrich and Marilyn Monroe.

In the years after World War II, studios demanded that their stars and starlets put on weight—men just home from the battlefield didn't want to see the lean and hungry look. They wanted something to hold on to. With Monroe, Jane Russell, and Jayne Mansfield to set the trends, the American public was being treated to legs, breasts, and voluptuous curves with each new movie produced. Many of the women started working out with bodybuilders from Santa Monica's Muscle Beach, men and women with sculpted bodies and pre-steroid musculature that had to be seen to be believed. Russell worked out with her own muscleman and husband, Bob Waterfield, and Jayne Mansfield married the man who helped mold her shape, strongman Mickey Hargitay. But about as soon as the public had broadened its beams and firmed its curves, along came Audrey Hepburn. Suddenly the full-hipped look was over. Audrey's rail-thin body was the mark of perfection.

Like any trends, movie-star bodies by necessity must be different from the public's. Right or wrong, the movie-star silhouette has always been something to aspire to, something to be glorified. So when the audience achieves it, it's unquestionably time to change the style. That's the Hollywood way.

Right: Back in the Hollywood Hills in 1967, Clint Eastwood exercised away any excess-pasta pounds after spending most of the decade in Italy making spaghetti westerns.

Opposite: When Marlon Brando played Stanley Kowalski in Tennessee Williams's *Streetcar Named Desire* (1951), the bulging muscles that protruded from his T-shirt became an immediate trend for young rebels.

Below: Clark Gable worked out throughout his career to keep his torso trim and his arms firm, a plus when he bared his chest in *It Happened One Night* (1934). Vain about his well-developed chest and narrow waist, he typically wore his shirts unbuttoned and his pants belted high and tight.

Below right: Rudolph Valentino works out in Santa Monica's Palisades Park and a camera just happens to be nearby to capture his muscles— and his varicose veins—on film.

MASTER OF THE MACABRE

BY ROGER CORMAN

There's more to a great horror film than a few scary surprises—just ask Alfred Hitchcock, or, as we did here, Roger Corman. Corman's the man who studied the works of Hitchcock and the stories of Edgar Allan Poe to shape his own modern form of macabre film. A magnet for talent in his long career, he hired the likes of Martin Scorsese, Jonathon Demme, Francis Ford Coppola, and Peter Bogdanovich in the earliest days in Hollywood. Here he shares how he mastered fright.   —The Editors

Three films from the Golden Age made a big impact on me at the time, and have been a lasting inspiration to me for their mastery of creating suspense and terror on screen. David Lean's *Great Expectations* (1946), with its opening graveyard sequence, Ingmar Bergman's *The Seventh Seal* (1957), and Alfred Hitchcock's *Psycho* (1960) showed me that the creation of suspense and terror is a matter not only of cinematic technique but also of understanding the symbolic power of film to tap into the unconscious fears of the audience.

However, the influences that propelled me into the horror-film genre were literary rather than cinematic. When I was in high school, I read Edgar Allan Poe's *The Fall of the House of Usher* and it so took hold of my imagination that I immediately asked my parents to give me the complete works of Poe as a birthday or Christmas present. Some years later, between 1960 and 1964, after I had made some low-budget movies in various genres, I directed eight films derived from Poe's macabre, psychologically unsettling tales and poems.

Freud was the second major influence on my approach to horror films. I read a great deal about Freudian psychoanalysis and the inner workings of the psyche. I believed that Poe and Freud had been working in different ways with the concept of the unconscious, so I tried to use Freud's theories to interpret the work of Poe. Poe was obsessed with symbolism and Freud was the master of symbolism. In fact, Poe's whole world of ruined sanctuaries, brooding trees, cawing ravens, cats, deaths, and funerals was a symbolic one. Horror (as in a nightmare) can be a re-enactment of our primal, suppressed fears of darkness, death, and sex. Our fears of darkness and death are paralleled by our childhood mixture of curiosity and fear about what is going on behind the parents' closed bedroom door, what those unfamiliar sounds in the night may be.

If you search for the most chilling moment in any horror film you will usually be able to relate it to a scene in which a character is seen either running away from or approaching some unspecified object of unparalleled terror. The moment before the revelation of the actual nature of that "thing" builds the tension. The frightened figure in terrified flight arouses more fear than anything that could lie at the end of that flight.

At the same time that I was reading Freud, I came across a book by a Beverly Hills psychiatrist who analyzed the connection between humor and horror, and realized that this could be applied to the construction and manipulation of suspense in horror films. An effective sequence in

One of Roger Corman's greatest hits was based on a story from Edgar Allan Poe, *The Masque of the Red Death* (1969). This lobby card features an intricately designed mask incorporating scenes from the film into Vincent Price's face.

horror depends on the building and release of tension. Sometimes it is good to build tension and give the audience a moment of release with a touch of humor, before building the tension again toward the climactic shock. One example of this can be seen in *The Masque of the Red Death* (1964) when Jane Asher, in a panic-stricken flight along dark corridors, comes face to face with a masked figure who suddenly steps out from behind a draped curtain. Fear is quieted when the mask reveals the smiling face of a practical joker, and provides a brief, temporary lull between the shudder-tactics of the story.

By the time I was preparing *The Raven* (1963), the fifth in the cycle of Poe movies I directed, both the writer, Richard Matheson, and I were getting a little burned out, and Dick suggested that we play it for laughs. I agreed, so long as we still delivered moments of real terror. Vincent Price, Peter Lorre, Boris Karloff, and Jack Nicholson played off each other brilliantly. In retrospect, I think, it was not until Anthony Hopkins played Hannibal Lechter in *The Silence of the Lambs* (1991) that anyone came along to really challenge these great horror actors in the ability to deliver both menace and wit.

3

"Real life" becomes a relative term when the subject is Hollywood. Where does the fantasy leave off and reality take over? Homes and cars reflect a person's taste and their eagerness to follow—or rebel against—trends and expectations, so they qualify in the "real" category, as do great marriages, the true reality check in Hollywood. Aspects that are out of a star's control, such as natural beauty, can't be argued about—makeup artists have recognized that reality factor from the earliest days of Hollywood. Other real-life challenges have turned people into stars—Billy Barty proves that nothing stands in the way of a great talent.

In 1952, Humphrey Bogart and Lauren Bacall bid goodbye to son Stephen before taking off in their XK120 Jaguar.

HOMES TO WRITE HOME ABOUT

862—Home of Bette Davis, North Hollywood, California

OB-H2560

For star-hungry tourists, finding the homes of the stars has always been relatively easy. In 1911, the first tour bus took sightseers to early Hollywood attractions, which were then limited primarily to pioneer film studios, growing residential districts, and picturesque orange groves, but in 1918 the first map of the stars' homes was published, listing mainly Hollywood homes. Two years later, Tanner Motor Tours organized the first sightseeing excursions of Beverly Hills using crowded double-decker buses.

Douglas Fairbanks and Mary Pickford, filmdom's glamour couple, were the first big stars to call Beverly Hills home. While not the first estate in the community—that was built in 1914 by Burton E. Green—their huge hillside estate, named Pickfair, was built in 1919 by Fairbanks, who brought his new bride to live there in 1920. Redesigned from 1924 to 1936 by Pickford's favorite architect, Wallace Neff (who would soon become Hollywood's most sought-after architect), Pickfair had a wall surrounding it to keep curious fans from sneaking onto the premises. While not all stars lived as lavishly, Beverly Hills offered an irresistible quiet charm. Its beauty lured Hollywood celebrities away from bustling Hollywood and staid Los Angeles. Gloria Swanson, Pola Negri, Tom Mix, and Richard Barthelmess followed Pickford and Fairbanks to the little town in the 1920s.

The official city limits of Hollywood have attracted many stars. But it wasn't

819—Beach Home of Cary Grant, Santa Monica, California

1B-H1017

824—Home of Tyrone Power, Brentwood, California

OB-H507

Top: Home of Bette Davis, North Hollywood, California
Middle: Beach home of Cary Grant, Santa Monica, California
Bottom: Home of Tyrone Power, Brentwood, California

Top: Marion Davies's Ocean House, Santa Monica, California **Bottom:** Rudolph Valentino's Falcon Lair, Beverly Hills, California

always a positive experience. Take, for instance, the imposing Craftsman-style house that was home to five well-known personalities. Situated on busy Hollywood Boulevard and built by grocery store magnate Albert Ralphs, the home was left empty when Ralphs was struck and killed by a falling boulder. In 1918, Fairbanks rented the house for a then-astronomical sum of five hundred dollars a month, but he left deeply depressed within months following marital problems with his first wife before he met Pickford. Then John P. Cudahy, son of the meatpacking mogul, purchased the estate. Hounded by lawsuits, the younger Cudahy committed suicide in the spring of 1921. Film producer Joseph Schenck took possession of the property for his protégée, Norma Talmadge, following their marriage. Norma separated from Schenck in 1928 and later filed for divorce. Emil Jannings, the esteemed actor, leased the house from Schenck for $1,250 a month. Although he was the first actor to win an Academy Award, he did not attend the ceremony held in 1929. He took refuge in his homeland, Germany, distraught by the advent of talkies, since his thick accent was no longer acceptable. He had had enough of that house and of Hollywood.

Other homes have become famous because they were immortalized in movies. The *Sunset Boulevard* (1950) house, at Wilshire and Irving Boulevards in Los Angeles, for example, was later used in *Rebel without a Cause* (1955). It has since been replaced by an office building. Also famed are the *Double Indemnity* (1944) house, at 6301 Quebec Street in Hollywood, and the *Whatever Happened to Baby Jane?* (1962) house at 172 S. McCadden Place in the Wilshire district of Los Angeles.

Tours are still available, and maps to stars' homes continue to be hawked on street corners. Ephemera collectors highly prize curiously tinted postcards—like those shown on these pages—from the early days of the film industry depicting the stars and their homes.

821 HOME OF HEDY LAMARR

John Hughes Photo

802 HOME OF BING CROSBY, TOLUCA LAKE, NORTH HOLLYWOOD, CALIF.

781. RESIDENCE OF JUDY GARLAND, BEL AIR, CALIFORNIA

FROM KODACHROME BY JUSMEY

787. HOME OF JANE WITHERS, WESTWOOD VILLAGE, LOS ANGELES, CALIF.

Opposite: Home of Hedy Lamarr
Left: Home of Jane Withers, Westwood Village, Los Angeles, California

816 HOME OF THE BENNYS (JACK BENNY AND MARY LIVINGSTON)

John Hughes Photo

Opposite: Home of Bing Crosby, Toluca Lake, North Hollywood, California
Left: Home of the Bennys (Jack Benny and Mary Livingston), Beverly Hills, California

785. RESIDENCE OF ERROL FLYNN, BEVERLY HILLS, CALIFORNIA

FROM KODACHROME

Opposite: Residence of Judy Garland, Bel Air, California
Left: Residence of Errol Flynn, Beverly Hills, California

PUBLIC FACES IN THEIR PRIVATE SPACES

I n the Golden Age of Hollywood stars didn't merely live in houses like normal folk; the studio moguls demanded that their human properties be surrounded by offscreen settings that were as dramatic as the movies they filmed. Though these homes were their private worlds, many stars bought the publicity prattle that surrounded them and opted to live in homes as big as their images—and their egos.

During the first two decades of the film industry, the film celebrities' homes that were photographed were as opulent as their fans hoped they would be. They were homes so special that they earned names of their own. Pickfair, the somewhat eponymous moniker of Mary Pickford and Douglas Fairbanks's domicile, was an opulent estate in Beverly Hills surrounded by a moat where the couple would sometimes canoe. Rudolph Valentino's Falcon Lair at the top of Benedict Canyon in Beverly Hills cost more than $175,000 to build in 1925, and then "the Sheik" filled it with more than sixty thousand dollars' worth of period furniture. But Harold Lloyd's Greenacres was the grandest estate of them all, a rambling Shangri-La befitting one of Hollywood's most successful actors. His forty-four-room Italian Renaissance mansion, which cost $2 million to build in 1928, was overshadowed by

Mae West's opulent apartment in Los Angeles, circa 1934, was as outrageously flamboyant as her image.

its abundant gardens that followed the slopes of Benedict Canyon. Fountains, pools, waterfalls, and a wooded entry drive that was nearly a mile long created a private world rivaled only later, perhaps, by Neverland Valley, the compound of the late-twentieth-century popstar turned movie star Michael Jackson, a home where the entertainer surrounded himself with his own amusement park, llamas, and armed guards.

In 1928, when William Randolph Hearst built a dream retreat for his mistress Marion Davies (who already had a huge home in Beverly Hills), he set out to make it the grandest on the coast. A 110-room mansion situated on the Pacific Coast Highway (when the house was built the thoroughfare was known as Beach Palisades Road) in Santa Monica, her beach house was a grand mélange of opulent this and gilded that. A miniature version of Hearst's own castle, San Simeon, the beach house featured a ballroom from a 1750 Venetian palazzo and a circa-1560 pub imported from Britian.

Outside, adjacent to the Pacific, was a 110-foot-long swimming pool inlaid with Italian marble, surrounded by Greek columns (and when guests used the pool, they had their choice of more than a thousand lockers to store their belongings). Her beach house sold in 1945 for $600,000, when Davies moved to San Simeon to live full time with the newspaper czar on his own turf. In 1949, the biggest building was remodeled and opened as a lavish hotel named Ocean House. Eight years later, that was demolished. Today, only a small portion of the beach manse remains on Santa Monica beach, ramshackle but filled with Hollywood history.

Stars were varied in their taste—some opted for the Hearstian, Valentinian, Lloydian, and Pickfordian style, while others chose to live closer to reality. A down-to-earth few—Jimmy Stewart in the 1940s, and in the 1950s, Marlon Brando, for instance—who could afford baronial environs, nixed grandiose mansions, even

Top: Joan Collins pauses in the ultra-classic foyer of her home to give a mod nod to the 1960s.
Above: John Barrymore admires the antique fireplace in his Beverly Hills home shortly before his death in 1942.
Opposite: Joan Crawford, posing at home in a gown by Adrian, circa 1928, overlooks her hand-decorated baby grand piano.

opted for simple bachelor pads, so they could honestly tell someone who might ask, that, indeed, they lived in private spaces, despite their public faces.

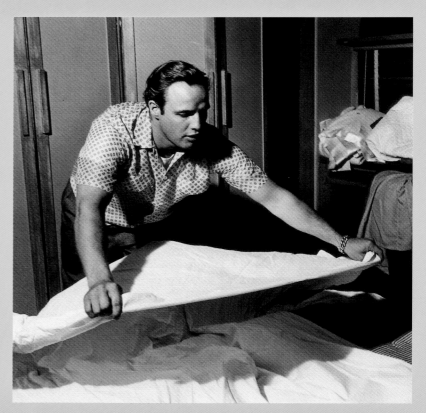

Top: Jimmy Stewart cracks nuts in his 1946 living room while his roommate, photographer John Swope, clicks away.
Above: Is Marlon Brando really making his own bed, or is he posing? Only photographer Sid Avery knows for sure.
Opposite: As if he just returned from the Bates Motel, Tony Perkins takes a rest in his 1950s living room.

MOVIES FULL OF "LIFE"

Movies are all about "real life," aren't they? The screenwriter is trying to capture it. The director is trying to re-create it. The actors are trying to put more life into their roles. The choreographers are asking dancers to add life to their step. And audiences are craving slices of life. Obviously, the people who name films are longing to get the point across, too. Hundreds of film titles contain the word "Life." Here's a selection of twenty films that begin with the four-letter word. (We list-makers just couldn't resist including *It's a Wonderful Life* (1946), because there's arguably no film that explains the meaning of the word better.)

Life (1920)
Life of the Party (1930)
Life Begins (1932)
The Life of Jimmy Dolan (1933)
The Life of Vergie Winters (1934)
Life Begins at Forty (1935)
Life Begins in College (1937)
The Life of Emile Zola (1937)
The Life of the Party (1937)
Life Begins for Andy Hardy (1941)
Life with Henry (1941)
Life Begins at Eight-Thirty (1942)
The Life of Jack London (1943)
Lifeboat (1944)
It's a Wonderful Life (1946)
Life with Blondie (1946)
Life with Father (1947)
The Life of Riley (1948)
A Life of Her Own (1950)
A Life in the Balance (1955)
Life Begins at 17 (1958)

Jimmy Stewart stars in one of the most sentimental movies of the 1940s, *It's a Wonderful Life*, which was nominated for four Academy Awards, including best picture.

SOUL MATES
BY SHEILA PERKINS

A marriage is difficult to maintain in the real world, where two people face normal, everyday stresses. But throw a celebrity or two into the coupling, and the marriage is catapulted into the limelight. With the pressures of fame—tabloids, paparazzi, and gossip columnists—most celebrity marriages dissolve after a few short years. Even in Hollywood's earliest days, when divorce was uncommon, holding a Hollywood marriage together was difficult. Mary Pickford and Douglas Fairbanks were the quintessential Hollywood glamour couple after they met on a Liberty Bond tour in 1920. Both were married, but quickly divorced their spouses so they could marry that same year. As they were making wedding plans,

HUMPHREY BOGART AND LAUREN BACALL:
Married May 21, 1945
Portraying a gangster on the silver screen was much easier for Humphrey Bogart than maintaining the perfect marriage. In the midst of his third failed marriage, Bogart met Lauren Bacall while shooting *To Have and Have Not* (1945). Their on-screen chemistry led to an offscreen marriage, based on intellectual conversation and witty humor. Bogie considered Bacall a "pal"—his highest compliment. Characteristic of their fierce devotion, they displayed the plastic bride-and-groom decoration from their wedding cake under a glass dome, right next to two other trophies: his Academy Award for best actor in *The African Queen* (1951), and the silver loving cup he earned racing his boat, *Santana*.

Mary asked Douglas, "What if the world doesn't approve? Will our love be strong enough if we both lose our careers? Will our love be sufficient for our happiness together?" To which Douglas strongly asserted, "I can't speak for you, Mary, but I know that my feeling for you is not of the moment. It has nothing to do with your career or your fame, or how other people feel about you. I love you for yourself. If you don't marry me you'll never see me again." Hollywood's most famous couple subsequently separated in 1933 and divorced in 1936.

King Vidor, the thrice-married director, once acknowledged with an intended double entendre, "Take it from me, marriage isn't a word, it's a sentence." But some Hollywood couples don't view it that way. Their happy unions have withstood the tests of time, paparazzi, children, and sexy costars. These couples embraced the loves of their lives, and stuck it out through thick and thin, without regard to their celebrity. Ask them their secrets to a happy marriage and inevitably the answer is a decided shrug. Ever the comedian, Bill Cosby explains a successful marriage this way: "For two people in a marriage to live together day after day is unquestionably the one miracle the Vatican has overlooked." Herewith, some Hollywood miracles. . . .

Right: JOANNE WOODWARD AND PAUL NEWMAN: Married January 29, 1958 Joanne Woodward first met a married Paul Newman at their mutual agent's office in 1952, but their attraction to each other only began after they worked together on Broadway. When he and his wife separated, Joanne and Paul publicly admitted their love. They married and continued to work side by side. When Paul made his directorial debut in *Rachel, Rachel* (1968), Joanne was nominated for an Academy Award in the lead role. Their union has lasted over four decades.

Right: SOPHIA LOREN AND CARLO PONTI: Married April 9, 1966 Teenage Sophia Loren met the very married producer Carlo Ponti when she entered a beauty contest. While living with Carlo, she gave him the ultimatum: marry her, or she was going off with Cary Grant, who was pursuing her. They married, but Italy's Catholic church wouldn't recognize the union. In Rome they lived under assumed names to avoid arrest. Carlo's other wife moved to France with them, where, as citizens, she could legally divorce him. Sophia said years later, "I could live very nicely without him. But I don't want to. The more years go by, the more I love him."

Left: CLARK GABLE AND CAROLE LOMBARD: Married March 29, 1939
Clark Gable, the king of Hollywood, with his irresistible sexual magnetism and his ability to seduce any woman in the business, said he only wanted to grow old with Carole Lombard. Cast together in the 1932 film *No Man of Her Own*, Gable and Lombard both were married when they fell in love. After each divorced and they lived together, the lovers finally married in 1939, after receiving an ultimatum from David O. Selznick, who was afraid that scandal about their romance would sully Gable's reputation and hamper the success of his *Gone with the Wind* (1939). Marriage didn't hurt Gable's sex-symbol status a bit. In fact, Lombard's raconteur style only helped him. When reporters asked for a new piece of Gable trivia, Lombard forthrightly responded, "Well, Clark isn't circumcised. Bet you didn't all know that." Their joy was short-lived, however. After finishing a tour selling war bonds in 1942, Lombard's plane crashed, killing all passengers. Gable said his life was ruined—he had lost his soul mate.

Right: GRACE KELLY AND PRINCE RAINIER: Married April 19, 1956
A fairy tale come true: the Prince of Monaco weds America's most glamorous movie star. Grace Kelly and Prince Rainier met briefly at a photo shoot in the south of France, but it took the matchmaking prowess of the prince's priest for the couple to fall in love. The holy man, who was an American assigned to the Monaco parish of St. Charles, orchestrated their second meeting, which did the trick. Married in Monaco with six hundred guests in attendance, the couple eventually had three children. Unbeknownst to her fans, Grace would have been forced to relinquish custody of their children to her royal spouse had she and the prince ever divorced. Princess Grace died in an automobile accident in 1982 and by the century's end, Prince Rainier had not remarried.

Left: BOB HOPE AND DOLORES READE: Married February 19, 1934
Bob Hope, applauded as the only performer who has triumphed in all five major media—vaudeville, stage, radio, motion picture, and television—has also achieved a marriage that has spanned seven decades, four children, and four grandchildren. Bob Hope met Dolores Reade during Broadway's *Roberta* (1933). Enraptured as Dolores sang "Did You Ever See a Dream Walking?" Bob soon proposed. In the 1940s, they entertained countless overseas U.S. troops, a tradition they continued through the Gulf War. The Hopes have been honored with charitable, congressional, political, and entertainment awards, and Bob has been labeled the "world's most decorated and honored man in entertainment." Broadcaster Larry King put him on the spot, asking about his fidelity during all those years of working with beautiful women. Bob fidgeted, and then admitted that temptation had crossed his path, "But I always wind up coming back to Dolores."

STARS WHO COOK

F ew Hollywood stars have turned their cooking skills into a burgeoning commercial food business the way Paul Newman has. Newman became famous as a chef making pasta and his special sauce for his friends. After so many of them urged him to market that sauce, Newman's Own was born in 1982. By the end of the twentieth century, Newman was producing not just pasta sauce and salad dressing, but popcorn, lemonade, salsa, steak sauce, and ice cream, profits from which benefit charities—"from salad dressing blessings flow," Newman once quipped. Numerous stars, including Dom De Luise and Sophia Loren, have produced best-selling cookbooks. Still others, including Dick Van Dyke and Brooke Shields, have put their kitchen skills to noncommercial use, volunteering to help prepare or serve food at homeless shelters.

Many celebrities simply like to tinker in the kitchen or to learn from their chief cooks the way Marilyn Monroe did from her longtime helper Eunice Murray. Doris Day, whose all-American image necessitated a strong-in-the-kitchen presence, frequently gave interviews in the 1960s that focused on food and cooking, and even contributed her favorite recipes to "all-star" cookbooks. Her celebrated costar in *Pillow Talk* (1959) Rock Hudson, was renowned for his parties in his Hollywood Hills home; whether it was a barbecue for a few friends or a sit-down dinner for 250 guests, Hudson was lead chef.

The history of stars in the kitchen

DORIS DAY'S GERMAN POTATO SALAD

6	medium potatoes, well scrubbed
1	large stalk celery, chopped
4	slices lean bacon
2/3 cup	water
1/2 cup	vinegar
3-4	scallions (white part only) choppped

1. Cook potatoes in skins until tender.
2. Cool slightly, peel, and slice into large bowl.
3. Add celery and scallions.
4. Cut up bacon into small strips and fry until crisp.
5. Add water and vinegar to bacon to create sauce.
6. Pour over potato, celery, scallion mixture and toss.
7. Cover and marinate several hours or overnight.

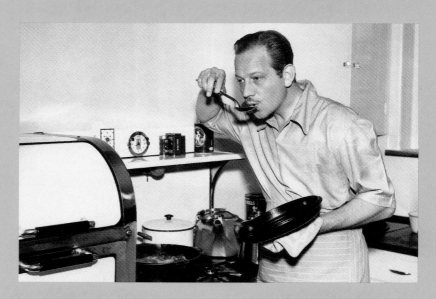

Above: Melvyn Douglas tastes his specialty, Hungarian goulash, while taking a break from filming *Our Wife* (1941).
Opposite: Rock Hudson barbecues California-style hamburgers in his backyard, circa 1952. "He had a great gift for putting everybody at ease, of making people feel comfortable and at home," noted Hudson's one-time roommate Tom Clark.

dates back to the earliest days of the film industry. Rudolph Valentino showing off his pasta-making skills in a studio publicity photo captures the Italian actor looking more natural than he looked in other promotional photographs of the day. Marion Davies's lavish home that W. R. Hearst built for her in Santa Monica featured a huge kitchen, large enough to prepare food for the hundreds—sometimes thousands—of guests who frequented the couple's parties. But did she cook? As she told *Movie Mirror* magazine in 1934, "I'm really not very good at cooking, but in Hollywood it's not essential. I just need to know when something tastes good."

Opposite: Rudolph Valentino offered the photographer a glimpse of the pasta he cooked, and flashed a smile—both rare sightings. A publicity man had found a unique aspect of Valentino's personality that had not been exploited before. But the down-home image didn't work. The Sheik never cooked in photos again.

Above: Paul Newman showed the makings of a chef in 1952, while Joanne Woodward played with kitty. His friends raved about his pasta sauce, so he finally marketed it, and a year later gave $100 million to charity from company profits.

Right: Marilyn Monroe examines the cooking of her housekeeper Eunice Murray in 1950. Murray was still working with Monroe when the actress died, but the housekeeper quietly disappeared to avoid interviews.

I WAS A HOLLYWOOD KID

BY BARBARA WHITING

It's never easy to be a kid in Hollywood. But that was especially true in the 1930s, 1940s, and 1950s, when parts for kids were taken by established stars such as Shirley Temple, Margaret O'Brien, Butch Jenkins, Natalie Wood, Dean Stockwell, Brandon De Wilde, and Elizabeth Taylor. So few kids counted on being stars or getting a break. But consider the pressure for the nonacting child in an entertainment family where big sister and Daddy are already Hollywood successes, growing up surrounded by "the business." Such was the world in which little Barbara Whiting grew up. And then one day, all of a sudden, the self-proclaimed "little monster" got discovered.
—The Editors

When I was a child, I never even dreamed about being in show business. I thought I already was. My father, Richard Whiting, wrote wonderful songs for the movies, songs like "Hooray for Hollywood," "Beyond the Blue Horizon," "On the Good Ship Lollipop," "Too Marvelous for Words," and "She's Funny That Way." My aunt, Margaret Young, had been a star in vaudeville, having toured with Al Jolson and Sophie Tucker. My mother, Eleanore, had managed her sister Margaret's career as well as Daddy's. And my older sister, Margaret, was a singer. (She still is.)

My best friends were the daughters of producers, directors, and writers. And our house always seemed to be filled with songwriters, such top musical talents as Frank Loesser, Harold Arlen, George Gershwin, Jule Styne, Jerome Kern, Johnny Mercer, Sammy Cahn, Jimmy Van Heusen, and Gus Kahn. But being the little monster that I was, I rarely saw much of them. I was usually in another room, locked safely out of sight. It was all right for sister Margaret to be with these important men. She was older, and because she sang, she got all the attention. Miffed, and definitely a brat, I wrote a poem in her honor called "I Hate Margaret." It went: "I hate Margaret. She'd make a good target. She sings, she thinks, but I think she stinks. I hate Margaret." My sister swore I would wind up in Tehachapi prison before I was twelve.

My best friend was the little girl next door, Judy Davies. Her father, Valentine Davies, was a screenwriter and a good friend of George Seaton, who had written and directed *The Song of Bernadette* (1943) for Jennifer Jones, and *Billy Rose's Diamond Horseshoe* (1945) for Betty Grable. Together, Valentine Davies and George Seaton would go on to win Academy Awards for *Miracle on 34th Street* in 1947.

By 1944 I had safely made it to age thirteen without landing in Tehachapi, even though I was still a terror. Little did I know that Judy's father was talking about me. He knew that George Seaton was preparing to film *Junior Miss* (1945), a comedy based on the hit Broadway show, and that Peggy Ann Garner had been cast as the teenage title character. "I still need a weird teenager to play Fuffy, her best friend," Seaton had told him.

"There's a weird thing living next door," Davies replied. It just so happened that Judy Davies was about to celebrate her thirteenth or fourteenth birthday, and her parents were throwing a big party to celebrate. I was

Top: Eleanore Whiting with her daughters, Margaret, and the pouty little "monster," Barbara
Above: Mabel Albertson, with Barbara and Margaret Whiting in CBS's *Those Whiting Girls*, circa 1956

invited along with some guys and gals from school. George Seaton and his wife were co-chaperones with Val and Liz Davies.

During the party the Seatons were everywhere, keeping the girls from kissing the boys and doing stuff teenagers do. They also had their eyes on me and another young girl, a budding actress, trying to decide which one of us might be weird enough to play Fuffy. The next thing I knew George Seaton was pulling me aside and asking questions. I guess I looked or acted "weird" enough for him to say, "Barbara, I'd like you to come and test for the part." Or maybe it was because my father was Richard Whiting and my sister was Margaret Whiting, who by then had a number of hit records to her credit. At any rate, he probably thought I knew something about show business.

I was floating on the day of the test, mostly because I didn't have to go to school. Instead, I was driven to Twentieth Century–Fox, where I had to read for George Seaton. Then I did a screen test, and when that was done, we went to the studio commissary for lunch. There I had my picture taken shaking hands with Fred MacMurray and William Bendix. Sitting at the next table were Betty Grable and Dan Dailey. When I arrived home that day and saw Margaret, I said, "You think you sing? Ha!" What a kid! To everyone's surprise, George Seaton loved my screen test and I became Fuffy in *Junior Miss* (1945). Looking back, I wasn't very good in the movie, but I did get laughs because the character had some funny lines.

I went on to appear in ten more movies, star as the title character in the hit radio series of *Junior Miss*, and teamed with Margaret for three seasons on TV in *Those Whiting Girls*, which was the summer replacement for *I Love Lucy*. That was great fun because I was able to be me and not another character. I loved working with Margaret and with Mabel Albertson, who played our mother.

In the late 1950s I was offered a television series with three other gals, but I said, "No, I'm going to marry a wonderful man and move to Michigan." That's what I did and I've never regretted the decision. Today it seems like I was lucky to have actually been in show business, but at the time it seemed like a natural thing. All my friends and young studio pals, such as Peggy Ann Garner, Beverly Wills, Lon McCallister, Connie Marshall, Roddy McDowall, and Elizabeth Taylor, were in show business, too. For us it was all a part of growing up in Hollywood.

HEAD FIRST INTO HOLLYWOOD
BY BILLY BARTY

The people who directed Austin Powers: The Spy Who Shagged Me *(1999) might never have found a little person brave enough to try acting if it hadn't been for Billy Barty. Billy remains the most famous actor in the world who's less than four feet tall. His career has spanned more than seventy years in the entertainment field and because of his talent and success, little people have been cast in numerous roles in Hollywood films. Here he shares the story of how a very little kid got his big start and how he remained a big star.* —The Editors

"Why don't you try your luck in Hollywood? It's a new line of opportunity."

When Rod Steiger, as W. C. Fields, posed that question to me, playing his sidekick, in the 1976 film *W. C. Fields and Me*, my reply was, "For me? Ridiculous!"

That would have probably been my answer in real life as well if someone had asked me the same question seventy years ago. After all, what possible opportunity could have existed in the film capital of the late 1920s for me, a three-year-old "little person," living in Millsboro, Pennsylvania, population four hundred?

And yet, my father, an enterprising fellow, who had grown weary of running his car dealership and who was eager to test the possibilities out West, packed the family into our Dodge and left the gray skies of our river town behind. On January 4, 1928, we set out for the renowned sunny climate of southern California.

Our first home in Hollywood was two blocks from Santa Monica Boulevard, then the site of a cluster of movie studios. One day, my father and I were out walking and we passed a movie company shooting on the sidewalk. The crew took notice of me, and my father, proud of my latest trick, said, "Spin on your head, Billy." I did. The director, Jules White, was amused and put me in the film *Wedded Blisters*, a tuxedo comedy released in 1928; thus began a career of more than seventy years in the entertainment business.

That head spin really served me well. I used it in *Soup to Nuts* (1930), *A Midsummer Night's Dream* (1934), and again, three decades later in *Harum Scarum* (1965). I haven't "spun" lately.

Over the years, I have played a variety of film roles, from the title role in *Rumpelstiltskin* (1987) to a tough newspaper vendor; from a Bible salesman to a German spy. I have portrayed circus performers, mythical beings, and an assortment of heroes and villains, often in prosthetic makeup and costumes that weighed almost as much as I did. In fact, in the 1933 version of *Alice in Wonderland*, in which I played the baby, the white pawn, and the pig, actor Ned Sparks walked into makeup one day, took one look at me, and asked the makeup artist, "What are you trying to do, kill the kid?"

In many films, I was cast as the "mischievous child" after having appeared in baby roles until I was almost eight. I then played eight-year-olds for five

Billy Barty's long career included the role of Ludwig in *W. C. Fields and Me* (1976), which also starred Rod Steiger.

years, which is one rare advantage to being a little person actor. One disadvantage is that a little person is not likely to be cast as a leading man, but nevertheless, I can claim to having been held in the arms of Bernadette Peters on-screen. Unfortunately it wasn't a romantic part; I was playing a baby.

I am forever indebted to a special-effects person on the *Foul Play* (1978) set who forgot to score a vase (to make it break easily) that Goldie Hawn was supposed to use to hit me over the head. First strike: it didn't break. Goldie struck again: it didn't break. Finally on the third blow, the vase began to crumble. Talk about seeing stars! Goldie was so upset that for the next half hour, she held me on her lap and applied ice to my forehead. Despite the pain, I found myself transported back to the time when "America's Sweetheart" Mary Pickford had held me on her lap after my appearance with the Hollywood Baby Orchestra at Pickfair.

Naturally, as a young child, I did not realize the importance of the directors I was working for; some were legends, others legends in the making. Today, I look back and realize my good fortune. James Whale, master of the horror film, put me in his now classic *Bride of Frankenstein* (1935). Producer/director Max Reinhardt never complained that I couldn't pronounce the word "Professor," as he was called on the set of *A Midsummer Night's Dream* (1934). I tried, but it came out "So-fessor." One of my favorite directors was Busby Berkeley. Before we were going to shoot one of the big production numbers in *Golddiggers of 1933* (1933), he asked me if I knew how to roller skate. I had never been on skates, but it looked easy enough, and whatever Mr. Berkeley asked me to do, I was going to do. I guess I managed to do all right because he hired me again, for *Footlight Parade* (1933).

In 1987, when I was cast in the George Lucas-inspired film *Willow* (1988), I was unsure about how I should address director Ron Howard. He had come a long way from television's *Andy Griffith Show* and *Happy Days* and had gained respect as a very talented film director. I was serious when I asked him, "How shall I address you, as Mr. Director or Sir?" He replied, "Billy, you've known me since I was nine years old. Call me Ronnie."

When I was handed the script for *The Day of the Locust* (1975), a chilling story about Hollywood in the 1930s, I was shocked by some of the language in the script. Here was an opportunity to work with the highly regarded director John Schlesinger, but for me, a Mormon, to use profanity—even in a film—posed a serious moral issue. At the reading, I was offered the role. I explained to Mr. Schlesinger and to the producer, Jerome Hellman, that I would have a difficult time with some of the dialogue. They generously offered to let me change any words that bothered me as long as it didn't interfere with the role or the story-line. It remains one of my favorite film roles because it took me out of comedy and allowed me to be recognized as a dramatic actor. I did all my own stunts in *Locust*, which included the handling of a crazed rooster for the cockfighting scene. A rooster can be very threatening to someone three feet nine inches tall.

Early on in my career I worked in dozens of the "Mickey McGuire" comedy shorts that starred my friend, Mickey Rooney. All of us kids did many stunts that child actors would not be allowed to do today. I remember having to shimmy down the side of a building on a rope for one scene, and for another, swinging à la Tarzan from rooftop to rooftop.

It would seem from the story that my work in films was continuous—not so. From 1934 to 1941 I traveled throughout the forty-eight states and parts of Canada with my family on the vaudeville circuit—we were "Billy Barty and Sisters." At age fourteen, I was too young to get a part in MGM's *The Wizard of Oz* (1939), which employed 125 little people (more than any film until *Willow*, which employed three hundred). By law you had to be eighteen to work the long hours that the film demanded. I was lucky I had a vaudeville career going strong already. When I got back to Hollywood, I took time off to attend Los Angeles City College (where I lettered in basketball—but that's another story).

After college, my dream was not to return to acting, but rather to be a sportswriter or a sportscaster. But one day in 1946, my friend, Jerry Maren, the "Lollipop Kid" in *The Wizard of Oz*, said, "Come on, Billy, let's go over to Metro and audition for *Three Wise Fools* (1946)." We were both hired for the film and I was off to follow the Hollywood road again.

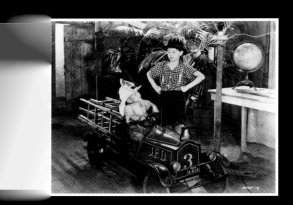

Above: Billy Barty, in the fire truck, appeared opposite Mickey Rooney, standing, in the early "Mickey McGuire" comedy serials.
Right: In the late 1920s, to become members of the official Hollywood Baby Orchestra, children five years old and under had to be able to sight-read music. Their playtime was spent rehearsing, and it paid off with a busy performance schedule. In this photo, taken on December 24, 1931, the youngsters are seen playing their miniature instruments at a party hosted by Marion Davies, whose handwriting is seen on the photo, on a sound stage at MGM studio in Culver City. The conductor, standing on a chair (center) is Billy Barty, a little person who, at eight years old, looked much younger than his years. Karl Moldrem led the group. (He and his wife can be seen at the piano.)

"Baby Orchestra" entertaining at M.G.M. Picture Studios — Hollywood Cal.

MAX FACTOR'S FABULOUS FACES

Below: Greta Garbo, whose natural eyelashes were, as Max Factor noted, "more lovely than any artificial lashes I can supply," became even more striking with the use of brown, not black, mascara and variegated shades of gray eye shadow.
Bottom: Maureen O'Hara, of the fiery red hair, helped promote Max Factor's "Color Harmony" makeup, the first cosmetics to show women how to select makeup based on a combination of hair color, eye color, and skin tone.
Opposite: Loretta Young, an elegant beauty, was a frequent visitor to Max Factor's salon in Hollywood. In 1953, when she started her television career after three decades on the big screen, Young surprised audiences by her still-youthful appearance. She credited Factor's cosmetics for her flawless skin.

Until Max Factor, nice women never wore makeup. (Even the word "makeup" was taboo in social circles.) But the genius of this young immigrant, who arrived in America in 1904, literally turned the image, as well as the business, of cosmetics upside down.

As the father of modern makeup, Max Factor changed the faces of the world. Beginning in the early days of cinema, he was responsible for countless innovations and helped define the standard of modern beauty. Because of Max, the movies began to take on a new glamour, and every woman soon wanted to look as flawlessly beautiful as her favorite star.

Born in Lodz, Poland, Max Faktor (the family name changed to Factor when he landed in the United States) launched his career at age eight when he became an apprentice to a wigmaker. By the time he was fourteen, he was a wigmaker to the Imperial Russian Grand Opera. And by age twenty-two, he was hairstylist and cosmetician to the royal family.

But even a link to the royal family was not enough to keep Max safe from increasing religious persecution. Max and his growing family fled to America in 1904. They settled in St. Louis, where Max exhibited hairpieces, creams, and perfumes at the St. Louis World Exposition. Four years later, he relocated to the theatrical district of downtown Los Angeles, where he opened "Max Factor's Antiseptic Hair Store," selling made-to-order wigs, toupees, and imported stage makeup, which was greasepaint in

stick form. It had to be applied one-eighth-inch thick, then powdered, forming a heavy mask. When it dried, it cracked. That was fine for the stage but not for the movies, where the cameras moved in for close-ups.

Early comedians, such as Ben Turpin, Louise Fazenda, and Charlie Chaplin, were the first film stars to come to Factor's little downtown store, requesting a makeup that was flexible enough to allow full facial movement and expression. The new makeup Max formulated was thinner and in cream form; it became the first makeup created specifically for movies.

Soon other film actors arrived with makeup requests: Rudolph Valentino wanted a special shade to compliment his olive skin; Douglas Fairbanks, whose athletic stunts thrilled movie audiences, needed a perspiration-proof makeup. Actresses, too, began flocking to Max with their own special requests. It wasn't much later that he created a line of makeup that for the first time coordinated with the color of a woman's hair, eyes, and complexion. Max Factor's "Color Harmony" would soon revolutionize the cosmetics business.

Max had unwavering standards for beauty, and he offered his beauty secrets to every star in Hollywood. For the actresses of the 1920s, Max created "Bee-Stung Lips," color on the bow and pout of lips, and then spreading color to the corners, known as "Cupid's Bow Lips." He gave "the smear" to Joan Crawford, a lipstick style that had no bow—color spread across her lips, which became her dramatic, trademark lip look. Bette Davis adopted "the smear" too.

For lovely Phyllis Haver, Max developed the first false eyelashes made from human hair. For Marlene Dietrich, he added real gold dust to her hair, which gave it a glow on-screen. Merle Oberon's naturally high forehead was dramatized by pulling back

Audrey Hepburn was partial to her heavy brows even though Factor had suggested she pluck and reshape them to look like every other star's in Hollywood. When she refused, he then showed her how to emphasize their lush beauty.

her hair, rather than covering up the forehead with bangs.

When Howard Hughes brought his young
starlet Jean Harlow to Max Factor her natural blond hair was made shockingly lighter.
Women everywhere rushed to copy the
shade. (Harlow credited Hughes's "clever
publicity man," Lincoln Quarberg, for coin-
ing the term "Platinum Blonde.")

Max's choice of makeup for gorgeous
Hedy Lamarr caused him to receive more
requests for her beauty secrets than for any
other star. The trick that worked for the
most women was to extend eye shadow onto
the sides of the bridge of the nose, minimiz-
ing the nose and making the eyes appear
larger. (She was Max Factor's "Girl of the
Year" in 1938.)

Of all the stars, Max Factor had his
favorites, "Fabulous Faces" as he called
them, whose beauty endured the test of
time. When Max died in 1938, his son, Max
Factor, Jr., continued this tradition of naming the top Hollywood beauties—Max Factor's
"Girl of the Year"—until the company
merged with a conglomerate in 1973. On
these pages are some of the actresses
dubbed as Factor's "Fabulous Faces."

Opposite top: Lena Horne, whose African-American skin was very light, was forced by her studio bosses to use a darker shade of Max Factor makeup to appear "more black" for a screen test.

Opposite bottom: Dolores Del Rio, born in 1905, was a celebrated starlet with stunning looks. Factor cooed and said there was little to do to her exquisite face but add highlights and thin her thick brows.

Below: Hedy Lamarr, nicknamed "the Most Beautiful Woman in Films," caused Max Factor to say that the Austrian's perfect complexion allowed her to get by without using foundation.

Below right: Lucille Ball credited her makeup to Max Factor from 1935 and throughout her TV career. Factor's makeup director, Hal King, left the Factor salon in 1960 to become Ball's personal makeup man.

Right: Rita Hayworth became a redhead under Max Factor's guidance. In 1938, Factor advised electrolysis to remove the hair growth on her temples and forehead, creating a widow's peak in the process.

STARS ON WHEELS

Certain accoutrements of stardom are *de rigueur*: a notable home, a good haircut, a swimming pool, diamonds, a fabulous wardrobe (or at least an expensive one), and, of course, a great set of wheels. Perhaps the greatest fantasy American movie fans have shared is the dream to one day drive cars like their favorite stars own. From Mary Pickford's brand new Model A, to James Dean's death-mobile, to Elvis's stable of wheels, an actor or actress's choice of transportation has always reflected his or her chosen image. Some, such as Steve McQueen, Peter Fonda, and Errol Flynn, selected two-wheeled vehicles to create temporary images during various phases of their lives. Paul Newman, who has long pursued a passion for race-car driving, elected to spend his seventy-fifth birthday racing around a professional track. Marlene Dietrich celebrated her thirty-first birthday with a new sixteen-cylinder Cadillac, which she had customized with a huge trunk to accommodate the numerous large pieces of luggage she carried. Although Hollywood studios demanded that stars drive luxurious vehicles, cars were at least one part of their lives that the celebrities could control, a four-wheeled reflection of their dreams.

James Dean gasses up his Porsche Spider 550. Dean was driving this car when he had his fatal accident on a central California roadway in 1955.

Right: Marlene Dietrich poses with her brand new 1932 Cadillac. In the winter her chauffeur Briggs, who always toted two revolvers, wore a uniform with a mink collar for extra warmth—and the necessary chic.
Below right: Mary Pickford received the first Ford Model A to roll off the assembly line. She and her husband Fairbanks were close friends of Henry Ford, so he made certain that Hollywood's A-couple had the appropriate model.
Opposite: Robert Montgomery takes aim for the photographer as he drives around the MGM studio backlot.

Above: Audrey Hepburn and Mel Ferrer admire their new 1953 Thunderbird.

Right: Elvis Presley bought this 1956 Ford Thunderbird shortly after his success with "Hound Dog" and "Don't Be Cruel," at a price of about $3,500. Dubbed "the personal luxury car," the two-seater T-Bird had power windows, a rare feature in the 1950s. Elvis could not keep all the cars he bought, so he simply gave them away.

4

Bottom line, what gets recorded on film is the essence of Hollywood and it can impact the world, a handful of fans, or an individual. If it hadn't been for her film career, one of America's favorite First Ladies never would have met her husband and might never have become queen of the free world. And if it weren't for the movies, would a billion people crowd around the television screen every spring to see "the Academy Award goes to . . ."? Four of Hollywood's most beloved stars share "reel life" stories in the pages that follow, emphasizing that what happens in the movies can change a life forever. . . .

Busby Berkeley choreographed the intricate "By a Waterfall" number for *Footlight Parade* (1933). His overhead camera positions became known as the "Berkeley top shot," a term still used in the film industry.

REEL LIFE

HOLLYWOOD KISSES

BY ROBERT STACK

Hollywood is a fickle lot. Kisses can be as cheap as the script they're written into, and often as meaningless. But some, a blessed few, are so filled with emotional power that they can never be forgotten. In 1939 an unknown Robert Stack was so convincing when he gave aging child star Deanna Durbin her first kiss in First Love *(1939)*, that his career was born.   —The Editors

One day, not long after my twentieth birthday, a friend asked me to go with him to watch Deanna Durbin on the set of her newest movie, *Three Smart Girls Grow Up* (1939). We were standing around listening to Deanna sing when a little guy with a heavy German accent walked up to me and said, "How would you like to be in pictures?" "Who, me?" I asked. "Yes, you. You make a little test with Helen Parrish." The man was Deanna's director, Henry Koster, so I made the test and wound up playing the lead opposite America's sweetheart in her next film, *First Love* (1939).

Deanna was a teenager who was fast becoming a woman. Her earlier films, *Three Smart Girls* (1936) and *One Hundred Men and a Girl* (1937), had made millions of dollars for Universal and had saved the studio from bankruptcy. The fact that she was growing up scared the hell out of everybody. They didn't know if audiences would show up to see a "maturing" Deanna. In other words, they really didn't know what to do with her—or with Mother Nature.

To ease Deanna into her grown-up

Above: Ready for the big kiss, Dolores Del Rio and Charles Farrell embrace with all the passion director Raoul Walsh could elicit from them in *The Red Dance* (1928).
Right: Sophia Loren blows a kiss to the camera—or the cameraman.

years, someone came up with the idea of "her first love" and, of course, her first kiss. It was a Cinderella story, with Deanna as Cinderella and me as a half-assed Prince Charming.

There were some rough moments in building up the romance between the two of us. It was my first picture, and I had no idea what I was doing. There was one scene when I was supposed to see Deanna and begin to fall in love with her. At that point, Henry said, "Are you ready?" "Where's Deanna?" I asked. "She's gone home," he replied. "What? But how..." "This is what you do," Henry said. He took a blackboard and put a big X on it. "Here she is," he added, pointing to the X. "You're an actor. It's Deanna. Now you see her. Now she's attractive. Now you think you're falling in love."

I kept looking at that X as we filmed and my eyes got kind of bleary. (So help me God, when the reviews came out, one critic noted: "Robert Stack, in his first picture, showed wonderful potential of passion. His eyes even seemed to glaze.")

The kiss lasted a nice three or four seconds—at least she was there! It was wonderful. Kissing a girl was easy for me. But audiences never saw our full kiss. When the movie was released, it had been trimmed to a millisecond peck. The studio got cold feet, afraid that all the publicity about Deanna growing up would backfire. They even turned down a cover of *Life* magazine, fearing negative public reaction.

Deanna's first kiss not only made worldwide headlines and solidified her stardom. It was also a great springboard for me. I wasn't prepared for the sudden fame.

Top right: Ann-Margret and Elvis Presley lock lips in *Viva Las Vegas* (1964).
Right: Charlton Heston gets a hold on Haya Harareet in *Ben-Hur* (1959).
Opposite: Burt Lancaster and Deborah Kerr smooch on the beach in *From Here to Eternity* (1953).

WEEPIES

They tear your heart out. "Weepies" are tearjerkers or movies rated by the number of handkerchiefs it takes to get through the final frames. "Chick flicks" today, they were "women's pictures" (and their directors were called "women's directors") in the Golden Age, mainly because their plot lines are often driven by either a doomed love affair, unrequited love, infidelity, or separation. If love isn't the issue, it's probably a family crisis, illness, amnesia, a life-threatening accident, death, or war ravaging the family unit—more reasons to reach for tissues.

A mother's love for her child can be overwhelmingly emotional in such films as *Stella Dallas* (1937), *Imitation of Life* (1934), and *To Each His Own* (1946). Men and women alike wept openly during *The Sullivans* (1944), the true story of five brothers from the same family who were lost when their ship was torpedoed during World War II. Through the years weepies have taught us that a good cry feels good. When our tears are over, we rejoice that "it was just a movie."

Olivia de Havilland received an Academy Award for her performance in *To Each His Own* (1946); here she dances with her "nephew" John Lund as the audience pulls out the hankies. A perfect "women's picture weepie," *To Each His Own* features de Havilland as the loving mother who gives up her illegitimate son for adoption, devotes her life to loving him as his "aunt," yet never reveals her deep, dark secret, despite their constant contact.

Back Street (1932)
Universal
Director: John M. Stahl
Cast: Irene Dunne, John Boles

Imitation of Life (1934)
Universal
Director: John Stahl
Cast: Claudette Colbert, Warren William,
Louise Beavers

Magnificent Obsession (1935)
Universal
Director: John M. Stahl
Cast: Irene Dunne, Robert Taylor

Camille (1937)
Metro-Goldwyn-Mayer
Director: George Cukor
Cast: Greta Garbo, Robert Taylor

Madame X (1937)
Metro-Goldwyn-Mayer
Director: Sam Wood
Cast: Gladys George, John Beal

Stella Dallas (1937)
Samuel Goldwyn
Director: King Vidor
Cast: Barbara Stanwyck, John Boles

Dark Victory (1939)
Warner Bros.
Director: Edmund Goulding
Cast: Bette Davis, George Brent

Love Affair (1939)
RKO
Director: Leo McCarey
Cast: Charles Boyer, Irene Dunne

The Old Maid (1939)
Warner Bros.
Director: Edmund Goulding
Cast: Bette Davis, Miriam Hopkins,
George Brent

The Grapes of Wrath (1940)
Twentieth Century-Fox
Director: John Ford
Cast: Henry Fonda, Jane Darwell, John
Carradine

Penny Serenade (1941)
Columbia
Director: George Stevens
Cast: Cary Grant, Irene Dunne

King's Row (1942)
Warner Bros.
Director: Sam Wood
Cast: Ann Sheridan, Robert Cummings,
Ronald Reagan

None but the Lonely Heart (1944)
RKO
Director: Clifford Odets
Cast: Cary Grant, Ethel Barrymore

The Purple Heart (1944)
Twentieth Century-Fox
Director: Lewis Milestone
Cast: Dana Andrews, Richard Conte

Since You Went Away (1944)
David O. Selznick
Director: John Cromwell
Cast: Claudette Colbert, Joseph Cotten

**The Sullivans or The Fighting
Sullivans (1944)**
Twentieth Century-Fox
Director: Lloyd Bacon
Cast: Anne Baxter, Thomas Mitchell

The White Cliffs of Dover (1944)
Metro-Goldwyn-Mayer
Director: Clarence Brown
Cast: Irene Dunne, Alan Marshal

Tomorrow Is Forever (1945)
RKO
Director: Irving Pichel
Cast: Orson Welles, Claudette Colbert

The Best Years of Our Lives (1946)
Samuel Goldwyn
Director: William Wyler
Cast: Fredric March, Myrna Loy

It's a Wonderful Life (1946)
RKO
Director: Frank Capra
Cast: James Stewart, Donna Reed

To Each His Own (1946)
Paramount
Director: Mitchell Leisen
Cast: Olivia de Havilland, John Lund

The Yearling (1946)
Metro-Goldwyn-Mayer
Director: Clarence Brown
Cast: Gregory Peck, Jane Wyman

I Remember Mama (1948)
RKO
Director: George Stevens
Cast: Irene Dunne, Barbara Bel Geddes

My Foolish Heart (1949)
Samuel Goldwyn
Director: Mark Robson
Cast: Susan Hayward, Dana Andrews

An Affair to Remember (1957)
Twentieth Century-Fox
Director: Leo McCarey
Cast: Cary Grant, Deborah Kerr

AMERICA'S ULTIMATE CO-STAR

BY BETTY GOODWIN

Opposite: Nancy Davis played a pregnant homemaker in *The Next Voice You Hear* (1950); her wardrobe test proved she could look unsophisticated.
Below: Just as she met Ronald Reagan, Nancy Davis was cast as a socialite in *East Side, West Side* (1949).

ancy Davis had every intention of making it big as an actress, even though she gained fame on another stage, opposite her husband, Ronald Reagan, fortieth president of the United States.

"I didn't have time to discover whether I could ever join the upper galaxy," she said dreamily in her autobiography, *Nancy,* written with Bill Libby, of her brief, forgettable film career, which she abandoned soon after she married Reagan.

In fact, Nancy was genetically disposed to acting. Her mother, Edith Luckett, was a flamboyant leading lady of the teens and 1920s. At fifteen, Edith joined the stock company managed by her brother Joseph and went on to work in companies around the country. She appeared in one road show produced by the famous showman George M. Cohan. While working one summer in Pittsfield, Massachusetts, she dazzled young Kenneth Robbins, descendent of a conservative New England family, and they married just before he enlisted in the army during World War I. The couple separated after their daughter Anne Francis—known familiarly as Nancy—was born on July 6, 1921.

Nancy was immersed in her mother's theatrical world. Her godmother was actress Alla Nazimova and her mother's many famous friends included Walter Huston, Spencer Tracy, ZaSu Pitts, Pat O'Brien, and Josh Logan. Nancy loved nothing more than playing dress-up in her mother's clothes and watching her work from the wings. When Edith married Dr. Loyal Davis, a Chicago physician, she retired from the stage but worked for many years in national radio soap operas. She also continued to surround herself and family with her theater friends. In 1938, Nancy asked Dr. Davis if he would adopt her, and her natural father signed the necessary documents.

In high school, Nancy began appearing in plays, carrying on the family tradition and, perhaps also foreshadowing her biggest role, she played the lead in the George S. Kaufman–Katharine Dayton comedy, *First Lady.* At Smith College, Nancy majored in drama and English and had parts in many college productions. During summers, she worked as an apprentice in summer stock theaters and playhouses in New England.

Through her mother's friend ZaSu Pitts, a Metro-Goldwyn-Mayer star, Nancy was hired for her first professional role in the touring play *Ramshackle Inn,* in which Pitts was starring. Nancy spoke three lines. When the play arrived in New York, Nancy decided to stay. Reportedly at the insistence of Mary Martin, one of Dr. Davis's patients, Nancy was cast in a small, nonspeaking part as a Chinese handmaiden in *Lute Song,* starring Martin and Yul Brynner, which had a six-month run on Broadway. Two more plays with Pitts, *Cordelia* and *The Late Christopher Bean,* followed. "Nicely sweetened without saccharin," one critic said of her performance in the latter. During the late 1940s, Nancy also counted among her accomplishments three dates with Clark Gable, whom she met through Spencer Tracy.

A dinner date with Benjamin Thau, a honcho at MGM, with whom she

PROD: 1488
NAME: NANCY DAVIS
WARD CHG # I
2/13/50

Above: Ronald Reagan married Nancy on March 4, 1952, and her future was determined. **Opposite:** In 1955, the Reagans were still living in southern California, both pursuing their Hollywood careers.

reportedly had a romance, led to the all-important Hollywood screen test. Her mother saw to it that Tracy—who had benefited from Dr. Davis's help for his deaf son, John—put in a good word for her daughter at the studio. Tracy did more than that. He asked the studio's top director, George Cukor, to direct the test and top cinematographer George Folsey to photograph it. Nancy was signed to a seven-year contract.

Nancy made eleven films from 1949 to 1956. *Variety* liked her in her first movie, *Shadow on the Wall*, noting her "standout performance as a child psychiatrist. Actress definitely is a comer." Three pictures later, Nancy's name went above the title in *The Next Voice You Hear* (1950), playing James Whitmore's pregnant wife in a low-budget, religious-themed movie. The *New York Times* noted that Nancy was "cheerful and considerate." Still, the movie closed after one week. She played Whitmore's wife again two years later in *Shadow in the Sky* (1951). Nancy believed her best picture was *Night into Morning* (1951), starring Ray Milland, in which she played John Hodiak's fiancée. It was one of the few times, Nancy admitted, she "wasn't a wife." Still, she wasn't exactly a femme fatale. She later played a schoolteacher opposite Fredric March in *It's a Big Country* (1951) and was George Murphy's wife in *Talk about a Stranger* (1952), which even Nancy admitted was a clunker.

Nancy met Ronald when another Nancy Davis—an ice skater who earlier had worked in Sonja Henie pictures—appeared on a list of Communist sympathizers in the *Hollywood Reporter*. The future Mrs. Reagan asked Mervyn LeRoy, who was directing her in *East Side, West Side* (1949), to call Screen Actors Guild president Ronald Reagan to help her distance herself from potential scandal. Ronald reported back to the director that there were four or five Nancy Davises working in Hollywood, only one of whom was an actress. He promised LeRoy that if she ever had any problems, the Guild would handle them on her behalf. "I didn't think that should be the end of it," Nancy said. She was frankly interested in meeting Ronald, who was considered a catch ever since his divorce from Jane Wyman. The next call LeRoy made was to suggest to Ronald that he take Nancy on a blind date.

On March 4, 1952, after a three-year courtship, Nancy became Ronald's second wife. Nancy wanted to quit acting as soon as they were married in order to devote herself to her husband and to start a family, but she says she was "talked into" making a few more films. The last movie she made was *Hellcats of the Navy* in 1957 so that she could work with her husband. Having played Ronald's fiancée in the film, Nancy recalled that a scene in which she had to say goodbye to him was extremely difficult for her and had to be reshot many times.

Once again, Nancy got decent notices, although she wasn't exactly setting the town on fire. Her final professional appearances were on the *General Electric Theater*, a weekly half-hour television series that her husband hosted. And before too long, she was costarring with him, first in the California governor's mansion, and then in the White House.

HOLLYWOOD MUSICALS

M ost fans equate the advent of sound movies with the premiere of *The Jazz Singer* (1927), despite the fact that sound on film debuted earlier. Al Jolson's classic was the first to put a full-blown musical on the screen complete with singing and dancing that everyone could hear.

The crowds that lined up at the box office to hear Jolson sing "Mammy" encouraged Hollywood to produce numerous musicals such as *The Rogue Song* (1930) and *Manhattan Parade* (1931), complete with chorines and hoofers, accordion-playing comedians and ballerinas, anything that would add some high notes to a soundtrack. Even Mary Pickford tried singing and dancing in *Kiki* (1931). But except for Jolson's, that first generation of musicals was a disappointment to Americans who had grown up on fine operettas. Despite the fact that MGM's *Broadway Melody* (1929) won the first Academy Award for sound, by the end of 1930, the musical was all but over at the box office.

Indefatigable Hollywood moguls weren't giving up, however. Especially MGM's production supervisor Irving Thalberg, who had asked Herb Brown and Arthur Freed to partner on music and lyrics, respectively, for *Broadway Melody*. Sam Goldwyn, an independent producer, had hired Busby Berkeley as dance director on *Whoopee* (1930)—the film that showcased a fifteen-year-old unknown named Betty Grable—and Rouben Mamoulian had hired Rodgers and Hart to score *Love Me Tonight*

Above: Carmen Miranda, the "Brazilian Bombshell," put her unique spin on the hit song "Chattanooga Choo Choo," in *Springtime in the Rockies* (1942). **Opposite:** Lucille Ball's outrageous pink feathered headdress and vibrant red hair are a Technicolor sensation in *Ziegfeld Follies* (1946). Ball's segment, introduced by Fred Astaire and highlighting a then-unknown dancer named Cyd Charisse, featured the song "Bring on the Beautiful Girls."

1932). Hollywood had shifted into high gear, determined to produce musicals.

Busby Berkeley—who had worked with Pickford on *Kiki*—knew what most filmgoers wanted: beautiful girls shown in close-ups on the screen and a roving camera that moved around and above the sets, creating unpredictable angles. "These are moving pictures," he once said, "so everything has to move." His films revolutionized musicals, turning them from simple song-and-dance films into kaleidoscopic extravaganzas that tested the limits of dancers, cameramen, and censors.

Fred Astaire was another import from Broadway who revolutionized the way dances were filmed. In *Flying down to Rio* (1933), he teamed not only with Ginger Rogers for the first time, but also with choreographer Hermes Pan, who would come to be known as Astaire's "alter ego." Astaire insisted that the camera be pulled back to capture his routines in full figure, (on occasion Pan danced as his double). With Rogers as Astaire's dancing partner, the popularity of Hollywood musicals sky-rocketed. By 1937, Bing Crosby was making films sing at Paramount; Jeanette MacDonald and Nelson Eddy had found each other in MGM's *Naughty Marietta* (1935); Disney put a song in Snow White's heart in the first animated musical; and Luise Rainer won the first Oscar awarded to an actress in a musical, *The Great Ziegfeld* (1936).

Throughout the 1940s and 1950s the musical attracted audiences eager for escapism. By 1961, the film version of the Broadway hit *West Side Story* proved that Hollywood could take a serious stage play to new heights and, by 1964, *The Sound of Music* became one of the most profitable movies in history. Musicals had proven to be, arguably, the most important legacy of Hollywood's Golden Age.

Fred Astaire, Lucille Bremer, and dancers in "This Heart of Mine" production number from *Ziegfeld Follies* (1946). The spectacular set-ting was created by Tony Duquette. Judy Garland, Lucille Ball, Esther Williams, and Gene Kelly also had featured roles in the film.

FOR THE LOVE OF OSCAR

BY ARMY ARCHERD

I've been covering the Academy Awards since March 13, 1947. That was the eighteenth year of the event and it was held at Los Angeles's Shrine Auditorium. The winning picture was *The Best Years of Our Lives* (1946), which is the story of veterans returning from World War II. Ironically, that was really the first year of movies for me after returning from serving in the navy in the war. Since then, I have covered the awards both inside and outside, as the master of ceremonies on the red carpet, interviewing the stars and movie makers at the Shrine, the Dorothy Chandler Pavilion, and the Santa Monica Civic Auditorium (where sometimes it was so foggy that I couldn't tell who the stars were until they were right under my nose). I've worked in the rain and been soaked; I've worked in the sun so hot that I even got a sunburn in the early evening.

I was inside the year Elizabeth Taylor

Army Archerd welcomed the new governor of California, Ronald Reagan, and his wife Nancy, as they walked the red carpet into the 1967 Academy Awards ceremony.

Academy Awards
1928-1999

1928
Picture: *Wings*
Director: Frank Borzage, *Seventh Heaven*
Actor: Emil Jannings, *The Way of All Flesh*
Actress: Janet Gaynor, *Seventh Heaven*

1929
Picture: *The Broadway Melody*
Director: Frank Lloyd, *The Divine Lady*
Actor: Warner Baxter, *In Old Arizona*
Actress: Mary Pickford, *Coquette*

1930
Picture: *All Quiet on the Western Front*
Director: Lewis Milestone, *All Quiet on the Western Front*
Actor: George Arliss, *Disraeli*
Actress: Norma Shearer, *The Divorcee*

1931
Picture: *Cimarron*
Director: Norman Taurog, *Skippy*
Actor: Lionel Barrymore, *A Free Soul*
Actress: Marie Dressler, *Min and Bill*

1932
Picture: *Grand Hotel*
Director: Frank Borzage, *Bad Girl*
Actor: (tie) Fredric March, *Dr. Jekyll and Mr. Hyde* and Wallace Beery, *The Champ*
Actress: Helen Hayes, *The Sin of Madelon Claudet*

1933
Picture: *Cavalcade*
Director: Frank Lloyd, *Cavalcade*
Actor: Charles Laughton, *The Private Life of Henry VIII*
Actress: Katharine Hepburn, *Morning Glory*

1934
Picture: *It Happened One Night*
Director: Frank Capra, *It Happened One Night*
Actor: Clark Gable, *It Happened One Night*
Actress: Claudette Colbert, *It Happened One Night*

1935
Picture: *Mutiny on the Bounty*
Director: John Ford, *The Informer*
Actor: Victor McLaglen, *The Informer*
Actress: Bette Davis, *Dangerous*

1936
Picture: *The Great Ziegfeld*
Director: Frank Capra, *Mr. Deeds Goes to Town*
Actor: Paul Muni, *The Story of Louis Pasteur*
Actress: Luise Rainer, *The Great Ziegfeld*
Supporting Actor: Walter Brennan, *Come and Get It*
Supporting Actress: Gale Sondergaard, *Anthony Adverse*

1937
Picture: *The Life of Emile Zola*
Director: Leo McCarey, *The Awful Truth*
Actor: Spencer Tracy, *Captains Courageous*
Actress: Luise Rainer, *The Good Earth*
Supporting Actor: Joseph Schildkraut, *The Life of Emile Zola*

1938
Picture: *You Can't Take It With You*
Director: Frank Capra, *You Can't Take It With You*
Actor: Spencer Tracy, *Boys Town*
Actress: Bette Davis, *Jezebel*
Supporting Actor: Walter Brennan, *Kentucky*
Supporting Actress: Fay Bainter, *Jezebel*

1939
Picture: *Gone with the Wind*
Director: Victor Fleming, *Gone with the Wind*
Actor: Robert Donat, *Goodbye, Mr. Chips*
Actress: Vivien Leigh, *Gone with the Wind*
Supporting Actor: Thomas Mitchell, *Stagecoach*
Supporting Actress: Hattie McDaniel, *Gone with the Wind*

1940
Picture: *Rebecca*
Director: John Ford, *The Grapes of Wrath*
Actor: James Stewart, *The Philadelphia Story*
Actress: Ginger Rogers, *Kitty Foyle*
Supporting Actor: Walter Brennan, *The Westerner*
Supporting Actress: Jane Darwell, *The Grapes of Wrath*

1941
Picture: *How Green Was My Valley*
Director: John Ford, *How Green Was My Valley*
Actor: Gary Cooper, *Sergeant York*
Actress: Joan Fontaine, *Suspicion*
Supporting Actor: Donald Crisp, *How Green Was My Valley*
Supporting Actress: Mary Astor, *The Great Lie*

1942
Picture: *Mrs. Miniver*
Director: William Wyler, *Mrs. Miniver*
Actor: James Cagney, *Yankee Doodle Dandy*
Actress: Greer Garson, *Mrs. Miniver*
Supporting Actor: Van Heflin, *Johnny Eager*
Supporting Actress: Teresa Wright, *Mrs. Miniver*

1943
Picture: *Casablanca*
Director: Michael Curtiz, *Casablanca*
Actor: Paul Lukas, *Watch on the Rhine*
Actress: Jennifer Jones, *The Song of Bernadette*
Supporting Actor: Charles Coburn, *The More the Merrier*
Supporting Actress: Katina Paxinou, *For Whom the Bell Tolls*

1944
Picture: *Going My Way*
Director: Leo McCarey, *Going My Way*
Actor: Bing Crosby, *Going My Way*
Actress: Ingrid Bergman, *Gaslight*
Supporting Actor: Barry Fitzgerald, *Going My Way*
Supporting Actress: Ethel Barrymore, *None But the Lonely Heart*

1945
Picture: *The Lost Weekend*
Director: Billy Wilder, *The Lost Weekend*
Actor: Ray Milland, *The Lost Weekend*
Actress: Joan Crawford, *Mildred Pierce*
Supporting Actor: James Dunn, *A Tree Grows in Brooklyn*
Supporting Actress: Anne Revere, *National Velvet*

1946
Picture: *The Best Years of Our Lives*
Director: William Wyler, *The Best Years of Our Lives*
Actor: Fredric March, *The Best Years of Our Lives*
Actress: Olivia de Havilland, *To Each His Own*
Supporting Actor: Harold Russell, *The Best Years of Our Lives*
Supporting Actress: Anne Baxter, *The Razor's Edge*

1947
Picture: *Gentleman's Agreement*
Director: Elia Kazan, *Gentleman's Agreement*
Actor: Ronald Colman, *A Double Life*
Actress: Loretta Young, *The Farmer's Daughter*
Supporting Actor:Edmund Gwenn, *Miracle on 34th Street*
Supporting Actress: Celeste Holm, *Gentleman's Agreement*

won for *Butterfield 8* (1960). When she came offstage she actually collapsed and was caught by her then-husband, Eddie Fisher. I was backstage when Joan Crawford was the grande dame hostess to the winners, nominees, and all the participants, with a huge Pepsi-Cola cooler in her dressing room—but the cooler was filled with vodka and other alcoholic drinks. I was in the theater in 1973 when I saw Sasheen Littlefeather head to the stage ready to reject Marlon Brando's Oscar, so I tipped off the producer that it was about to happen. At the 1967 Academy Awards nominee Walter Matthau, for *The Fortune Cookie* (1966), arrived with his arm in a sling. When I asked him about the sling, he said, "Please don't talk about it. I don't want my mother to know I broke my arm." I said, "How did you break your arm?" And he said "Riding my bicycle on Pacific Coast Highway." I said, "Walter, sorry, but your mother will know just by looking at her television set."

Introducing the stars has brought some memorable moments, like when Shirley Temple arrived in 1998. I introduced her to the fans in the stands and had them all sing "Happy Birthday" to her because her seventieth birthday was coming up. Similarly, I had the fans in the stands sing "Happy Birthday" to Warren Beatty the year his birthday was the day after the awards.

Jimmy Stewart always received the most tumultuous applause. The crowd went wild for Ingrid Bergman upon her triumphant return after having been practical-

Shirley MacLaine gets silly at the 38th Academy Awards in 1966. Brother Warren Beatty saves her from a tumble.

1948
Picture: *Hamlet*
Director: John Huston, *Treasure of the Sierra Madre*
Actor: Laurence Olivier, *Hamlet*
Actress: Jane Wyman, *Johnny Belinda*
Supporting Actor: Walter Huston, *The Treasure of the Sierra Madre*
Supporting Actress: Claire Trevor, *Key Largo*

1949
Picture: *All the King's Men*
Director: Joseph L. Mankiewicz, *A Letter to Three Wives*
Actor: Broderick Crawford, *All the King's Men*
Actress: Olivia de Havilland, *The Heiress*
Supporting Actor: Dean Jagger, *Twelve O'Clock High*
Supporting Actress: Mercedes McCambridge, *All the King's Men*

1950
Picture: *All about Eve*
Director: Joseph L. Mankiewicz, *All about Eve*
Actor: Jose Ferrer, *Cyrano de Bergerac*
Actress: Judy Holliday, *Born Yesterday*
Supporting Actor: George Sanders, *All about Eve*
Supporting Actress: Josephine Hull, *Harvey*

1951
Picture: *An American in Paris*
Director: George Stevens, *A Place in the Sun*
Actor: Humphrey Bogart, *The African Queen*
Actress: Vivien Leigh, *A Streetcar Named Desire*
Supporting Actor: Karl Malden, *A Streetcar Named Desire*
Supporting Actress: Kim Hunter, *A Streetcar Named Desire*

1952
Picture: *The Greatest Show on Earth*
Director: John Ford, *The Quiet Man*
Actor: Gary Cooper, *High Noon*
Actress: Shirley Booth, *Come Back, Little Sheba*
Supporting Actor: Anthony Quinn, *Viva Zapata!*
Supporting Actress: Gloria Grahame, *The Bad and the Beautiful*

1953
Picture: *From Here to Eternity*
Director: Fred Zinnemann, *From Here to Eternity*
Actor: William Holden, *Stalag 17*
Actress: Audrey Hepburn, *Roman Holiday*
Supporting Actor: Frank Sinatra, *From Here to Eternity*
Supporting Actress: Donna Reed, *From Here to Eternity*

1954
Picture: *On the Waterfront*
Director: Elia Kazan, *On the Waterfront*
Actor: Marlon Brando, *On the Waterfront*
Actress: Grace Kelly, *The Country Girl*
Supporting Actor: Edmond O'Brien, *The Barefoot Contessa*
Supporting Actress: Eva Marie Saint, *On the Waterfront*

1955
Picture: *Marty*
Director: Delbert Mann, *Marty*
Actor: Ernest Borgnine, *Marty*
Actress: Anna Magnani, *The Rose Tattoo*
Supporting Actor: Jack Lemmon, *Mister Roberts*
Supporting Actress: Jo Van Fleet, *East of Eden*

1956
Picture: *Around the World in 80 Days*
Director: George Stevens, *Giant*
Actor: Yul Brynner, *The King and I*
Actress: Ingrid Bergman, *Anastasia*
Supporting Actor: Anthony Quinn, *Lust for Life*
Supporting Actress: Dorothy Malone, *Written on the Wind*

1957
Picture: *The Bridge on the River Kwai*
Director: David Lean, *The Bridge on the River Kwai*
Actor: Alec Guinness, *The Bridge on the River Kwai*
Actress: Joanne Woodward, *The Three Faces of Eve*
Supporting Actor: Red Buttons, *Sayonara*
Supporting Actress: Miyoshi Umeki, *Sayonara*

1958
Picture: *Gigi*
Director: Vincente Minnelli, *Gigi*
Actor: David Niven, *Separate Tables*
Actress: Susan Hayward, *I Want to Live!*
Supporting Actor: Burl Ives, *The Big Country*
Supporting Actress: Wendy Hiller, *Separate Tables*

1959
Picture: *Ben-Hur*
Director: William Wyler, *Ben-Hur*
Actor: Charlton Heston, *Ben-Hur*
Actress: Simone Signoret, *Room at the Top*
Supporting Actor: Hugh Griffith, *Ben-Hur*
Supporting Actress: Shelley Winters,
The Diary of Anne Frank

1960
Picture: *The Apartment*
Director: Billy Wilder, *The Apartment*
Actor: Burt Lancaster, *Elmer Gantry*
Actress: Elizabeth Taylor, *Butterfield 8*
Supporting Actor: Peter Ustinov, *Spartacus*
Supporting Actress: Shirley Jones, *Elmer Gantry*

1961
Picture: *West Side Story*
Director: Robert Wise and Jerome Robbins, *West Side Story*
Actor: Maximillian Schell, *Judgment at Nuremberg*
Actress: Sophia Loren, *Two Women*
Supporting Actor: George Chakiris, *West Side Story*
Supporting Actress: Rita Moreno, *West Side Story*

1962
Picture: *Lawrence of Arabia*
Director: David Lean, *Lawrence of Arabia*
Actor: Gregory Peck, *To Kill a Mockingbird*
Actress: Anne Bancroft, *The Miracle Worker*
Supporting Actor: Ed Begley, *Sweet Bird of Youth*
Supporting Actress: Patty Duke, *The Miracle Worker*

1963
Picture: *Tom Jones*
Director: Tony Richardson, *Tom Jones*
Actor: Sidney Poitier, *Lilies of the Field*
Actress: Patricia Neal, *Hud*
Supporting Actor: Melvyn Douglas, *Hud*
Supporting Actress: Margaret Rutherford, *The V.I.P.s*

1964
Picture: *My Fair Lady*
Director: George Cukor, *My Fair Lady*
Actor: Rex Harrison, *My Fair Lady*
Actress: Julie Andrews, *Mary Poppins*
Supporting Actor: Peter Ustinov, *Topkapi*
Supporting Actress: Lila Kedrova, *Zorba the Greek*

1965
Picture: *The Sound of Music*
Director: Robert Wise, *The Sound of Music*
Actor: Lee Marvin, *Cat Ballou*
Actress: Julie Christie, *Darling*
Supporting Actor: Martin Balsam, *A Thousand Clowns*
Supporting Actress: Shelley Winters, *A Patch of Blue*

y barred from Hollywood. The same for Charlie Chaplin. In recent years those new-yweds, Barbra Streisand and Jim Brolin, got the biggest applause—they were so enthusiastic about attending the awards right after their marriage. Another big crowd pleaser was Cher in 1986, showing up in a Bob Mackie dress that was the most exotic ever seen before or since. The most exuberant person I have ever introduced has to be the one and only Roberto Benigni, who actually leaped into my arms when he came up to my microphone in 1999. The nights on the red carpet have been the most exciting nights in Hollywood, and the viewing audience has increased from a few million to a billion. I've always been proud to be part of the Academy Awards.

Below: Rod Steiger won the Oscar for his lead in *In the Heat of the Night* (1967). Wife Claire Bloom shares the joy at the 49th Academy Awards in 1968.
Bottom: Robert Wagner and Natalie Wood attend the 32nd Academy Awards in 1960. The following year she was nominated for an Oscar for *Splendor in the Grass*.

1966
Picture: *A Man for All Seasons*
Director: Fred Zinnemann, *A Man for All Seasons*
Actor: Paul Scofield, *A Man for All Seasons*
Actress: Elizabeth Taylor, *Who's Afraid of Virginia Woolf?*
Supporting Actor: Walther Matthau, *The Fortune Cookie*
Supporting Actress: Sandy Dennis,
Who's Afraid of Virginia Woolf?

1967
Picture: *In the Heat of the Night*
Director: Mike Nichols, *The Graduate*
Actor: Rod Steiger, *In the Heat of the Night*
Actress: Katharine Hepburn, *Guess Who's Coming to Dinner*
Supporting Actor: George Kennedy, *Cool Hand Luke*
Supporting Actress: Estelle Parsons, *Bonnie and Clyde*

1968
Picture: *Oliver!*
Director: Sir Carol Reed, *Oliver!*
Actor: Cliff Robertson, *Charly*
Actress: (tie) Katharine Hepburn, *The Lion in Winter* and Barbra Streisand, *Funny Girl*
Supporting Actor: Jack Albertson, *The Subject Was Roses*
Supporting Actress: Ruth Gordon, *Rosemary's Baby*

1969
Picture: *Midnight Cowboy*
Director: John Schlesinger, *Midnight Cowboy*
Actor: John Wayne, *True Grit*
Actress: Maggie Smith, *The Prime of Miss Jean Brodie*
Supporting Actor: Gig Young, *They Shoot Horses Don't They?*
Supporting Actress: Goldie Hawn, *Cactus Flower*

1970
Picture: *Patton*
Director: Franklin J. Schaffner, *Patton*
Actor: George C. Scott, *Patton*
Actress: Glenda Jackson, *Women in Love*
Supporting Actor: John Mills, *Ryan's Daughter*
Supporting Actress: Helen Hayes, *Airport*

1971
Picture: *The French Connection*
Director: William Friedkin, *The French Connection*
Actor: Gene Hackman, *The French Connection*
Actress: Jane Fonda, *Klute*
Supporting Actor: Ben Johnson, *The Last Picture Show*
Supporting Actress: Cloris Leachman, *The Last Picture Show*

1972

Picture: *The Godfather*
Director: Bob Fosse, *Cabaret*
Actor: Marlon Brando, *The Godfather*
Actress: Liza Minnelli, *Cabaret*
Supporting Actor: Joel Gray, *Cabaret*
Supporting Actress: Eileen Heckart, *Butterflies Are Free*

1973

Picture: *The Sting*
Director: George Roy Hill, *The Sting*
Actor: Jack Lemmon, *Save the Tiger*
Actress: Glenda Jackson, *A Touch of Class*
Supporting Actor: John Houseman, *The Paper Chase*
Supporting Actress: Tatum O'Neal, *Paper Moon*

1974

Picture: *The Godfather, Part II*
Director: Francis Ford Coppola, *The Godfather, Part II*
Actor: Art Carney, *Harry and Tonto*
Actress: Ellen Burstyn, *Alice Doesn't Live Here Anymore*
Supporting Actor: Robert DeNiro, *The Godfather, Part II*
Supporting Actress: Ingrid Bergman, *Murder on the Orient Express*

1975

Picture: *One Flew over the Cuckoo's Nest*
Director: Milos Forman, *One Flew over the Cuckoo's Nest*
Actor: Jack Nicholson, *One Flew over the Cuckoo's Nest*
Actress: Louise Fletcher, *One Flew over the Cuckoo's Nest*
Supporting Actor: George Burns, *The Sunshine Boys*
Supporting Actress: Lee Grant, *Shampoo*

1976

Picture: *Rocky*
Director: John G. Avildsen, *Rocky*
Actor: Peter Finch, *Network*
Actress: Faye Dunaway, *Network*
Supporting Actor: Jason Robards, *All the President's Men*
Supporting Actress: Beatrice Straight, *Network*

1977

Picture: *Annie Hall*
Director: Woody Allen, *Annie Hall*
Actor: Richard Dreyfuss, *The Goodbye Girl*
Actress: Diane Keaton, *Annie Hall*
Supporting Actor: Jason Robards, *Julia*
Supporting Actress: Vanessa Redgrave, *Julia*

1978

Picture: *The Deer Hunter*
Director: Michael Cimino, *The Deer Hunter*
Actor: Jon Voight, *Coming Home*
Actress: Jane Fonda, *Coming Home*
Supporting Actor: Christopher Walken, *The Deer Hunter*
Supporting Actress: Maggie Smith, *California Suite*

1979

Picture: *Kramer vs. Kramer*
Director: Robert Benton, *Kramer vs. Kramer*
Actor: Dustin Hoffman, *Kramer vs. Kramer*
Actress: Sally Field, *Norma Rae*
Supporting Actor: Melvyn Douglas, *Being There*
Supporting Actress: Meryl Streep, *Kramer vs. Kramer*

1980

Picture: *Ordinary People*
Director: Robert Redford, *Ordinary People*
Actor: Robert DeNiro, *Raging Bull*
Actress: Sissy Spacek, *Coal Miner's Daughter*
Supporting Actor: Timothy Hutton, *Ordinary People*
Supporting Actress: Mary Steenburgen, *Melvin and Howard*

1981

Picture: *Chariots of Fire*
Director: Warren Beatty, *Reds*
Actor: Henry Fonda, *On Golden Pond*
Actress: Katharine Hepburn, *On Golden Pond*
Supporting Actor: John Gielgud, *Arthur*
Supporting Actress: Maureen Stapleton, *Reds*

1982

Picture: *Gandhi*
Director: Richard Attenborough, *Gandhi*
Actor: Ben Kingsley, *Gandhi*
Actress: Meryl Streep, *Sophie's Choice*
Supporting Actor: Louis Gossett, Jr., *An Officer and a Gentleman*
Supporting Actress: Jessica Lange, *Tootsie*

1983

Picture: *Terms of Endearment*
Director: James L. Brooks, *Terms of Endearment*
Actor: Robert Duvall, *Tender Mercies*
Actress: Shirley MacLaine, *Terms of Endearment*
Supporting Actor: Jack Nicholson, *Terms of Endearment*
Supporting Actress: Linda Hunt, *The Year of Living Dangerously*

Below: Eddie Fisher and Elizabeth Taylor attended the the 32nd Academy Awards ceremony in 1960, the same year he appeared with her in *Butterfield 8.*
Below middle: Elizabeth Taylor won an Academy Award for her work in *Butterfield 8* at the 33rd Academy Awards in 1961.
Bottom: At the 42nd Academy Awards ceremony in 1970, Liz Taylor and Richard Burton showed off the Taylor-Burton diamond on a precious cushion.

1984
Picture: *Amadeus*
Director: Milos Forman, *Amadeus*
Actor: F. Murray Abraham, *Amadeus*
Actress: Sally Field, *Places in the Heart*
Supporting Actor: Haing S. Ngor, *The Killing Fields*
Supporting Actress: Dame Peggy Ashcroft, *A Passage to India*

1985
Picture: *Out of Africa*
Director: Sydney Pollack, *Out of Africa*
Actor: William Hurt, *Kiss of the Spider Woman*
Actress: Geraldine Page, *The Trip to Bountiful*
Supporting Actor: Don Ameche, *Cocoon*
Supporting Actress: Anjelica Huston, *Prizzi's Honor*

1986
Picture: *Platoon*
Director: Oliver Stone, *Platoon*
Actor: Paul Newman, *The Color of Money*
Actress: Marlee Matlin, *Children of a Lesser God*
Supporting Actor: Michael Caine, *Hannah and Her Sisters*
Supporting Actress: Dianne Wiest, *Hannah and Her Sisters*

1987
Picture: *The Last Emperor*
Director: Bernardo Bertolucci, *The Last Emperor*
Actor: Michael Douglas, *Wall Street*
Actress: Cher, *Moonstruck*
Supporting Actor: Sean Connery, *The Untouchables*
Supporting Actress: Olympia Dukakis, *Moonstruck*

1988
Picture: *Rain Man*
Director: Barry Levinson, *Rain Man*
Actor: Dustin Hoffman, *Rain Man*
Actress: Jodie Foster, *The Accused*
Supporting Actor: Kevin Kline, *A Fish Called Wanda*
Supporting Actress: Geena Davis, *The Accidental Tourist*

1989
Picture: *Driving Miss Daisy*
Director: Oliver Stone, *Born on the Fourth of July*
Actor: Daniel Day-Lewis, *My Left Foot*
Actress: Jessica Tandy, *Driving Miss Daisy*
Supporting Actor: Denzel Washington, *Glory*
Supporting Actress: Brenda Fricker, *My Left Foot*

1990
Picture: *Dances with Wolves*
Director: Kevin Costner, *Dances with Wolves*
Actor: Jeremy Irons, *Reversal of Fortune*
Actress: Kathy Bates, *Misery*
Supporting Actor: Joe Pesci, *Goodfellas*
Supporting Actress: Whoopi Goldberg, *Ghost*

1991
Picture: *The Silence of the Lambs*
Director: Jonathan Demme, *The Silence of the Lambs*
Actor: Anthony Hopkins, *The Silence of the Lambs*
Actress: Jodie Foster, *The Silence of the Lambs*
Supporting Actor: Jack Palance, *City Slickers*
Supporting Actress: Mercedes Ruehl, *The Fisher King*

1992
Picture: *Unforgiven*
Director: Clint Eastwood, *Unforgiven*
Actor: Al Pacino, *Scent of a Women*
Actress: Emma Thompson, *Howards End*
Supporting Actor: Gene Hackman, *Unforgiven*
Supporting Actress: Marisa Tomei, *My Cousin Vinny*

1993
Picture: *Schindler's List*
Director: Steven Spielberg, *Schindler's List*
Actor: Tom Hanks, *Philadelphia*
Actress: Holly Hunter, *The Piano*
Supporting Actor: Tommy Lee Jones, *The Fugitive*
Supporting Actress: Anna Paquin, *The Piano*

1994
Picture: *Forrest Gump*
Director: Robert Zemeckis, *Forrest Gump*
Actor: Tom Hanks, *Forrest Gump*
Actress: Jessica Lange, *Blue Sky*
Supporting Actor: Martin Landau, *Ed Wood*
Supporting Actress: Dianne Wiest,
Bullets over Broadway

1995
Picture: *Braveheart*
Director: Mel Gibson, *Braveheart*
Actor: Nicolas Cage, *Leaving Las Vegas*
Actress: Susan Sarandon, *Dead Man Walking*
Supporting Actor: Kevin Spacey, *The Usual Suspects*
Supporting Actress: Mira Sorvino, *Mighty Aphrodite*

1996
Picture: *The English Patient*
Director: Anthony Minghella, *The English Patient*
Actor: Geoffrey Rush, *Shine*
Actress: Frances McDormand, *Fargo*
Supporting Actor: Cuba Gooding, Jr., *Jerry Maguire*
Supporting Actress: Juliette Binoche,
The English Patient

1997
Picture: *Titanic*
Director: James Cameron, *Titanic*
Actor: Jack Nicholson, *As Good as It Gets*
Actress: Helen Hunt, *As Good as It Gets*
Supporting Actor: Robin Williams, *Good Will Hunting*
Supporting Actress: Kim Basinger, *L.A. Confidential*

1998
Picture: *Shakespeare in Love*
Director: Steven Spielberg, *Saving Private Ryan*
Actor: Roberto Benigni, *Life is Beautiful*
Actress: Gwyneth Paltrow, *Shakespeare in Love*
Supporting Actor: James Coburn, *Affliction*
Supporting Actress: Dame Judi Dench,
Shakespeare in Love

1999
Picture: *American Beauty*
Director: Sam Mendes, *American Beauty*
Actor: Kevin Spacey, *American Beauty*
Actress: Hilary Swank, *Boys Don't Cry*
Supporting Actor: Michael Caine, *The Cider House Rules*
Supporting Actress: Angelina Jolie, *Girl, Interrupted*

HI YO SILVER! AND AWAY . . .

BY CLAYTON MOORE

The masked man and Silver appeared in 169 episodes of *The Lone Ranger* for television and two feature films.

Until the latter part of the twentieth century, a great Western with a great cowboy hero had one prevailing plot line: the triumph of virtue over evil; the white hat over the black hat. Sheriffs and outlaws might have reversed moral codes from time to time, but whoever the good guy happened to be, he damned near always won. The first white hat was "Bronco Billy" Anderson, a silent screen cowboy, and of course William S. Hart, Tom Mix, Roy Rogers, and Gene Autry taught us what it meant to be a true good guy of the West. But none was purer, none was kinder, and none protected the American Way better than that Superman on horseback, the Lone Ranger. For a half century Clayton Moore was that masked man. In his last interview, he tells us how he came to don his white hat.

—The Editors

When I was a kid, my father used to give my brothers and me a nickel each for Saturday matinees and I would stay and watch my favorites: Ken Maynard, William S. Hart, and Tom Mix. I would sit there in the dark and dream of being up there with them. At that age, all I knew is that I wanted to grow up to be either a policeman or a cowboy.

I wasn't really "discovered" in the sense that most people think of it. I was Jack Moore, a former trapeze artist in the Chicago World's Fair, when I headed off to model for the John Robert Powers agency in Chicago and New York. Then my friend, actor Tom Neal, called me from Hollywood to say, "Why don't you come out? The picking is good." My mother had a friend at Columbia studios who agreed to meet me. So I went west.

It was then that I made a screen test at MGM (as Jack Carlton) with Claire Owen, whom producer Eddie Small was considering for the lead in his next film. I guess I made an impression so Mr. Small put me under contract. I don't remember what happened to Miss Owen; I hope she got the part! (I felt like I had made it when this was reported in Louella Parsons's column.)

I got a few parts at first in feature films at MGM and Warner Bros., then I started to get steady work in serials at Republic. Working in those serials was different from features because you were chosen less for your acting talent than for your athletic skills and ability to do as you were told. They were cranked out fast and inexpensively. The directors only wanted actors who did their own stunts and could get the job done. I think this is why I was dubbed "King of the Serials" during my years at Republic. I actually did more serials than Buster Crabbe.

After the war, Republic started doing many more Westerns. I felt pretty lucky to work with Gene Autry (*The Cowboy and the Indian* in 1949, also featuring Jay Silverheels, the man who played Tonto), Rex Allen, Alan Lane, Roy Rogers (*Heldorado* in 1946 and *The Far Frontier* in 1949), and many other matinee favorites of the time. Then when George Trendle, the producer of the new TV series, *The Lone Ranger*, asked if I would like the lead, I tried to stop my knees from shaking and I said, "Mr. Trendle, I am the Lone Ranger." More than two hundred actors tried out, but Trendle had just seen me in a mask in the *The Ghost of Zorro* (1949) and, I later found

Above: The Republic serial *The Ghost of Zorro* (1949) starred Clayton Moore and was the first film in which he wore a mask.

Left: Moore and his wife Sally meet the president of the Lone Ranger fan club at their home in Tarzana, California, in 1949.

Above: During the press tour for the film *The Lone Ranger and the Lost City of Gold* (1958), Moore visited children all over the world, like this young girl in London.
Opposite: In 1932 Clayton Moore, née Jack Moore, modeled for a milk advertisement in Chicago.

out, had decided before I even walked in.

You know, I never felt any competition between myself and, say, Gene or Roy. Honestly, we all felt lucky to be where we were and we were all just doing our jobs. When I was away from the *Lone Ranger*, I played heavies on Gene's TV show at Republic in the serials. Playing the heavy is always fun, but once I got the white hat, I never wanted to take it off again.

Because locations were expensive, most filming was done in the studio. But in a Western, of course, there needed to be some outdoor shots. The *Lone Ranger* features were filmed in what is known as Monument Valley in Moab, Utah. However, all the TV serials were filmed in California: Bronson Canyon in the Hollywood Hills, the Alabama Hills in Lone Pine, but mostly in Chatsworth at Iverson's Ranch. There is a rock formation there called "Garden of the Gods" that I rode Silver through many a time. Jay especially loved that area. He had been cast as Tonto before the Lone Ranger's role had been filled and was happy to be in a weekly series. A full-blooded Mohawk, Jay had started out as an athlete—a boxer, wrestler, and lacrosse player—before he became an actor. He was a wonderful friend.

Everybody always asks me about the mask and if I may say so, it has become a symbol of Americana. But, it was very uncomfortable at first. I did most of my own stunt work and it was very difficult to see properly: like where a punch was coming from or where a rock was during a fall. Then I worked with the costumer and we took a plaster mold of my face to create a mask perfectly fitted to the exact contours of my face. That solved the vision problem. But it was still very hot. Whether we were filming inside with the bright lights or outside in the heat, the sweat would just pour out from that mask. I have been blessed with the recognition I have had in my career—especially from the kids. It has been a humbling but joyful experience. I fell in love with the Lone Ranger character and I never wanted to play any other role after that.

A daughter's note: This was the last interview my father ever did. It was Christmas Day 1999. Three days later he was gone "to the big ranch in the sky," as he would say. The incredible outpouring of love since his death has given me pause to consider why he touched so many people so profoundly. I always knew what a great guy he was (considerate husband and loving, supportive father) but to the rest of the world, he represented everything that was right and just. Fans knew he strove to live the Lone Ranger Creed, not just preach it. While Roy Rogers and Gene Autry enjoyed tremendous success and were loved by millions, it was a different kind of hero worship. Fans knew that Roy was a family man with great kids and a beautiful wife, and Gene was a savvy businessman—talented performers, but mortals who put their pants on one leg at a time. Not the Lone Ranger—he was no mortal. He had the moral strength and ethical integrity of nothing less than a super being; a deity. He received mail every day from his fans—and still does. He was always grateful and I am grateful to have the opportunity to say, "thank you." —Dawn Moore

GETTING CREDIT

For decades, movies could actually carry the words "The End" because the credits ran before the start of the film, offering only a short list of individuals involved in the production such as actors, producer, director, art director, screenwriters, cinematographer, hair stylist, and film editor. In time, as studios began to rely on independent contractors to fill jobs that were once staff positions, strong entertainment industry unions and guilds demanded extensive and specifically worded recognition for their members. Today, moviegoers who sit through a film to its end, the very end, know that the closing credits may run three minutes or longer, filled with job titles that are totally inexplicable (who determines who's a "best boy"? does a "gaffer" specialize in mistakes? and does a "foley artist" draw?). The terminology is jargon to an in-crowd called the entertainment industry; those on the outside don't speak the language. The following little glossary should help strangers in the strange land of credits.

Right: The film editor is one of the unsung heroes of every film and it was one important behind-the-scenes job open to women early in the industry's history.
Opposite: The stars on the set of *The Garden of Allah* (1936) (left to right, Charles Boyer, C. Aubrey Smith, Joseph Schildkraut, and Marlene Dietrich) and part of the crew (including director Richard Boleslawski) surround the huge Technicolor camera.

ART DIRECTOR
—one who plans interior or exterior sets or locations.

BEST BOY
—one who serves as the assistant to the chief electrician, better known as the gaffer.

BOOM OPERATOR
—one who determines best placement of the movable telescopic "boom" or arm that holds either a microphone, a camera, or a light during filming. The mobility of the boom allows the operator to follow characters through a scene while keeping the apparatus out of camera frame.

CINEMATOGRAPHER
—one who creates a specific ambience, feel, or look of a film through images, works with the director on light and shadow combinations to create atmosphere, drama, or mood. Sometimes referred to as a director of photography or cameraman. The remainder of the team of camera operators is referred to as first, second, third, etc.

DAILIES TIMER
—one who times the dailies or rushes, which are the day's shooting on film when it comes back from the laboratories and is ready for viewing by the director, cinematographer, etc.

DOLLY GRIP
—a stagehand who lays tracks used in dolly shots, or scenes photographed from a mobile platform on wheels.

FILM EDITOR
—the artist who assembles various strips of film into their final sequence.

FOLEY ARTIST
—a sound effects technician.

GAFFER
—the chief electrician in a film or TV production crew.

GRIP
—one who rearranges scenery, props, and heavy equipment.

KEY GRIP
—one who directs the stagehands or grips.

LOCATION MANAGER
—one who scouts suitable sites for filming away from the studio and gains permission to use them.

PROPERTY MANAGER
—one who oversees objects that are to be used to furnish a scene during the production of a film.

RIGGER
—one who places lighting equipment and erects the scaffolding and catwalks needed to support the sets.

SET DESIGNER
—one who literally designs the sets in a film, making the necessary drawings and specifications from the sketches supplied by the art director.

FURRY FRIENDS TO THE RESCUE

BY JON PROVOST

TIMMY: "Lassie! Lassie! Quick, get help!"

CUT TO: Lassie running miles across fields, leaping over crevasses, climbing mountains, and finally arriving at the farmhouse . . .

LASSIE: "Bark! Bark, bark!!!"

RUTH MARTIN: "Paul! Hurry, Timmy's in the well!"

PAUL MARTIN: "I'll get the pickup!"

How I ever wandered that far from home during a half-hour television show, I'll never know. Lassie always managed to rescue me and, on rare occasions, I saw her through danger, too. Seems like most TV and movie animals find themselves in some kind of life-threatening situation eventually. Daring dogs, crafty cats, heroic horses, brave bears—all of them have looked death in the eye and stared him down. A tragic few have succumbed to save their young or their masters. Their unconditional love, their loyalty, and courage won our hearts. Of course, Lassie will always be uppermost in my heart, but I do have room in there for a few others, like the ones pictured here.

One of my favorite episodes was when the Lone Ranger visited and I rode his stallion, Silver. What a thrill! I remember think-

Pete the Dog, with the obviously painted-on ring around his eye, poses with the Our Gang kids, including Jackie Cooper, far left, who joined the group of rascals in 1929. Renowned makeup master Max Factor created Pete's special eye makeup.

ing that Western stars had the greatest horses. They ran like the wind and never flinched, even when they were being shot at. Galloping through canyons, they outran the bad guys and whisked their masters to safety. These steeds were as famous as their riders: Tonto's Scout, Joey's Fury, Annie Oakley's Target, Hopalong Cassidy's Topper, Roy Rogers's Trigger, Dale Evans's Buttermilk, and one of the bravest, Tony the Wonder Horse, who belonged to Tom Mix. If it hadn't been for these brave broncos, the West would still be wild.

Television also gave us Gentle Ben, an eight-foot Canadian bear that weighed 630 pounds, a mountain compared to the boy he protected. Smokey Bear—the forest ranger bear—began as a drawing on a poster, but became so popular, the public looked for a live counterpart. A black bear cub—a real-life survivor of a fire found badly burned—became the embodiment of the very lesson the Forest Service was teaching. He became the star attraction at a zoo in Washington, D.C., and inspired a cartoon show in which Smokey saved countless lives. Smokey also recruited thousands of "Junior Forest Rangers"—including me!

When I was about ten, I was wandering around the Desilu lot where we made Lassie. I sneaked into the prop building where I loved to get lost examining all the models of battleships, planes, and submarines. On the second floor staring back at me from a high shelf was one of my all-time heroes, King Kong. I was sad to see that the gigantic fearless ape was just a little moth-eaten model, not more than eighteen inches high. He will always be bigger than life to me.

The invincible bond between man and animal has been forged over centuries. We have come to love them in all shapes and sizes. When they're in trouble, we worry. When they're hurt, we cry. So why do Hollywood writers always put our animal friends in peril? They recognize a good love story when they see one.

Opposite top: Lee Aaker played Rusty, Rin Tin Tin's boy, and several generations of German shepherds played Rinty, whose career began as a silent-movie star. Rin Tin Tin was a real war hero who participated in thirty-six combat missions in World War I. Safely back home in the good old United States, this brave German shepherd became a silent-screen superstar. He earned more than $300,000 in his fourteen-year career on the screen. His descendants came to the rescue on radio, in films, and on TV for more than four decades.

Opposite bottom: Lassie and the author, Jon Provost, worked together for seven seasons on TV's most beloved animal series. The first film at movie theaters to feature a collie was *Lassie Come Home* (1943), followed by six sequels, all starring male dogs who were descendants of the first "Lassie"—whose real name was Pal. The television series began in 1954, changing boy actors and dogs as nature demanded (kids grew; dogs died).

Below: City dogs could be pretty brave, too. Asta, the wire-haired terrier who costarred with William Powell and Myrna Loy in *The Thin Man* (1934–37) series, helped his masters find stolen loot, solve murders, and even recover from hangovers. The first dog in films was Jean "the Vitagraph Dog," who starred in early silents prior to 1920. But the first canine star was Strongheart, whose eponymous 1914 film also featured Lionel Barrymore.

LEAPING TO THE TOP

BY ANN MILLER

What a cast: Fred Astaire, Gene Kelly, Rita Hayworth, Cyd Charisse, Ann Miller, Bill Robinson, Eleanor Powell, Jimmy Cagney, Donald O'Connor, the Nicholas Brothers, Dan Dailey, Gene Nelson, Vera-Ellen, Sammy Davis, Jr., Bobby Van, Debbie Reynolds. They were the star Hollywood dancers who kept America's toes tapping. But it was Ruby Keeler who started it all when she starred in 42nd Street (1933). Now as we watch Hollywood's first great dancing star in that role, she appears heavy-footed and rather awkward. But audiences loved her—she could dance. On Ruby's heels came Eleanor Powell, MGM's machine-gun-quick tapper, who made audiences dizzy with her nonstop whirls. Hollywood was attracting the nation's top dancers, and studios were snapping them up. Ann Miller was seventeen when she tapped into Hollywood, but thirty before she made it to the top and thirty-four when she made the film she discusses here.   —The Editors

The best thing I ever did at MGM was "I've Gotta Hear That Beat," the Busby Berkeley number in *Small Town Girl* (1953). It was a cute picture, with Jane Powell and Farley Granger, but it should have been in a

Right: Ann Miller came to Hollywood from Texas and danced in a dozen MGM musicals.
Opposite: Judy Garland and Gene Kelly rehearse a number for Kelly's first film, *For Me and My Gal* (1942).

166

big, big picture, because all of a sudden there I was dancing in this huge number with rows of disembodied arms, hands, and musical instruments poking up through holes in the dance floor. It was so different—and out of this world.

It was such a great thrill working for Busby Berkeley. But I had no idea he was such a perfectionist or taskmaster. I had developed a blister rehearsing for that number and during the filming it started to bleed. I said, "Mr. Berkeley, can't we just stop for a minute and let me change stockings? There's blood in my shoe." "We have no time for that," he replied. "It's costing thousands of dollars for all these musicians and crew. Just keep dancing." I didn't want to cause an uproar, so I did it. But I couldn't walk for a week.

Top right: The amazing Nicholas Brothers, Harold and Fayard, were known for their high-energy jumps and splits learned from their days dancing at New York's Cotton Club and in Broadway musicals.

Opposite: Fred Astaire and Eleanor Powell, in *Broadway Melody of 1940*, set the screen on fire with their fast tapping to Cole Porter's "Begin the Beguine."

Bottom right: Bill "Bojangles" Robinson, vaudeville and musical stage star, was fifty-six years old when he appeared with six-year-old Shirley Temple in two 1935 films, *The Little Colonel* and *The Littlest Rebel*.

Below: Fred Astaire and Ginger Rogers, the most beloved and famous dance team in movie history, perform "The Yam" in *Carefree* (1938).

5

Fantasy intersects reality rarely, except in Hollywood, where it's a collision course—Einstein encounters the film industry, fans write to a star for advice, a car crash helps launch the career of the most famous actress and sex symbol of all time. The Kennedy name finds its way to the film capital. Little Shirley Temple writes a letter to Santa Claus, to show just exactly what a real little girl she is—the only difference is that her letter gets published in *Photoplay*. But real-world concerns sometimes took precedence over fantasies: World War II meant that many big stars were shipped off to the battle. Those who stayed home, like a 4-F Orson Welles or a too-old Bob Hope, devoted time to entertaining enlistees, making certain that morale stayed high. The entertainment industry took it upon itself to communicate the real messages of democracy and the hope of peace.

Raising morale: Bob Hope waves as he brings a touch of home to servicemen during the Korean War, 1950. Hope ranked among the top ten Hollywood moneymakers that year, but still made time for the troops.

EINSTEIN IN HOLLYWOOD

It was a mismatch indeed: Albert Einstein and Hollywood. Each was as curious as could be about the other. The difference was that for the genius Einstein, the only film industry person of real interest to him was Tinseltown's resident genius, Charlie Chaplin. Conversely, in Hollywood, everyone was interested in Einstein; everyone wanted to rub elbows with the man who was famous for explaining that mass and energy were related. It didn't matter that they couldn't understand his theory; Einstein was famous.

Professor Einstein and his wife toured Hollywood in 1931 as a side trip when they visited the hallowed halls of the California Institute of Technology in Pasadena. Certainly he was more comfortable in Cal-Tech's physics labs than at Universal Studios, where mogul Carl Laemmle's celebration commemorating twenty-five years of moviemaking was getting under way. Laemmle, a native of Germany, decided that an appearance at a Hollywood party by the famed physicist would be just the kind of news that would generate headlines internationally. And so it did. Among the glitterati were Mary Pickford, Gary Cooper, and Will Rogers. Einstein hadn't heard of any of them, but his wife filled him in on their fame and he responded cordially at each introduction. When face to face with Mary Pickford, Einstein stared blankly at the woman who was called "Queen Mary" in her environs. Frau Einstein quickly spoke for her husband, noting that "We came to America in the same state room on the *Belgenland*

in which your husband traveled." The star was delighted and Einstein was saved from embarrassment.

At the party, studio promoters bombarded the new "star" with on-the-spot movie contracts and fans begged for introductions and autographs. Disgusted, Einstein reminded all, via interpreters that Laemmle had provided, that he spoke poor English and had no time in his life for acting or autographs. As a fan magazine of the day reported, at one point the scientist said to his wife, *"Jetzt gehen wir zum nachsten ring!"* ("Now we're going to the next ring!") It was indeed a circus.

The next ring happened to be Warner Bros.–First National Studios, where Jack Warner was not to be outdone by Laemmle. On one of the sets, Warner convinced the Einsteins to sit behind the wheel of a roadster affixed to a motorized scaffold in front of a blue screen. Cameras rolled, the car began to bounce, and within hours Warner had footage of the couple driving through the streets of Paris, Berlin, and Hollywood, thanks to early technicians who were perfecting trick-photography techniques.

At the same studio, as *Photoplay* magazine noted, Einstein unwittingly insulted its biggest star, John Barrymore, by refusing to sign an autograph (he was far too shy) for one of the actor's assistants, shortly after he had refused to make a trip to the Barrymore set. The two slights enraged the actor, who then refused to leave his set to meet the scientist.

The tours and the premiere had left the scientist without explanations for the world's fascination with what he viewed as the shallowness and fakery he had experienced in the film capital. But most bewildering of all, as *Photoplay* reported, was the news he received the morning after he and his wife had spent a quiet evening in a Pasadena bungalow. He learned that he had been spotted the night before at a Hollywood party. "He" was there in the form of a double, a German actor hired when the scientist had turned down another invitation. And nobody who met "him" that night knew the difference.

Preceding pages: For Einstein the highlight of the Hollywood visit was finally meeting Chaplin. Together with Mrs. Einstein, they attended the premiere of *City Lights* (1931) and were greeted by more than 25,000 spectators. Police had to escort them through the mob into the theater. Stoic through it all, Einstein finally confided to Chaplin that "I have visited the world's famous laboratories. I have looked through the greatest telescopes. I have seen science's wonders. But never have I seen anything like that. And never, I hope, shall I again."

Opposite: Einstein speaks in German with film producer Carl Laemmle at Universal Studios. So many members of Laemmle's family were at his anniversary party, legend has it, that he wisecracked to Einstein, "You're telling *me* about relativity?" Laemmle also invited Einstein to a screening of *All Quiet on the Western Front* (1930). Unbeknownst to Einstein, Laemmle invited every major star to meet the scientist, and posted photographers at every door.

Below: Mrs. Einstein, actor and future director William Dieterle, Einstein, Col. Nugent H. Slaughter, an unidentified man, and Henry Blake stop for a photo opportunity on the Warner Bros. lot.

WHAT SHOULD I DO?

BY BETTE DAVIS

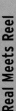

Beginning in December 1942, Bette Davis lent her name to the following advice column, which helped push Photoplay-Movie Mirror *to the top of the movie magazine heap. The actress was a master of public relations and worked closely with both movie magazine editors and the studio flacks who concocted publicity opportunities like this. Other stars such as Betty Grable, Humphrey Bogart, and Joan Crawford lent their bylines to articles in the magazine, but Davis was the first to do a regular advice column. Her column soon became the most heralded "star" column in the history of the magazine. Studio writers probably wrote the letters and the answers, then turned them over to Davis for editing. An excellent writer herself, however, the actress undoubtedly did heavy editing, if not major rewrites. Contrary to the Editor's Note from* Photoplay-Movie Mirror *staff that accompanies this reprint from the old magazine, don't try sending letters to Ms. Davis, since she died in 1989. And* Photoplay-Movie Mirror *went out of business in 1980.*

—The Editors

YOUR PROBLEMS ANSWERED BY BETTE DAVIS

Photoplay-Movie Mirror **institutes the greatest advice feature of the year.**

Believing that there is great need for wise counsel in this troubled world, *Photoplay-Movie Mirror* has persuaded Bette Davis, the woman who is Hollywood's famous advice star, to act as consultant to its readers. So every month Miss Davis will study the letters you send her and give her answers on these pages. Naturally she cannot cover every individual query; she will of necessity have to choose those problems which seem most universal. But you may rest assured your letter will be read personally by her and, as proof, each one of you will receive her acknowledgment. Address your letters to Miss Bette Davis, c/o *Photoplay-Movie Mirror*, Hollywood, California. And have no fear that your identity will be revealed to the world, for no names of towns are given and all names of persons are changed to protect the writers. From her personal mail Bette Davis has selected these letters as the ones to be answered this month through the pages of *Photoplay-Movie Mirror*.

—The Editors

DEAR Miss Davis:

My husband has been drafted and sent to a training camp nearly two thousand miles away. A good many girls have had to give up their husbands to the Army, but I wonder how many of them face the same problem that I do. You see, I had only known my husband six months before we were married. And we were married chiefly because he was going to be drafted and he said he couldn't bear to leave me unless he knew that I belonged to him.

He didn't know that for two years before I met him I had been going steady with a nice boy, Tom, in our town. Tom won't be taken into the Army because he was blinded in one eye during a hunting accident.

He has telephoned me several times, asking for dates. I told my mother at first that I didn't want to talk to him but she says I'm foolish. I'm still in love with my husband and I write to him every day, but I'm only twenty-two and I'll have to admit that I think I'll go crazy sitting at home night after night.

What do you think I should do? Refuse to see Tom? Or go out with him on a strictly friendly basis? If I do that, should I tell my husband about the dates or just keep it quiet?

Eleanor J.

Dear Eleanor J.:

You are probably only one out of the hundreds of girls who married in haste because of the war.

My deduction is that you are more in love with Tom than you are with your husband, in spite of what you say. However, let us suppose that you don't realize that fact yourself.

In a way, it seems selfish for a boy to want to marry just before he leaves for camp; this is a man's way of putting a girl on the shelf for the duration although he can do nothing for her, not even offer her companionship. It is, in fact, a type of hoarding.

I think you want me to say that it is quite all right for you to go out with Tom. Personally, that is exactly what I would do under the circumstance, being careful to keep our relationship entirely friendly—if you could manage it that way.

Every girl has to look down the road of the future and decide upon one of two paths for herself. She has to foresee the consequences of any given act. In this case there is a chance that townspeople are not going to understand your going out with Tom and that you may suffer from undue criticism. Also, Tom may get out of hand.

If you don't tell your husband you have been seeing Tom, he will learn of it in time, make no mistake about that. Then pray that your husband is an understanding soul.

Finally, beware of propinquity. Being with Tom a great deal may create even greater problems than loneliness and boredom.

Sincerely yours,
Bette Davis

DEAR Miss Davis:

This is not the typical "fan" letter. I have never before written a stranger a letter, but I suppose there is a first time for everything.

I'm a widow, Miss Davis. I'm only twenty-seven, financially independent, and I have a rather good education. But I can't seem to meet the right sort of man. I try not to be too particular; I've done all the usual little stunts such as going out with a perfect bore of a man just on the chance that I might meet someone interesting. Alas, I meet only more bores.

Worse, practically every man who takes an interest in me eventually works around to the old cliché—"Well, well, are you a merry widow." In the town in which I am now living only a girl who will try anything once is considered a good sport.

I don't intend to sacrifice my ideals for cheap companionship. Yet I don't want to live my life alone. So my problem is this: How can I meet a "good" man?

How does one attract a man one meets casually? And how does a girl who has been married keep a man interested while refusing to grant him certain taboo favors? I shall appreciate any advice you care to give me.

Most cordially yours,
Mary-Jo G.

Dear Mrs. G.:

In any woman's life, she meets only a few men who really appeal to her, so she must be careful not to drive those away. Life has a way of solving itself, if one doesn't push it too impatiently.

Apparently you are trying too hard to find a man to marry. Men can sense this hunting quality instantly and are frightened away by it. A man friend of mine once said, "Why do women let that acquisitive gleam come into their eyes after they have known a man for an hour and learned that he has a decent job, has pleasant manners and is free?"

Let that be a warning. If I were you, since you have a good education and are only twenty-seven and financially independent, I should travel about the country.

For some reason, a newcomer to town has special charm. If I were you, I'd take advantage of that fact. I think the only way to secure and hold a man's respect is to be good spirited company, interested in everything he says, but to also keep him guessing.

The best of luck to you,
Bette Davis

DEAR Miss Davis:

I just saw *The Man Who Came to Dinner* for the third time. I liked the way you played Maggie Cutler very much, probably because I am a secretary myself.

I am now doing my hair up high the way yours was done, but still I'm no prize package. A beautiful, famous, elegant lady like you probably has no idea what it means to be awkward and self-conscious. I just know, to look at your hands, that you've never bitten your fingernails. I'm ashamed to admit it, but I have an awful time keeping my nails above the quick.

I might as well tell you all the things that are wrong with me in hopes you will be able to help me. Whenever a man pays attention to me—and that isn't very often—I can't think of a thing to say. I feel all tied in knots and I just stand there sort of grinning and wishing the floor would open and drop me into a well.

I'm not exactly a dumb bunny because I got good grades in school and my three older sisters nag at me and say I wouldn't be bad-looking if I weren't such a goof.

I'm twenty-two years old, 5'8" tall and I only weigh 115 pounds.

I won't take up any more of your time, dear Miss Davis, but I thought you might be able to help me. I get so blue sometimes. This is what I want to know—how can I gain poise?

Anxiously yours,
Ruth Ann W.

Dear Miss W.:

In the first place, since you are working and are, therefore, financially independent, if I were in your place I'd take a room in a guest house, so moving away from those older sisters who, by their nagging, would probably give even beauty Hedy Lamarr an inferiority complex.

Paint your nails with the brightest red polish you can find and see if you aren't too pleased with the effect to spoil it by nibbling.

You are tall. Do you stoop when you walk? Some of the loveliest girls in pictures are tall—Alexis Smith, Gail Patrick, and Rosalind Russell, for instance—and each of them is as straight as a ramrod.

Finally, the best way I know of gaining poise is to forget yourself entirely and to direct your attention at the person with whom you are talking. Wonder, if you can't divert yourself otherwise, how he or she would look in a bathing suit. Remember those celebrated lines:

When pompous people squelch me with cold and snooty looks
It makes me happy to conjecture how they'd look in bathing suits.

Develop a system of controversial topics to put the other fellow at his ease and you'll be surprised at your resultant calm. Ask, "What picture could you bear to see once a week for an entire year?" or "What was the most frightening thing you ever saw?"

Relax, and you'll be all right.

Sincerely yours,
Bette Davis

DEAR Miss Davis:

You've played the roles of so many girls in serious trouble that I thought you might be able to give me some good advice.

I am a country girl who came to the big city and met a very nice boy. Everything I have ever had I have worked for very hard; he has an elegant job that was simply handed to him on a silver platter.

What I am getting at is this, Miss Davis, he has always had everything he wanted. I've learned that there are some things out of reach. Now he is going into the Army. He asked me to marry him when he gets out and I said I would because I love him with my whole heart and soul.

The only trouble is that we are feuding all the time over a very important matter. He thinks I should give him the things that go with marriage right now, before he goes away to war, instead of waiting until he comes home and the wedding is held. He says he doesn't know what is in store for him and that I should be generous and noble instead of thinking only of myself.

I am seventeen and he is twenty-four. Please, please tell me what to do.

> Your friend,
> **Betty L.**

Dear Miss L.:

At seventeen, one is likely to think that the present love is the one and only, but take my word for it—life is just beginning. The argument that men use, "Don't be selfish; be patriotic, be generous—I may not live long," is not new. From my reading, I judge that stone-age men used the same type of persuasion.

A girl facing this decision, as I have said before, has to consider the consequences of action in either direction. The consequences, if she listens to her soldier boy, are likely to be extremely serious.

On the other hand, if she says "no" life will go on much the same for her—without regrets. Never forget this: It takes a frightfully strong character to be a weak woman.

And always remember, there are more ways than just one of showing love and devotion. The promise of daily letters, cigarettes every week, surprise packages of writing paper, razor blades and sweets, as well as visits to camp may not be as "all-out" for victory as he would like, but in that way you will be telling your soldier how much he means to you without endangering your own future.

> Sincerely yours,
> **Bette Davis**

STARS IN UNIFORM

From World War I to the close of the twentieth century, Hollywood and its stars have played a major role in the various confrontations around the world. Whether they were at war fronts overseas or at military bases at home, entertaining troops in Europe or in the Pacific, raising morale or money during War Bond drives, the stars were there—on land, at sea, in the air, on desert and jungle stages, and in military hospital wards. At the famed Hollywood Canteen in Hollywood, and its East Coast counterpart, the Stage Door Canteen in New York City, and USOs worldwide, the stars donated their time and talent to offer returning and departing servicemen a touch of home. Bette Davis served as president of the Hollywood Canteen. The USO-run nightclub, housed in a livery stable on Cahuenga Boulevard, was a haven for soldiers who were about to be

Opposite: Clark Gable joined the Air Force soon after Carole Lombard's shocking death. For flying bombing missions over Germany, he was awarded the Distinguished Flying Cross and Air Medal.
Below: The Andrews Sisters—Maxine, Patti, and Laverne—chat with servicemen before their singing turn on stage at the Hollywood Canteen.

STARS WHO SERVED STARS

This "Gallery of Stars" salutes in words and pictures many of the Hollywood celebrities who put their careers on hold to serve their country during times of peril. There were hundreds more, as well. (Unless noted, service was during World War II.)

John Agar — Army
Eddie Albert — Navy
Herbert Anderson — Army
Desi Arnaz — Army
Roscoe Ates — Army Air Corps
Gene Autry — Army Air Corps
Lew Ayres — Army Medical Corps
Richard Barthelmess — Navy
Freddie Batholomew — Army Air Corps
John Beal — Army Air Corps
Wallace Beery — Navy
Turhan Bey — Army Air Corps
Tom Brown — Army
Bruce Cabot — Army Air Corps
MacDonald Carey — Marine Corps
John Carroll — Army Air Corps
Broderick Crawford — Army Air Corps
Donald Crisp — Army Intelligence
Robert Cummings — Civil Air Patrol
Tony Curtis — Navy
Dan Dailey — Army
Tom D'Andrea — Army
Richard Denning — Navy
Kirk Douglas — Navy
Melvyn Douglas — Army
Leif Erickson — Navy
Douglas Fairbanks, Jr. — Navy

shipped off to war. There they could dance and talk with their favorite stars such as Betty Grable, Rita Hayworth, and Judy Garland. Davis also recruited stars such as Frank Sinatra, Mickey Rooney, Tommy Dorsey, and many others to entertain.

Bob Hope, who was riding the crest of being one of Hollywood's top ten performers during World War II, was nearing forty when the war broke out, so instead of enlisting, he devoted weeks at holiday time to entertaining servicemen and women overseas. His Christmas tours became legendary and continued through the Persian Gulf conflict in 1990 and 1991. For his work he received the Presidential Medal of Freedom.

Hollywood civilian contributions to the war effort at home paled in comparison to the individual efforts of the men who took time off from their film industry jobs to join less-famous men on the battlefields. Actor Audie Murphy became World War II's most decorated soldier, earning two dozen medals, including the Congressional Medal of Honor. But he was only one of dozens of less-celebrated actors who headed for the war front.

Charles Farrell — Navy
Fritz Feld — Army
Henry Fonda — Navy
Glenn Ford — Marine Corps
Clark Gable — Army Air Corps
James Garner — Army (Korean War)
Farley Granger — Navy
Huntz Hall — Coast Guard
Jon Hall — Coast Guard
Sterling Hayden — Marine Corps
Peter Lind Hayes — Army
Louis Hayward — Marine Corps
Van Heflin — Army
Charlton Heston — Air Force
William Holden — Army
Sterling Holloway — Army Coast Artillery
Jack Holt — Air Force
Tim Holt — Air Force
William Hopper — Coast Guard
John Howard — Navy
Richard Jaeckel — Navy
Gene Kelly — Navy
Arthur Kennedy — Army
Alan Ladd — Air Force
Jeffrey Lynn — Air Force
Ben Lyon — Air Force
Guy Madison — Navy
Tony Martin — Air Force
Victor Mature — Army
Lon McCallister — Air Force
Tim McCoy — Army
Burgess Meredith — Air Force
Cameron Mitchell — Air Force
George Montgomery — Air Force
Robert Montgomery — Navy
Wayne Morris — Navy
Audie Murphy — Army
Barry Nelson — Army
Paul Newman — Navy
Richard Ney — Navy
Edmond O'Brien — Army
Orry-Kelly — Army
Sidney Poitier — Army
Tyrone Power — Marine Corps
Elvis Presley — Peacetime Army
Ronald Reagan — Air Force
Sabu — Army
Robert Stack — Navy
James Stewart — Air Force
Ezra Stone — Army
Robert Taylor — Navy

Opposite top: Audie Murphy, who rose from private to lieutenant to become World War II's most decorated GI, wrote a book in 1949, *To Hell and Back*, which chronicled his days on the battlefront, and in 1955, he played himself in the film version. He died in a small plane crash in 1971.

Opposite middle: Robert Taylor served as a flight instructor with the Navy's air transport during World War II. In addition to work in the field, Taylor narrated and directed military training films.

Opposite bottom: Elvis Presley poses with his guitar in his Army uniform, 1958. It was during the Cold War, and Elvis felt he ought to do his part by joining the service when his number came up.

Above: Bob Hope broadcasts his popular radio show from the famous Hollywood Canteen during World War II.

SHIRLEY TEMPLE'S LAST LETTER TO SANTA

BY SHIRLEY TEMPLE

In 1939, Photoplay *magazine printed Shirley Temple's last letter to Santa. The legendary child star was almost twelve and almost a has-been, despite the fact that the year before she had been ranked as the country's top box-office attraction. Adolescence was her career's downfall and by 1940 her contract at Twentieth Century-Fox was dissolved. No other studio could convince the public that a gawky preteen was as cute as the "real" Shirley Temple they had forged in their mental image banks. Fortunately Santa was not affected by Shirley's stardom and was probably impressed by her gracious mentions of gifts for her brothers Sonny and Jack—nobody else had ever talked about them. —The Editors*

MRS. TEMPLE says that Shirley is "on the edge" in her belief in Santa. This is probably the last Christmas she will ever write to him and we are proud to present her letter. We sincerely hope he'll bring her everything she asks for. . . .

DEAR Santa:

Every year I write you a letter and on every Christmas you've always remembered what I ask for. I know it's not nice to ask for things but I've decided that telling you what I want might save you a lot of trouble. So this is a sort of shopping list and if you have time to get around to me after taking care of all the other little girls I'll be very glad if you take this list along.

But there is something I have to explain first. It is about last year. I didn't mean to play a trick on you. I just wanted to see you, Santa. Just once. That's why I put the bell on the toe of my stocking and hung it by my bed (instead of the usual place on the mantel) so I'd be sure to hear it. But I didn't. You filled it without ever making a sound—with those candy nuts I love so, and the little glass figures for my collection and the small silver tea set. Remember?

And maybe I'd better explain about that stocking too. Mine isn't very big. Sonny and Jack (they are my brothers) only wear socks but they hold more. So I told a friend of mother's and she made me that glazed chintz stocking two feet long. I hope you don't mind because I'd like to use it again this year.

What I want more than anything Santa (even more than a double-folding sleeping bag and one of those jiffy tents) is another Jimmy. Oh I know it will be hard to find and you will have to look all over because Jimmy was the dearest baby doll in the world. He went to Honolulu with me and he was so good. But on the trip we took last summer I left my Jimmy sitting in the car right in the sun when we went to the Grand Canyon. I never should have done that because my dad locked the car and it got pretty hot. When we came back Jimmy's cheeks were cracked. The paint had run onto his little white rompers and when I picked him up his lashes fell out. I just could not help crying. My dad sent him back to the doll hospital in Hollywood but they couldn't fix him. When I got home I buried Jimmy in our backyard and Mary Lou Isleib (she is my best friend

and stand-in) was pallbearer. So please let me have another Jimmy.

And I would like to have:

1 pr dungarees (blue)

1 shirt (blue and red check like Bill's the cowboy

at Hillsdale ranch)

1 pr 6-shooters

That is to wear when I ride the pony Mr. Schenck gave me.

(We play G-men of the West. The pony is awful smart.)

And if it's not asking too much I certainly would like the wardrobe that goes with Lottie. I bought Lottie myself last week with money I saved up. But when I went to the store after her the clerk said "This doll's clothes are extra." And I did not have enough. They are on the fourth floor so you will know and they are in a big hatbox marked "My Dates." She has a dress for every day in the week. A blue one with a brown fur jacket (my favorite) and a red snow suit.

Last year I went to that store to see a man who said he was you. But I told mother "He is not the real Santa because he said—'Well, Shirley, I see all your pictures'—and I know you cannot do that up at the North Pole." But mother said, "He is a stand-in for Santa." I guess you have a lot of stand-ins.

We had a swell time last Christmas. I went to the Assistance League the day before and they let me help push the wagons and fill the baskets. Then we went home to supper but I could not eat much. We always have the tree on Christmas eve. A big green one (I do not like the white, they smell so funny) with electric candles and balls on it. My dad puts it on a turntable which plays "Silent Night." Only it did not work last year. The tree was too heavy.

Did you see the Star of Bethlehem lit up on the pine tree outside? Sonny put that up. He nearly fell.

We never open presents before Christmas morning but one kind of opened itself up. There was a terrible scream in the kitchen and we all ran out and sitting right on the floor in a cage was a big red macaw. Somebody had brought him for me around by the back and he had pecked through his paper covering. He was screaming at Elizabeth May (she is our cook) and Elizabeth May was screaming right back at him with a broom. My brother Jack said "Ha ha" and the macaw said "Ha ha" too and everybody laughed.

Once I got a very nice cow for Christmas. It was from the children of Tillamook where the cheese comes from. The Xpressman brought it to the studio and mother said "My goodness where are we going to keep it?" We tied it to the little fence outside my bungalow but it ate all the tops off the flowers and the studio gardener was pretty mad. I wanted to take it home it was so beautiful, only we lived in the house on 19 Street in Santa Monica then and when we phoned dad about it he said "Well, it is a case of keeping the cow or the car. We have not room for both!" So a milk farm man came and got it. It has little cows now.

Every Christmas morning when I was a little girl mother woke me with sleigh bells. Now she lets me ring them. My dad says 5 is too early so I wait till 6. We all go in the room together where the family presents are (the other presents are downstairs). Granny gave me a green sweater she knitted herself last year. And there was the nicest kitchen store from you with tiny jars and little potatoes and lemons and everything for my play-house. I am just learning to knit. I made my dad a tie but he has not worn it yet. He says he is saving it.

I love Christmas dinner. Sometimes Elizabeth May lets me help. I cannot cook much except biscuits. I make those on my little stove out in the playhouse. I did when Miss Carrie Jacobs Bond came to tea last Monday. (She is coming to visit me on the set of *The Little Princess* too.)

But Santa, when I was washing my dishes afterwards my dog Rowdy jumped up and broke three cups and the teapot cover. I would like very much to have another tea set if it is not too much trouble. There is a pretty one (blue with yellow flowers) on the fourth floor of that store I told you about. And in case you're not in a hurry could you just sort of look over the new *Wizard of Oz* book? And some of the Ranger series?

Mother says Christmas is a family day so we do not go out. We play and open presents and it is the Best day of the year. But the next day Mary Lou and my friends come over. We make Christmas last the whole week! In the evening my dad drives us around to see all the trees lit up outdoors and they are so beautiful. One house in Beverly Hills has studio snow piled all over the yard and reindeer in front. Sometime I would like to see real snow on Christmas.

Did you see our wreath? A Lumberjack man up north made it for me with my name on it. It must have been hard because holly pricks. People are awful good. So are you. Please give all my friends (like the crippled boy in Spokane and the lady from Detroit who writes me every week) extra presents. Thank you Santa.

Love,
Shirley Temple

P.S. Mother says "Please don't bring any more rabbits." I got two darling Chinese ones last year and when we came back from Honolulu there were forty-five.

MARILYN IN FOCUS

BY TOM KELLEY

I *n 1949, my father photographed a young model named Marilyn Monroe for a beer ad. It was his later session with her, however, when she posed nude, that created a stir. He was known for his celebrity and commercial advertising photography, not nudes, and he wanted none of the notoriety. It wasn't until 1964, two years after Marilyn died, that he agreed to discuss his moments with her. At that time he wrote a detailed draft for a proposed article in a photography magazine. Before my father passed away in 1984, he recorded his story. Here is his account.* —Tom Kelley, Jr.

I first met Marilyn Monroe by accident, or rather, because of an accident. It was a hot autumn afternoon in 1947 and I was driving east along the Sunset Strip in Hollywood. At Sunset Plaza Drive, near the front of LaRue restaurant, I spotted a crowd of people standing around two battered cars. My years of working as an Associated Press photographer got the best of me. I had to pull over and take a look.

Among the onlookers was Marilyn, blond and lovely, appearing even younger than her twenty-one years. She was wearing a dress that was too tight and heels that were too high, and she was on the verge of tears. A policeman was asking her questions and an irate older man was yelling at her. From what I could gather, Marilyn had rear-ended the man's car, and she had done a good job of it. Her car was out of commission.

I waited until things calmed down a bit before I approached Marilyn to ask what had happened. She was on her way to try out for a little theater play, she said, when the accident occurred. Now she was without a car, and she didn't have any money.

I gave her five dollars, my card, and told her to get a cab. "Pay me when you can," I said. She seemed grateful. She thanked me over and over.

Almost two years passed before I saw Marilyn again. It was in the spring of 1949 when she walked into my small studio, a pink stucco cottage on Seward Street in Hollywood. She stood in the tiny reception room looking about at the cameras, spotlights, and props. Natalie, my assistant, greeted her.

Marilyn had been sent by an agency to pose for a Pabst beer billboard ad. I had forgotten about our earlier meeting. In fact, I felt I was seeing her for the first time. There wasn't anything in particular to distinguish her from many of the other models who came into the studio. Her hair was now reddish-blond, worn long, curly and fluffed around her face, a style popular in the late 1940s. Natalie took Marilyn into the dressing room and had her change into a bathing suit. Once her makeup was toned down and her hair pulled back with a scarf, I asked her to pose holding a beach ball over her head. She had held that position for about an hour when we asked her if she wanted to rest, but she said she would hold it until we got all the shots we wanted. I'm sure she must have ached, if not at the time, then later. But she never complained.

After we finished and Marilyn was ready to leave, I asked her if she would consider posing for artistic nude color shots. We had clients who requested them for calendars. Reluctantly, Marilyn said, "I don't think so."

She admitted that she desperately wanted a career in films, but that she had already been dropped by two studios and she was taking all the work she could get to make ends meet. But pose nude? Again, she said no. She left without ever having mentioned that we had met earlier.

Two days later Marilyn was on the phone telling Natalie she had thought over my offer of posing for the calendar shots. "I'll do it," she said, finally. An appointment was made for 7:00 on Friday evening, May 27.

I didn't know what I was going to use as props for the session, but I knew I didn't want anything elaborate that would detract from Marilyn. She was too lovely for that. Keep it plain, keep it simple, I told myself. I sent Natalie to a prop house to pick up a pair of deep red velour drapes.

By the time Marilyn arrived on Friday evening, the red velour had been carefully draped on the floor of the studio. Natalie had her change into a robe from her street clothes—she was wearing rolled-up blue jeans, a low-cut blouse, and red high heels—and requested that she tie it loosely around her waist so there wouldn't be any marks on her body. Natalie worked on her makeup and combed out her hair as we sat at our lunch table for a few minutes. I thought I'd try to put her at ease in case she was nervous.

She didn't seem to be. In fact, she had more to say to me than I had to say to her. As I poured us each a cup of coffee, she said, "There's something I have to tell you, but I'll save that for later."

"Sure, that's fine," I said.

"But, and I hope you won't take this the wrong way . . ." She stopped and looked at me with sad eyes.

"Are you okay?" I asked.

"Oh, I'm fine . . . but it's the money, the modeling fee."

"You'll get paid tonight."

"Oh, thank you so much," she said with a smile. "The thing is, I'm behind on my rent and I really need the fifty dollars."

"Don't worry. You'll have it before you leave."

She smiled again. "You are a very dear person, Tom. Now I feel better."

"Good," I said. "Now we have work to do."

Marilyn Monroe in a variation of the stretch pose for the calendar

Marilyn left for the restroom while I set up a tall ladder, which had to be secured, checked the lighting and the cameras. As she returned, I put on a record of Artie Shaw's "Begin the Beguine."

Tossing her robe aside, Marilyn stretched out on the red velour drapes. Her body appeared longer and leaner than it actually was, and with her coloring, she looked sensational against the velvety fabric. She needed direction only for positioning. I had her turn more on her side, since we were not allowed to show pubic hair.

From then on, Marilyn was on her own, and she knew exactly what to do. Rather shy and insecure away from the cameras, she became the perfect model under the lights, moving instinctively from one provocative pose to another. She was so graceful, so feminine, so sensuous.

We worked together for two hours, and when we were done, I grabbed a smaller camera and had her move around, shooting her from all angles, including full, frontal nudity. I shot four rolls of film in the little camera. The shots were extraordinary. Marilyn later asked me for copies, and I gave them to her. She, in turn, gave them to Joe DiMaggio as a wedding gift following their marriage in January 1954. The original color transparencies of that night's work were all stolen from my studio.

It wasn't much later that Marilyn, Natalie, and I went to Barney's Beanery for chili and coffee. While we were there Marilyn said, "I've been saving something I have to tell you, remember?" I did.

"Well, you're not the first person to ask me to pose naked. I've been asked before, but I've always refused. I said yes to you because of something nice you did for me. I'll bet you've forgotten."

"Something I did? When?"

"The accident . . . with the car. On Sunset."

It suddenly clicked. "That was you?"

Marilyn smiled and nodded. "You were so wonderful to me that day, and I've never been able to pay you back. And, you know, the time we worked together before, I was too embarrassed to say anything. So what we did tonight, well, that was my way of thanking you."

Just before leaving Barney's Beanery, Natalie handed me an envelope. In it was a check for fifty dollars and the model release for the calendar session. Marilyn was in a playful mood now. She signed the release as "Mona Monroe," then she kissed me lightly on the cheek.

I thought that night might be the last I'd see of Marilyn, but I was wrong. Even though she went on to become queen of Twentieth Century-Fox and America's top sex symbol, she continued to drop by my studio on occasion, always unannounced. That was fine. We'd sit at the lunch table, drink cups

A rare double exposure, showing Marilyn in a reclining stretch pose as well as a sitting position

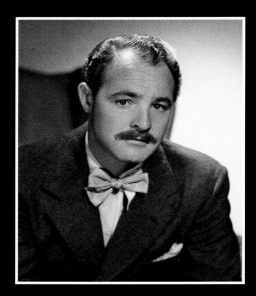

Above: Portrait of Tom Kelley, taken in 1949, the year he photographed Marilyn Monroe for her famous calendar
Opposite: Alternate sitting pose, one of the many unused shots taken on May 27, 1949

of coffee, and talk about that night with me on the ladder and her stretched out on the velour-covered floor. One time she confessed that she was petrified at having posed for me, fearing that someone in the film industry would recognize her once the calendar was released. As it turned out, she blew the whistle herself. It certainly didn't hurt her.

Like Marilyn, the calendar created a sensation. It's been reported that I shopped the photos after they were taken, but I had a waiting client. His name was John Baumgarth. A lithographer, he ran an art calendar print shop (John Baumgarth & Son) in the Chicago suburb of Melrose Park. John paid $300.00 for the color shots and complete rights for reproduction. I'd say John made a fortune on his small investment, especially after the identity of the reclining subject became known. I don't know how many copies of the calendar were sold, but it must be in the millions, and it's still selling. I imagine it will be selling for years to come.

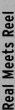

GLORIA SWANSON AND JOE KENNEDY IN LOVE

BY BETTY GOODWIN

Gloria Swanson never spoke of loving Joseph P. Kennedy, but instead commented on his fine manners and breeding. It never bothered her that his wife Rose would not give him a divorce. Joseph Kennedy was intoxicated with Gloria Swanson's power in the movie capital. At last he had met a woman who wasn't interested in his money—she had plenty.

Joseph P. Kennedy was a Harvard-educated banker who was looking to make a fortune in the movie business. Gloria Swanson was one of Hollywood's reigning stars, with driving ambition to match. But she lacked business acumen; in fact, she was seriously in debt. When their paths crossed in 1927, he took over her finances and set her up with a new production company. They also launched into an illicit personal relationship that lasted for several years.

Having Gloria in his stable provided Joe with an entrée into the upper echelon of moviedom. She was box-office gold, one of the most alluring stars of all time. When a studio friend hooked them up to see if Joe could help her finance her movies, Joe, thirty-nine, wasn't exactly in Hollywood's major leagues. He was an owner of Film Booking Offices of America, a small movie distribution and production company, and soon became chairman of the Keith Albee Orpheum corporation, a chain of seven hundred movie theaters, which he sold to RCA. He was also chairman of Pathé Exchange when it merged with RKO. With each transaction, Joe was getting richer and richer. Gloria, twenty-eight, had been Paramount's biggest star, but bolted under the restrictions of the studio to become an independent producer. She desperately needed money to support her lavish lifestyle and the movies she wanted to make. A year before, she became an owner with Charlie Chaplin, Mary Pickford, Douglas Fairbanks, D. W. Griffith, and Joseph Schenck of United Artists, which would release her movies.

"I had no doubt in my mind that I had stumbled on the right business partner to straighten out my career," Gloria wrote in *Swanson on Swanson: An Autobiography*.

Gloria, the mother of two, was recently married to her third husband, a charming but otherwise unremarkable French nobleman, Marquis Le Bailly de la Falaise de la Coudraye, who worked as her interpreter on the movie *Madame Sans-Gêne* (1925) in France. As for Joe, he had a reputation as a ladies' man regardless of the fact that he was a married man with a brood of seven children (Jean and Ted came later), including a future president of the United States. Joe acted with abandon, inviting Gloria to visit his family at their rambling, white house in Hyannis Port on Nantucket Sound in Massachusetts. Nearly every biography of the senior Kennedy repeats the scandalous tale, authentic or not, about the time he and Gloria snuck off for an assignation on his sailboat, the *Rose Elizabeth,* and, unbeknownst to them, twelve-year-old John was hidden below the deck. Whatever young John witnessed, he jumped overboard to swim back to shore—followed by Joe. On another occasion, Joe and his wife Rose traveled to Europe with Gloria. Many Kennedy watchers speculate that Joe's outrageous behavior sent his sons a clear-cut message that cheating was acceptable.

Joe quickly established Gloria Productions Inc. and dispatched her husband overseas as European director of Pathé studios. Joe also proposed that he back her next picture, *Queen Kelly* (1928), to be directed by Erich von Stroheim. It would be the first major movie with which Joe was associated. However, every aspect of the film was a disaster and Gloria was constantly pouring her own money into it. *Queen Kelly* was never released in the United States. (Ironically, twenty years later, Gloria starred in *Sunset Boulevard* with von Stroheim playing her butler, a washed-up director. In the movie, they actually watch clips from *Queen Kelly*.)

Joe wasn't enthusiastic about their next collaboration, *The Trespasser* (1929), and no thanks to him, it became an unqualified hit, earning Gloria her second Oscar nomination (her first was for *Sadie Thompson* in 1928). "Much as I cared for Joseph Kennedy, he was a classic example of that person in the arts with lots of brains and drive but little taste or talent," wrote Swanson. Shortly thereafter, her French husband left her for Constance Bennett, a rising star at Pathé.

Around this time, Gloria was called upon by Boston's Cardinal O'Connell. He asked that she stop seeing Joe. Gloria never knew who put him up to this task. The cardinal did, however, say that Joe had "sought permission to live apart from his wife and maintain a second household with her," according to Axel Madsen in the book *Gloria & Joe*.

In 1930, Joe and Gloria made a third picture, a farce called *What a Widow!*, which was another flop. Joe sold Pathé to RKO. Joe and Gloria's relationship ended on a sour note. He had charged a Cadillac to Gloria's personal account; he had given the car to screenwriter Sidney Howard as a gift. As soon as Gloria confronted him, Joe disappeared from her life. When she went over her books, she learned that Joe had also charged her for a fur coat he had given her as well as for the bungalow he had built for her on the Pathé lot.

In a short time, Joe was spotted with Nancy Carroll, an actress who resembled Gloria. He and Rose had two more children, and Joe dropped out of the film business. Gloria and the marquis were divorced and he married Constance Bennett. Gloria became pregnant after a fling with a young playboy, Michael Farmer, and married him at his insistence, and their daughter was born a few months later. In 1945, she married her fifth husband, William Davey, an alcoholic stockbroker, and divorced him a month later. In 1976, she entered into her sixth and final marriage, this time to writer William Dufty.

ALSO KNOWN AS . . .

They are that rare group of Hollywood royalty, stars who have been crowned with adoring nicknames by their fans—or studio publicists—because of that special "something" that sets them apart from all the others.

It really all began after the turn of the century when Florence Lawrence was known only as "the Biograph Girl" in honor of her studio, Biograph, where she was the recurring leading lady. In the earliest days of silent films, players were anonymous until audiences demanded to know the names of their favorites. Lawrence became the first film star to be known to the public by name.

Then along came "the Girl with the Golden Hair" and "America's Sweetheart" (Mary Pickford), "the Little Tramp" (Charlie Chaplin), "the Vamp" (Theda Bara), "the Great Profile" (John Barrymore), "the Girl Who Was Too Beautiful" (Barbara LaMarr), and "the IT Girl" (Clara Bow).

With the advent of talkies, new faces began to catch the public's fancy. Among them were new stars who were labeled with nicknames that would become forever associated with them. Jean Harlow was tabbed "the Platinum Blonde" and "Blonde Bombshell." Myrna Loy, after years of playing vamps and exotic characters, was named "the Perfect Wife" when she was teamed opposite William Powell in the sophisticated film adaptation of Dashiell Hammett's mystery, *The Thin Man* (1934).

Clark Gable became "the King," thanks to a joking remark by Spencer Tracy in the MGM studio commissary, and a sixteen-year-

old unknown named Lana Turner was dubbed "the Sweater Girl" when she filmed a brief scene in *They Won't Forget* (1937). As director Mervyn LeRoy, who discovered Turner, recalled, "When she walked down the street, in the film, her bosom seemed to move in rhythm, a rhythm all its own. When I added the musical score to the picture, I made sure that the composer emphasized that rhythm. She wore a sweater in that scene, and that's how she got her reputation as the Sweater Girl."

Dorothy Lamour, an overnight sensation as queen of Hollywood's South Seas island pictures, became "the Sarong Girl." Betty Grable, a favorite of GI's during World War II, was "the Pin-Up Girl," while Marie MacDonald attracted attention as "the Body." Lauren Bacall's nervousness before the cameras gave rise to "the Look," a suggestive, come-hither glance. Handsome John Payne competed as "the Body Beautiful" with beefy, buff Victor Mature, who was knighted "the Hunk."

Carmen Miranda, a Technicolor treat from her platform shoes to her ornate, towering turbans, raced onto the scene in 1940 as "the Brazilian Bombshell," even though she was actually born in Portugal. Frank Sinatra crooned his way into America's hearts as "the Voice" and "Old Blue Eyes," while Bill Robinson danced his way as "Bojangles." John Wayne became forever "the Duke."

In more recent years, audiences have come to know Madonna as "the Material Girl," Belgian-born Jean-Claude Van Damme as "the Muscles from Brussels," and Jack Nicholson (who named himself) as "the Great Seducer." But fewer recent stars have been tagged with nicknames. Perhaps that is because stars are no longer tied to studios and their publicity machines. Perhaps it is also because today's stars are missing that "something" that would set them apart. Or maybe it is simply because many—Cher, Barbra, Whoopi, Oprah, Liza, Bette, Goldie, Sly, Sting—have names unlike those of the past: instantly recognizable single names that light up a marquee.

Preceding page: Ann Sheridan was so sexy in her late 1930s films that she became known as "the Oomph Girl."
Opposite left: Clara Bow's nickname, "the IT Girl," lived on much longer than she as the symbol of the Roaring Twenties.
Opposite right: Marie MacDonald was known as "the Body" once people noticed her perfect curves.
Left: "The Great Profile," John Barrymore, was a matinee idol in both silent films and early talkies.
Opposite bottom: Carmen Miranda became the kitsch symbol of the 1940s and carried the title of "the Brazilian Bombshell."
Below: Once audiences saw Lana Turner wearing a sweater in *They Won't Forget* (1937), she became "the Sweater Girl."

READY-TO-WEAR STARS

BY HEIDI DVORAK

T o the horror—and delight—of fans, Marlene Dietrich wore a tuxedo to the premiere of *The Sign of the Cross* (1932). Back then, pants were considered menswear, and the actress's then-provocative fashion selection was the talk of Hollywood. Nevertheless, women began scouring stores for pants. One clothing manufacturer begged Dietrich to promote a pantsuit, but she adamantly refused. "I'm no crusader," she said. "I wear what I like and expect other women to do the same . . . It would be a pity if American women took to trousers."

It was a greater pity that Dietrich did not come up with a signature label for what turned out to be the biggest and longest-lasting fashion craze in history—she might have been an even bigger and richer star, though that's difficult to imagine. She also might have been a trendsetter in a business sense as well as a fashion sense. Despite Dietrich's refusal, celebrities have been lending their names to sell clothing since the 1930s.

Once the studio system ended, and stars and their agents started making the deals, most celebrities were no longer content to just endorse a clothing item. Business savvy taught them that when endorsing a signature line, it paid off to review fabric selections, color palettes, fit, and styling. The more fashion-savvy have even submitted sketches, and a rare handful began fulfilling lifelong dreams of being designers.

A winner of the Neiman-Marcus style

Opposite: Alexis Smith and Joan Leslie modeled Demoiselle dresses for day and evening in 1945 while helping to promote their latest film, *Rhapsody in Blue*.
Above: Lucille Ball put her stamp of approval on *I Love Lucy* apparel in 1952. Since the Lucy character embodied middle-American values over Hollywood glamour, Ball wanted her clothing to be simple and practical. Aprons, Monsanto raincoats, blouses, pajamas (with Lucy and Ricky caricatures), jackets, and sweaters were snapped up by fans. Here she poses in the late 1940s modeling one of the sun suits the public could copy.

Rhapsody in Blue

Reflecting the rhythm and romance of the great Warner Bros. production in which they star, Alexis Smith and Joan Leslie wear Dorothy Phillip's Demoiselle evening creation and Lynn Lester's Western Fashions daytime classic fashioned from "Rhapsody in Blue", an original California Authentics hand-screened print on Verdugo rayon. Featured with matching handbags and millinery at a select few of the nation's leading stores.

award in 1950, *Sunset Boulevard*'s Gloria Swanson began by designing some of her own gowns. The 5'1" actress then became a consultant for Puritan fashions, creating "Forever Young," a line of clothes scaled for large-sized women. According to Patty Fox, author of *Star Style: Hollywood Legends as Fashion Icons,* Swanson advised Puritan's designer Rene Huber to "shorten sleeves so they don't look like old lady dresses," adding, "a waistline is not straight. It should dip down in the back." Her twenty-year association with Puritan turned a $10 million business into a $100 million success.

In 1958 swimmer-turned-MGM aquatic star Esther Williams endorsed signature swimming pools but didn't get her feet wet in fashion until 1988, when she teamed up with Excelsior swimsuits. Incorporating her expertise into suits, Williams picked fabrics that would hold up when wet, styles that would allow for maximum movement while covering strategic areas. In 1991 her own ten-piece collection, inspired by her films *Dangerous when Wet* (1953) and *Million Dollar Mermaid* (1952), featured Lycra one-pieces, a bikini with a bandeau top, boy-leg bottoms, and a halter dress suit. At seventy-five, she was still overseeing manufacturing and design.

Using only her name and squeaky-clean, but sexy image, Doris Day endorsed her women's clothing label in the 1950s. The feminine attire consisted of dresses with coordinating sweaters and sweater sets. Day's line was a huge success, appealing to every blond girl-next-door in America.

As the years passed, celebrity endorsements became more numerous, and the bigger the star, the bigger the financial rewards of an apparel endorsement. But those numbers have always been held close to the vest. It can be assumed that with Hollywood stars as adored as Madonna and sports stars as beloved as Michael Jordan lending their names to the labels in clothes, there's enough money in it to keep the stars—and their fans—dressing very well, well into the twenty-first century.

Above: Ever since Sears Roebuck created its first Shirley Temple line of kids' clothes and featured Joan Crawford costume copies for women—both endorsed by the stars and featuring their images in the catalog—fashion marketers have understood that stars and apparel can be a perfect fit.
Opposite: Sears Roebuck featured Ginger Rogers's signature on the label of this felt fedora and captured her face in the ad.

$1.00

B

beauty hint: eyes look lovelier under a brimmed hat .. with a veil!

C

$1.98

hand made! of fine felt petals!

A

wool crepe "tucker" draped by hand

$1.49

A A sleek, snug fitting turban of fine wool crepe! With just a suspicion of draped width at the sides to make it becoming to all! The tucked band sweeps back in a bow end tailored to the crown beneath a pearlized pin. And a delicate, fine veil casts alluring shadows over the eyes!

78 F 7390—Fits 21¾ to 22¼ inches headsize.
78 F 7391—Fits 22½ to 23 inches headsize.......... **$1.49**
Colors: Black, Dark Brown or Navy Blue. *Measure and state color.* Shipping weight, 8 oz.

B Here's the typical hat for Fall 1934! With the shallower crown and the mushroom brim, the dip in front and the flattering veil! Makes you look modern; up to the minute! Made of fine quality all wool full body felt. Metal ornament. A wonder value that will surprise and delight you.

78 F 7385—Fits 21¾ to 22¼ inches headsize.
78 F 7386—Fits 22½ to 23 inches headsize.......... **$1.00**
Colors: Black, Jaffa (Dark) Brown, Cruise (Navy) Blue or Rubytone (dk. wine red). *State color.* Shpg. wt., 1 lb.

C These small leaf shaped petals are made of very fine supple all wool body felt (*not felt cloth*), skillfully overlapped and sewn by hand into a sleek snug-fitting turban. Fine and smart enough for your loveliest dresses. A stiffened visor veil flares gaily over the eyes.

78 F 7300—Fits 21¾ to 22¼ inches headsize.......... **$1.98**
Colors: Black, Jaffa (Dark) Brown, Cruise (Navy) Blue or Scotty (Dark) Green. *State color.* Shipping weight, 10 oz.

this stunning hollywood fashion is fur felt — a beautiful quality

$1.98

When Ginger Rogers O.K.'s this hat, you can be sure it has the gay dash and glamour that she demands in her clothes! That *you* like in your fashions! Sears have the identical hat shown in this photograph! And you don't have to be "in the money" to own it! Made of genuine *Fur* felt, that soft, supple quality that takes lovelier lines than ordinary wool felt. The new, one-sided fedora crease gives a rakish, tilted effect to the crown. The rich ribbon band ends in a whisk of fringe at the side. This fine Fur Felt hat is included in Ginger Rogers' new Fall wardrobe. It deserves a place in *yours,* too!

78 F 7310—Fits 21¾ to 22¼ inches headsize.
78 F 7311—Fits 22½ to 23 inches headsize.
Colors: Black, Jaffa (Dk.) Brown, Cruise (Navy) Blue or Rubytone (dark wine red). *State color.* Shpg. wt., 1 lb.

Autographed
AUTOGRAPHED *Fashions*
WORN IN HOLLYWOOD BY
Ginger Rogers REGISTERED

CELEBRITY AUCTIONS

BY SHEILA PERKINS

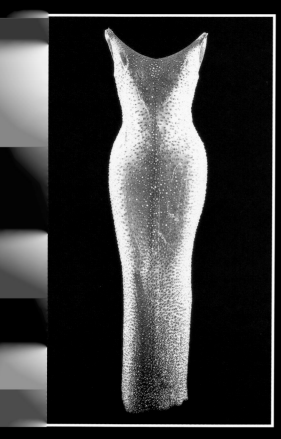

Dyed-in-the-wool Marilyn Monroe fans had a mixed bag of emotions when they exited the first night of the 1999 Christie's auction during which belongings of the century's most desirable woman were offered to the highest bidders. Sure, they got to see the goods, up-close and personal. Some even got to hold up their bid cards. But that was the upside. The downside was that there wasn't really a chance to buy—not when somebody like 1990s sportswear designer Tommy Hilfiger was forking over $42,550 for three pairs of JC Penny jeans and $85,000 for the cowboy boots she wore in *The Misfits* (1961). Or, God forbid, that an antique collectibles house pays $1.26 million for The Dress. This was the Kennedy birthday party dress—the one studded with rhinestones in all the right places, the one a real fan would die for, not simply pay for. The real fans who've spent their hard-earned dollars on all the books and photos and things she touched didn't have a chance.

The serious bidders were out to capture their slice of history, and perfection didn't matter. Nobody seemed to care that the eternity band DiMaggio gave her after they wed was missing a diamond. It went for $772,500 in its state of humble disrepair. And no one minded that the red *Prince and the Showgirl* (1957) gown wasn't really the gown that she actually wore in the movie, but the one worn for publicity stills. It still went for $150,000. So what does that make the white *Seven Year Itch* (1955) dress worth that Debbie Reynolds owns? A million bucks? More? Is its icon status enough to make it more valuable than the birthday dress used to woo the midcentury's favorite president? Indeed the Marilyn auction was the appropriate way to end the century that introduced movie-star memorabilia auctions. Certainly no celebrity auction matched this one's frenzy, but Sotheby's sale of Jacqueline Kennedy Onassis's personal items in 1996 came close. And perhaps it was the Onassis auction that opened the door for the Monroe extravaganza. When the former First Lady's triple strand of faux pearls went for $211,500, was it really a surprise that a thousand items reflecting almost every aspect of Marilyn's life would garner more than $13 million? Back in the days when Jack Warner, Louis B. Mayer, Darryl F. Zanuck, and Harry Cohn ruled Hollywood, nobody thought about auctioning off costumes. Costumes once worn by their stars were packed away for future use and studios swapped the clothes at will, never realizing the dollars those pieces might be worth down the road. What was worn by Rita Hayworth in one film for Columbia could just have easily been worn by Marilyn Monroe ten years later in a different film for Fox. If something had been worn in a movie, it held no value beyond its next rental.

To reduce the mounting storage costs of old film costumes, MGM was the first major studio to hold an official public auction, dubbed the "Star Wardrobe," in 1970. To the short-sighted bean counters who worked at MGM, the guys who valued a few bucks over a warehouse full of Smithsonian quality American nostalgia, the MGM costumes were considered a burden. They decided to sell off whatever "junk" they could. But MGM hadn't counted on the response, especially the response to a pair of thirty-one-year-old red shoes. An anonymous bidder paid the then unheard of sum of $15,000 for the famous ruby slippers worn by Judy Garland in *The Wizard of Oz.*

Suddenly studio executives caught on: it wasn't the garments themselves that were selling at such high prices, but rather the memories those costumes evoked. In the case of the ruby slippers, what price was too high for a cherished childhood memory, the fantasy of clicking your heels together and making dreams come true? But by the time the message was clear, it was too late, prices had zoomed. By 1988, when Christie's secured a second pair of ruby slippers (duplicates had been made for the 1939 film, which is still common and necessary practice for all Hollywood costumes), the glittering shoes drew the staggering sum of $165,000. In the post-Marilyn days of auctioneering, the red shoes commanded $666,000 at a Christie's East auction, in May 2000. The shoes were the first important piece of film-history memorabilia to be publicly auctioned in the twenty-first century. Until Marilyn's rhinestoned birthday dress, no other piece of Hollywood clothing had held the auction bidders, as well as the general public, in such enchanted reverence.

The Dress and the ruby slippers aside, however, other pieces of personal property that belonged to stars or have made appearances in their films have commanded equally astonishing bids. Sometimes it didn't even have to be a huge star, just a huge memory. For instance, on a scale of zero being an unlucky starlet and ten being Monroe, Dorothy Lamour was surely just a four or five. Yet one of the *Her Jungle Love* (1938) sarongs (designed by Edith Head), which eventually became Lamour's silver-screen signature, garnered $4,600 at Sotheby's. Considering that the 14-karat gold money clip Marlene Dietrich, who ranks between eight and nine on the subjective fame scale, gave to French star Jean Gabin as a token of her love went for a whopping $6,325 (Gabin returned the money clip when their relationship fell to pieces), the price for Lamour's sarong is very respectable. Gary Cooper had given Dietrich a 14-karat gold cigarette case, which sold for $10,925.

Stars' jewels sparkle on their new owners at the turn of the century just as brightly as they did sixty years earlier. Ella Fitzgerald's signature gold hoop earrings went for $3,737, while the 14-karat gold engraved ID bracelet given to Count Basie from Ella Fitzgerald sold for $4,887. The band was inscribed with "Chief" on the front, with "Love, Ella" on the back. Joan Crawford's brass and enamel twelve-charm bracelet, made in China in the 1930s, sold for $920. Possibly most unwearable, however, was the Medal of Courage, given to Burt Lahr as he played the beloved Cowardly Lion in *The Wizard of Oz* (1939), yet it was another piece that sold for the nostalgia factor. Valued by Sotheby's in 1999 at between $15,000 to $20,000, the medal sold for an astonishing $33,350.

Fashions will always hold their own appeal, but the highest bids are dependent on who wore them: Gene Kelly's famed dancing shoes worn during *An American in Paris* (1951), $3,220; Errol Flynn's shirt worn in *The Adventures of Robin Hood* (1938), $5,175; Natalie Wood's dress from *West Side Story* (1961), $3,450; Elizabeth Taylor's dress from *National Velvet* (1945), $4,025; Charlton Heston's *Ben-Hur* loincloth, $10,350; and Judy Garland's dress from *In the Good Old Summertime* (1949), $2,760.

Anything with a signature automatically raises the auction price. Marilyn's annotated script for *Some Like It Hot* (1959) went over the $50,000 mark at Christie's. Sotheby's landed $3,220 for Greta Garbo's 1943 handwritten letter to Gilbert Roland. A collection of Bette Davis's handwritten letters from the 1960s, discussing financial situations, "thank you" notes, and several referring to everyday things such as tea and scones, garnered $2,990, almost twice the asking price. But even more grandiose than handwritten letters was the autographed copy of Margaret Mitchell's *Gone with the Wind*. Inscribed in 1938 to the governor of Virginia, the book contained over one hundred signatures, most notably those of Clark Gable, Vivien Leigh, Leslie Howard, and Olivia de Havilland. This book collected $5,175 at Sotheby's. But who's to say it's less valuable than Clark Gable's Oscar for *It Happened One Night* (1934), given to him as best actor, which earned $607,500 at Christie's in 1996.

Old stars from the glory days of the Hollywood studio system are not the only ones to command high bids from loyal fans. The 1990s celebrities have just as much to offer in terms of movie nostalgia. Winona Ryder's costume from *Boys* (1996), including a sweater, skirt, tights, boots, and a pair of underwear, went for $2,070. Steve Martin's *Sgt. Bilko* (1996) costume, worn as Bilko cruised the Las Vegas strip in a tank, went for $3,335. Tom Hanks's military uniform worn as the irresistible *Forrest Gump* in 1992, $3,625; Michael J. Fox's radiation suit worn as Marty McFly during flying DeLorean scenes in *Back to the Future* (1985), $3,105.

Big dollars go for props that masquerade as characters. One such example is the flying saucer from the movie *Independence Day,* which took on an extraterrestrial life of its own. The saucer, painted gray with black "window holes," propped on legs with antennae, sold at Sotheby's for $2,530.

No matter what the auction price for celebrity fashions, furniture, jewels, movie props, or even Marilyn Monroe's personal property, most fans agree that there can be no price tag for memories. Fortunately, MGM learned that lesson with their public auction in 1970, and it was proven again by Marilyn's fans in 1999. When it comes to Hollywood nostalgia, the bottom line is never the actual bottom line.

6

From the earliest days of cinema, a gifted handful of actors and actresses elicited smiles on their audiences' faces and laughter that echoed through theaters. They continue to make us laugh as we look back at their movies, learning firsthand in our merriment that what was funny then, is still funny now and always will be funny. Anyone for a pie in the face?

Danny Kaye first attracted attention when he appeared with Gertrude Lawrence on Broadway in *Lady in the Dark* (1941). By 1943, he was under contract to Samuel Goldwyn and was starring in a string of lavish Technicolor musical-comedies, often opposite beautiful Virginia Mayo. Kaye's versatile comedic talents (he could sing tongue-twisting lyrics at a rapid clip without a slip) and winning personality soon established him as an international favorite, particularly in Great Britain.

FUNNY FACES

Once sound became more common to films in the late 1920s, every studio filled its roster with funny men and women from the stages of burlesque and vaudeville. No longer were pantomime and body language the keys to comedy. All those one-liners that had worked on stages across America were now made available to moviegoers—and audiences were happy to pay the 35 cents to 85 cents it cost to see a talking film, especially if it made them laugh. After the stock market

Right: The Marx Brothers—Zeppo, Harpo, Chico, and Groucho—honed their slapstick in vaudeville before they made it to the screen in *The Cocoanuts* (1929). Groucho became a star on his own as author and TV host.
Below: The Three Stooges—Larry, Curly, and Moe—were a rock 'em, sock 'em, pie-in-the-face trio of "nut cases" whose humor tickled everyone's funny bones. Their popularity began to soar in 1934 with a long-running series of two-reel comedies, and later when a new generation of fans saw them on TV.

crashed in 1929, people needed to laugh, so comedies became part of Hollywood's war against the Depression. Comedians came to town in droves, as solo artists or as teams, all trying to make it as lead performers or supporting cast members. Women, who had traditionally been relegated to dramatic or light romantic leads, became known for their comedic skills; the 1930s spawned Mae West, whose humor challenged the censors and opened doors for women to say outrageously funny things on the screen.

Individual comedic greats were in a class by themselves, and their appeal and jokes spanned decades: Bob Hope, Joe E. Brown, W. C. Fields, Mae West, Joan Davis, Red Skelton, Marion Davies, Martha Raye, Eve Arden, Milton Berle, Jackie Gleason, Jack Benny, Danny Kaye, Patsy Kelly, ZaSu Pitts, Thelma Todd, Lucille Ball, and Ann Sothern. The top teams included Laurel and Hardy, Burns and Allen, the Marx Brothers, the Ritz Brothers, the Three Stooges, Abbott and Costello, and Martin and Lewis.

Below: Stan Laurel and Oliver Hardy had met by accident in 1917 during the filming of *Lucky Dog*, but they were not teamed until 1926. The British-born Laurel, known as the "thin man" of the duo, and the "chubby," cherubic-faced Hardy went on to enjoy unprecedented popularity, becoming what has been called "the most fabulously successful comedy duo the screen has ever known."

Opposite: Dean Martin and Jerry Lewis teamed up in 1946 after making little headway on their own as solo performers. Three years later, thanks to their popularity in nightclubs and theaters, they were starring in movies. With Dean as the crooning, handsome babe magnet and Jerry as the goofy, childlike clown, they became overnight sensations, one of the most incredible success stories in show business. Their partnership lasted until 1957, when each man set out on his own.

Below: Vaudevillians Eddie Cantor, left, and George Jessel entered films during the silent era. Cantor continued in front of the camera, on both film and television, until the early 1950s. Jessel was behind the lens as a producer of musicals for Fox and was renowned for his skills as emcee cum jokester, becoming known as "America's Toastmaster General."

DIMPLED FLESH

D imples. Where would Shirley Temple have been without 'em? Could the ringlets jumpstart a career as fast as those little indentations at either corner of her mouth? And Clark Gable—would women's hearts have melted over him had his cheeks not been hollowed with a touch of humanity? No way. Dimples are symbols of true power in old Hollywood—only the most powerful stars faced the screen with them.

That they accompany a smile causes immediate reciprocal behavior; so for many years it was Hollywood's way to eradicate dimples on its major stars unless a star was out to evoke riotous laughter. No serious actress or big-screen beauty had dimples in the 1930s or 1940s, or if she did, makeup artists, cameramen, still photographers, and directors worked their magic to eliminate them. A dimple was a sign of humor, not beauty and drama.

Then along came Gable—the sex symbol of the 1930s. Gable's tough/tender masculinity made his dimples as sexy as his piercing eyes. In time, females could show dimples occasionally—Marilyn Monroe, for instance. But even the divine Miss MM learned to smile without displaying them when necessary.

Opposite: One look at Red Skelton's indented cheeks and audiences broke into laughter.

Below Left: Even when Clark Gable was telling Scarlett that he didn't give a damn, there was a trace of a dimple showing. Those trademark dents were proof positive that he was the king of Hollywood.

Below: Shirley Temple's dimples were undoubtedly the most famous in the history of the film world. As a child, hers was the best-known smile in the world.

SILENT CINEMA'S MOST NORMAL GUY

BY ANNETTE D'AGOSTINO LLOYD AND
SUZANNE LLOYD HAYES

I n the realm of silent film comedy, the name Harold Lloyd holds many traces of magic. Not only did Lloyd redefine the standards of comic film, but his work still thrills and amazes audiences with his wide scope of character offerings. He dangled from clocks; he hung off streetcars; he scaled buildings; he rode horses through city streets; he was poor, rich, cowardly, brash. Realistic comic diversity was his cinematic trademark. All this from a fellow who was trained on the dramatic stage in the rural Midwest.

Born in Burchard, Nebraska, on April 20, 1893, Harold Clayton Lloyd was reared in a nomadic, poverty-stricken, and ultimately broken family. His penchant, from an early age, was acting, and he whetted his appetite for histrionics in theater. He arrived in Los Angeles in 1912 and found early entry into the relatively new medium of film. After a 1913 on-screen debut, he proceeded to work for many companies, including Edison, Universal, and Keystone. His real career began, however, after joining forces with Hal Roach in 1914. Three years after their initial collaboration, Lloyd created his immortal "Glass Character," and it soon became his claim to fame. This persona, shedding the industry's then-standard eccentric makeup and wacky get-ups and costumes, simply presented a normal boy in common clothes doing ordinary things—revolutionizing comedy by allowing audiences to see themselves in the character.

This character would carry Lloyd throughout the rest of his career, which

spanned thirty-four years of active filmmaking, 201 comedies (mostly ten- and twenty-minute-long short subjects, including eleven silent and seven sound features), one 1928 Oscar nomination, and a 1953 Honorary Academy Award.

The "normality" of Lloyd's character meant that romance, among other plot choices, was more believable, and Lloyd's female costars (chiefly Bebe Daniels, Mildred Davis, and Jobyna Ralston) each went on to bigger and better careers after training with Lloyd. Davis took on a uniquely great role: on February 10, 1923, she became Mrs. Harold Lloyd.

Lloyd was a fabulously active and curious human being. Complementing his film career (he not only acted in, but he also produced all his pictures after 1924), Harold had a staggering number of hobbies and always mastered any avocation he touched. He greatly enjoyed Great Dane breeding and won numerous best in show ribbons. He pioneered film preservation by maintaining his own private film vault and was fascinated by color research and painting. In his later years, stereo (3-D) photography dominated his interests, and he shot upward of 300,000 color slides. Lloyd was also a founding member of the Actors' Branch of Academy of Motion Pictures Arts and Science in 1927. In 1949 he was elected Imperial Potentate, the highest national office of the Shriners, which he had joined in 1924. He produced "The Harold Lloyd Comedy Theatre" radio series in 1944–45. He owned the Llo-Da-Mar bowling establishment in Santa Monica—and, above all this, Harold was a devoted and playful husband and father, who truly personified the inscription on his Academy Award: "Master Comedian and Good Citizen."

Lloyd remained active in lecturing and traveling until cancer cut his life short, on March 8, 1971, at age seventy-seven.

Previous pages: Harold Lloyd alongside one of the many pools at Greenacres, his Beverly Hills estate. A true testament to his career, Lloyd's estate befitted cinematic royalty: sixteen lush acres, a nine-hole golf course, an Olympic-sized swimming pool, a waterfall leading to a canoe run and duck pond, seven separate gardens, tennis courts, and an indoor handball court. The central feature of the estate was the Italian Renaissance mansion, modeled after Rome's Villa d'Este. Prime among its forty-four rooms was a master bedroom suite (the size of a small house), which held two of the mansion's twenty-six bathrooms. The home's fourteen-inch-thick walls were designed to withstand the fiercest earthquake Mother Nature could offer. In 1984, the mansion was named to the National Registry of Historic Places.

Below: Lloyd and family in 1934. From left to right: Peggy, Harold, Harold, Jr., Gloria, and Mildred. Lloyd's lifestyle reflected his growing affluence (by the 1920s, he was the wealthiest performer in the world). In 1924, Harold and his wife Mildred built a swank home in L.A.'s fashionable Hancock Park district. Then, in 1929, the Lloyds moved into their magnificent estate, Greenacres, in the Benedict Canyon of Beverly Hills, and raised their three children.

Opposite: Harold Hickory (played by Lloyd) is having a grand time pretending to be the town sheriff in *The Kid Brother* (1927). Lloyd's career was almost halted in tragedy in 1919: right as Lloyd was gaining his greatest fame, a bomb blew up in his right hand, severing his thumb and index finger, and causing him temporary blindness. In the greatest tradition of the Lloyd comedies, which featured a boy who laughed at obstacles and always strove for success, Lloyd recovered his sight and his health, and he hid his deformity within a prosthetic glove. Harold came back, better than ever, leading popularity and box-office polls throughout the 1920s, as the most popular comedian in the world.

Charlie Chaplin, Harold Lloyd, Buster Keaton . . . the great clowns of the silent screen. They were the funnymen, the mimes, who made us laugh and even shed a tear or two, without a spoken word.

Portraying the common man, they did the impossible with a facial expression, a body posture, a walk, a run, or a pratfall. When Charlie Chaplin reflected on the first day creating his famous Tramp, circa 1914, he recalled that wearing baggy pants, a tiny mustache, and derby allowed him to shape the character: "This fellow is many-sided, a tramp, a gentleman, a poet, a dreamer, a lonely fellow. . . . He would have you believe he is a scientist, a musician, a duke, a polo player. However, he is not above picking up cigarette butts or robbing a baby of its candy." With those few words that he used to describe his Tramp to director Mack Sennett, he expressed the secret of his art. He intellectualized each character first and then let his body take over.

There were others who kept America laughing through good times and bad, including Roscoe "Fatty" Arbuckle, Polly Moran, Minta Durfee, Mabel Normand, Louise Fazenda, Ben Turpin, Chester Conklin, Marion Davies, Ford Sterling, Marie Dressler, and the sassiest of flappers, Clara Bow.

Above: Louise Fazenda began her career at age eighteen in 1913 in Universal's Joker shorts, in which she played wacky characters. From there she joined Mack Sennett's Keystone players, famous for its slapstick two-reel comedies and bathing beauties. In later years, she became an accomplished character actress.

Left: Buster Keaton's unsmiling deadpan expression earned him the title of "the Great Stone Face." An accomplished acrobat as a child, he was raised in medicine shows and vaudeville as part of a family comedy act known as the Three Keatons. With his keen sense of timing, he entered films in 1917 at age twenty-one as a supporting player and found enormous fame as the game little fellow who always came out on top, whatever the odds. Seen here with Kathyrn McGuire in *The Navigator* (1924).

FRANCIS THE TALKING MULE

BY PHILLIP DYE

Below and right: Although many mules played Francis in his seven eponymous films, only two actors played his pal—Donald O'Connor in six and Mickey Rooney in the finale. Donald O'Connor didn't have an easy task playing opposite a talking mule. But the series showcased the actor's remarkable comedic talent and turned him into a star.

In the 1940s and early 1950s, a popular part of any double bill was a feature comedy. With the same actors and directors from a successful movie under contract, it was cheap and easy for a studio to utilize the same characters and situations in a sequel—if the sequel was a hit, subsequent films were scheduled and a series was born.

There were many series: *Blondie*, derived from the popular comic strip; *Andy Hardy* at MGM, which was in turn imitated by the Henry Aldrich series at Paramount; *Maisie*, starring Ann Sothern as a showgirl involved in various humorous entanglements; the *Bowery Boys*, following the screw-ups and foibles of juvenile delinquents as portrayed by middle-aged actors. But the most unusual was the Universal Studios series about a talking mule.

Animals who chat are a sure sign of either a children's movie or demonic possession. The *Francis* movies were neither, though the series had elements of both. The original 1949 movie *Francis* was based on a novel by David Stern (the book is shown at the beginning of the movie to show its respectable origin; no Hollywood screenwriter came up with this idea, they want you to know, although Stern did write the screenplay). The story was set in Burma during World War II. Lost in the jungle, a bumbling army officer, Lt. Peter Stirling—played by comic Donald O'Connor, who had started acting at age eleven—encounters an army mule. Much to his astonishment, the mule talks, identifying itself as "Francis" ("that's Francis with an 'i,' " the mule insists in a gravelly voice only character-actor Chill Wills could have created), lambasting the officer's stupidity, and finally helping the wounded man to safety. This set the pattern of their relationship, with Francis getting Stirling in and out of trouble, insulting the hapless human every step of the way.

Francis was an unexpected smash hit at the box office, so Universal came out with a sequel. It started where the original movie ended, but otherwise the series paid little attention to continuity. Studios often used a series to try out new actors and aspiring starlets to test acting skills and public appeal. While some actors found it merely a pause on the road to obscurity, a few notable stars received a boost from the *Francis* series. Future *Fugitive* David Janssen appeared in three films of the series. *Francis Joins the Navy* (1955) featured Jim Backus as an officer, and, in his second screen appearance, Clint Eastwood as a sailor.

A number of different mules played Francis, their training limited to going into a stall or "mouthing" words on cue. Often, an off-camera hand jostled the mule's head to mimic the movements of speech. Nevertheless Francis the talking mule became a popular star in Hollywood, though the mules were indifferent to the acclaim. Francis won the first "Patsy" for animal stars, an award virtually created for the purpose of promoting Francis movies, although many other animal stars would later win. A peeved O'Connor complained that the mule got more fan mail than he did.

In *Francis and the Haunted House*, the original creative team of director Arthur Lubin, O'Connor, and Wills had left the series for greener pastures, and were replaced by director Charles Lamont and actors Mickey Rooney and Paul Frees. Best remembered as the voice of Boris Badenoff in the *Rocky and Bullwinkle* cartoons, voice-over specialist Frees had a distinctive voice on par with Wills. Former child star Rooney had beaten out promising new actor Ken Berry for the role of Francis's new pal. Rooney could summon the frantic energy of O'Connor for befuddled excitement. But lacking a better script, this replacement team couldn't save the series from the mire. After this box-office dud, Universal finally put the *Francis* series out of its misery.

His career revived by the series, O'Connor had moved on to bigger things, including a scene-stealing performance in *Singin' in the Rain* (1952). His greatest success would be in television in his own variety shows. Wills continued his career as a character actor in dozens of films, earning an Oscar nomination for supporting actor for his role in *The Alamo* (1960).

It's commonly held knowledge that a mule is the offspring of a donkey and a horse, but in Hollywood, a talking mule sired a talking horse. When director Arthur Lubin left movies to work in television, he created, produced, and directed the entire *Mister Ed* TV series, starring a talking horse. Of course, of course.

WILL ROGERS IN HOLLYWOOD
BY JOSEPH H. CARTER

I n 1918, superstar Will Rogers arrived in Hollywood from Broadway accompanied by the only wife he ever had or wanted, four kids, and two horses named Dodo and Dopey. Samuel Goldwyn quickly constructed a corral on his movie lot for the horses and adroitly launched MGM upon the folksy film fame of this man who would become an American legend.

Goldwyn put Rogers on the silver screen after the former Wild West and vaudeville showman had spent more than a decade in the *Ziegfeld Follies*. Rogers's first movie was a silent six-reeler, *Laughing Bill Hyde* (1918), filmed in New Jersey. Rogers baffled stardom, nurtured studios, and exploded stereotypes while starring in fifty silent features and twenty-one talkies for various studios, and even tried his hand at producing.

No matter what the character's name, he essentially played Will Rogers, an affable frontier Cherokee born on a ten-thousand-head cattle ranch in Indian territory. In cinema, he was Everyman. Rogers's cowboy roles were mainly parodies on Wild West cinema, even though he had driven, branded, and nurtured cattle herds on the real frontier without need of firearms. He willed shoot-'em-up Westerns to others.

Even more significant to American history than his career in film was his impact on the public. His acting days were interspersed with other roles as a syndicated newspaper columnist, author of six books, advisor to presidents, friend of kings and

Above: The face of an unidentified man in a crowd telegraphs recognition of Spencer Tracy and Will Rogers wearing matching fedoras. Tracy was so saddened by Will's death that he never played polo again.

Opposite: Will Rogers uses a break from filming at Fox Studios to type his newspaper column. Broadway resurrected the cowboy humorist in 1991 by handing six Tony awards to *The Will Rogers Follies: A Life in Revue,* which had nearly a thousand Palace Theater performances.

senators, world traveler, and $1000-a-speech after-dinner humorist. Rogers invented the role of radio commentator, tossing uncanny barbs dulled by folksy wit. Both in person and in talking films, his contagious humor and his sardonic wit won the hearts of Americans. He went on to become one of the biggest stars of his era.

Rogers's home life was also a main priority. Settling first in a mansion in newly founded Beverly Hills, he soon needed a large enough spread for his passions: family and animals. Betty and Will Rogers hacked out a $500,000, 300-acre ranch near Santa Monica with a sprawling frame house, roping arenas, cow pastures, a horse barn, and deluxe polo field. Rogers's three-goal polo handicap attracted most Hollywood stars to benefit games during the 1920s and 1930s.

The beloved star, who was fascinated with all facets of aviation, died in a plane crash in 1935 while flying with renowned pilot Wiley Post. Fifty thousand mourners passed Rogers's bier on his estate. The nostalgic ending of Rogers's last picture, *Steamboat 'Round the Bend* (1935), was reedited and toned down for its final showings, to console his distraught public. Nine years later and facing her own death from cancer, widow Betty quietly had the body moved to a hillside tomb in Claremore, Oklahoma—near the Indian village where he was born in 1879—and where the lovers now rest side by side.

Many of Rogers's witty quotes survive—unchallenged—more than half a century after he uttered them. Witness: "I never met a man I didn't like"; "If you live life right, death is a joke as far as fear is concerned"; and "The income tax has made liars out of more people than golf has." Another of his quotes is more ominous: "This acting thing don't last long. People get wise to you mighty quick and you never know what morning you might wake up without an audience." Therefore, Rogers advised, "retain your humor."

Below: Poster for *State Fair* (1933) fails to credit Rogers's favorite costar Blue Boy, a nine-hundred-pound Hampshire boar. His work in films was such a success that Rogers abandoned his $1000-a-week Broadway career for twice the pay in Hollywood, which grew into a top salary over the next seventeen years. The money was a resource to boost charities and environmental causes. He also bought a mile of Pacific shoreline and donated it to the state for a public beach that still bears his name.

Left: The Rogers family and their pet calf share a quiet evening in the living room of their Pacific Palisades ranch house, circa 1927. From left: Will, Jr., Jim (with calf), Betty, Mary (with dog), Will. Rogers was master of the cattleman's lariat. He performed spectacular rope tricks in his unparalleled 1922 two-reel silent film *The Ropin' Fool* (1922). It was a first in slow-motion photography. Because of his extraordinary skills, Will Rogers was dubbed the "poet lariat."

Below: Will Rogers, Irvin Cobb, center, and director John Ford confer on the set during the filming of *Judge Priest* (1934), which director John Ford dubbed as his own finest work. Bare-faced and ad-libbing were Rogers's style as he shunned stage makeup and wouldn't memorize or recite lines composed by screenwriters.

QUACKING UP THE OLD MASTERS

T he renowned film historian Ronald D. Haver, to whom this book is dedicated, was not bestowed with a middle name. He assumed the initial "D" later in life, and when asked what it stood for, he paid homage to his favorite Walt Disney character: "Duck," he explained, "Ronald Duck." Like so many others 'round the world, he felt the Duck was his man.
—The Editors

On April 16, 1945, *Life* magazine paid tribute to the world's most famous duck by showing a gallery of paintings devoted to him. The Duck was then only a bit more than ten years old, yet newborn babies had already been named in his honor, his quack was the most recognizable voice in the world, and one of his starring vehicles—the anti-Nazi film *Der Fuehrer's Face*—had won a 1943 Academy Award, so it was fitting that *Life* show another of his many sides. He was Donald Duck, the feathered friend of Peter Pig, introduced in *The Wise Little Hen* (1934). The film was the last we ever saw of Peter, but the Duck lived on. And on. The first Walt Disney character to show off a range of personality and emotion, be he mad, frustrated, or, if just for a moment, evil, Donald Duck was a versatile character.

So versatile, indeed, was Donald, as the *Life* article conveyed, that the team of artists who drew him celebrated him in their

Right: *Tahitian Ducks* are really sitting ducks à la Gauguin.

own renditions of fine art. John Dunn, Phil Klein, and Ray Patin turned out a new eight-minute animated film every three weeks in the 1930s and 1940s and then, anxious for relief from their daily toil, in their spare time, they fashioned a collection of "paintings" with the Duck as the central character. The artists used colored pencils in an attempt to simulate pastels, tempera, oil, and watercolors. Over the course of the four years that it took to complete the collection of seventeen works known in the Walt Disney Archives as the "Donald Duck Old Masters Collection," it hardly mattered whether the painting was *Pinkie or Blue Boy*, Degas's *Two Dancers*, Rembrandt's *The Noble Slav*, Gauguin's *Two Tahitian Women on the Beach*, or that the quacker was lost in the cubism of Picasso. The web-footed wonder had the perfect face to suit the Old Masters' frames.

The artists' diversion began in the animation room after they produced a Leonardo da Vinci–style take-off on *Mona Lisa* called *Madonna Duck*—a humorous prop in *The Reluctant Dragon* (1941), a film in which humorist Robert Benchley takes the audience on a behind-the-scenes tour of the Disney studios' creative spaces. With that, the artists let their minds run wild, finding not just predictable works in which

Don with a Pink painted in the manner of Quentin Massys

Harem Duck is an impressionistic tribute to Matisse.

Modern Quack would certainly make Picasso quack up.

El Quacko is a tribute to El Greco.

to incorporate their dear Donald, but eclectic pieces such as Brueghel's *Wedding Feast* and Massys's *Man with a Pink.* When the artists grew tired of turning Donald into classic art, they began casting him as the lead in famed films, including a beaky version of Rhett Butler, who would have starred in *Gone with the Duck* if the artists had had their way.

The honors bestowed upon Donald were echoed by his fans; by 1961 there were two feature-length D. D. movies and 136 cartoon shorts. His comic books and comic strips have been translated into at least twenty-one languages in some seventy-five countries. And honored by peers and fans alike, in 1984 he was inducted as a Screen Actors Guild member. Clarence "Ducky" Nash, who quacked for Donald for fifty years, died in 1985. The Duck, though, will never die; he has been immortalized by his progenitors, much as Leonardo spawned Mona Lisa.

Right: *Two Duck Dancers* as Degas might have seen them
Below: *The Blue Duck* has a quacky similarity to *Blue Boy* by Gainsborough

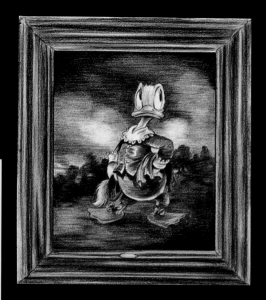

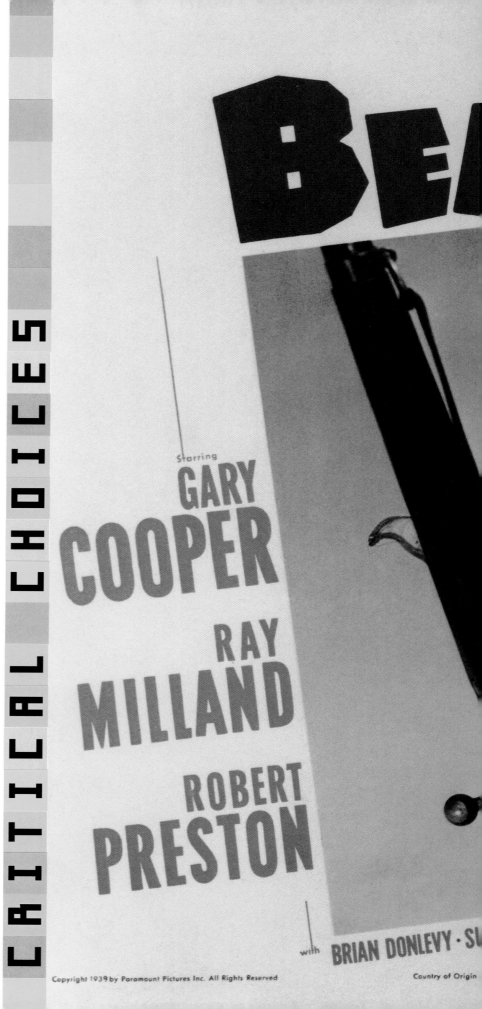

Film critic and celebrated classic-movies expert Robert Osborne evaluates the first five decades of filmmaking and says everything (almost) that he was always too polite to say on television. Osborne has the lucky task of concentrating on classic films, films that made a statement—or didn't—in a specific time in history. He thus can explain why a film is a notable in an archive. And unlike many modern critics on modern films, he provides the perspective that may convince viewers to look again at films they have forgotten. Before he reminds us of those films, Osborne tells us about old Sara Hamilton and how she inspired him to be a critic.

A favorite film of Robert Osborne, *Beau Geste* (1939) featured four future Oscar winners—Gary Cooper, Ray Milland, Susan Hayward, and Broderick Crawford—but Crawford missed his billing on the *Beau Geste* lobby card.

Starring
GARY
COOPER

RAY
MILLAND

ROBERT
PRESTON

with BRIAN DONLEVY · SL

Country of Origin

AU GESTE

N HAYWARD · J. CARROL NAISH · DONALD O'CONNOR · JAMES STEPHENSON · Produced and Directed by WILLIAM A. WELLMAN

Screen Play by Robert Carson   Based on the Novel by Percival Christopher Wren   A Paramount Picture

CRITIC ON A CRITIC
BY ROBERT OSBORNE

Growing up in a small town as I did (Colfax, Washington; population 2,500), I didn't have access to the movie reviews in *The New York Times*. No Internet access in those days. So, in order to get tips on what movies I should anticipate the most, when, and if, they ever arrived at my local Rose Theatre, I fervently turned every month to a magazine called *Photoplay*.

There a salty writer named Sara Hamilton regularly held forth, dispensing her opinions about which films must be seen and which should be avoided. After Sara waxed on about a movie, she'd always end with a capsule critique that began "Your reviewer says." Sara never held back. About the Ann Sheridan–Ronald Reagan movie *Juke Girl* (1942), my reviewer said "It should be plowed under." Regarding a 1944 Deanna Durbin musical called *Can't Help Singing,* Sara quietly—but lethally—let everyone know that Deanna had packed on a few pounds by finishing with "Your reviewer says: What a pleasure to see a plump heroine again."

Most of the time I agreed with the rascally Sara. She wrapped her opinion of *Anchors Aweigh* (1945) with "Your reviewer says, 'Miss this and you'll be sorry.'" But sometimes Sara and I were on a different

Frank Sinatra and Gene Kelly, center, both have eyes for Kathryn Grayson in *Anchors Aweigh,* a film *Photoplay* magazine's film critic gave the 1945 equivalent of "two thumbs up."

wavelength altogether. About a Fox musical called *Nob Hill* (1945), she wrote "It's Corn on the Nob." (Hey, I loved *Nob Hill*.) About a comedy titled *Murder, He Says* (1954), she finished, "One wonders what the writer's I.Q. is." (I thought the movie was hilarious.)

But that's what critics do and have always done—create controversy when they give their opinions. What follows are mine. If you find them foolish and off-base, it is your right. I understand because Sara Hamilton and *Photoplay* taught me eons ago that when judging movies there is no right and wrong. Only different sentiments. Your reviewer says: Relax and take what follows as one movie nut's opinion. Period.

Bing Crosby and Joan Fontaine in *The Emperor Waltz* (1948)

THE BEST MUSICALS WITHOUT FRED, GENE, OR JUDY

T he Musical. America's ultimate movie art form. With few exceptions, the musicals of the Golden Age have never been equaled; they were the best of the best. They raised war-torn spirits and kept America humming. Three stars have become synonymous with great musicals—Judy Garland, Gene Kelly, and Fred Astaire— but critic Osborne contends that unless someone speaks up for numerous others, history may overlook these classics. In this chapter he selects the Golden Age's best. —The Editors

SEVEN BRIDES FOR SEVEN BROTHERS, 1954

MGM's surprise musical hit of the year, *Seven Brides for Seven Brothers* was a true sleeper because the leads at MGM hadn't expected it to make a nickel. The studio thought *Brigadoon* would be its big box-office musical of 1954, going so far as to take a hefty amount of the initial budget away from *Seven Brides* to pump it into the Gene Kelly-Cyd Charisse musical. But *Brig* tanked and *Seven Brides* went on to break records and receive an Oscar nomination for best picture of the year. It was the sensational choreography of Michael Kidd that set everyone on their ears; looking at it all these years later, the dancing's still sensational, especially in the rousing "Challenge Dance" sequence. But now it's the quiet, sturdy, and honest performance of Jane Powell as the first of the seven brides that really holds the film together.

Above: Howard Keel and Jane Powell in *Seven Brides for Seven Brothers*
Opposite: Deborah Kerr and Yul Brynner in *The King and I*
Following pages: Busby Berkeley's dancers in *42nd Street*

THE KING AND I, 1956

Few musicals created for the stage have played better on film than they had on Broadway: *The King and I* was one of those rare exceptions. Deborah Kerr was perfectly cast in a role lusted after by many actresses, and Yul Brynner gave what turned out to be an Oscar-winning performance (a prize he won despite stiff competition from Laurence Olivier in *Richard III* [1955], Kirk Douglas as Van Gogh in *Lust for Life* [1956], and both Jimmy Dean and Rock Hudson in *Giant* [1956]). The film almost included Dorothy Dandridge as the King's unfaithful wife; Fox had wanted her to do it as a follow-up to her sensational movie performance in *Carmen Jones* (1954), but the man in her life, director Otto Preminger, convinced her it would be a step down for her, so Rita Moreno played the part. The brass at Fox never quite forgave Dandridge and thereafter did nothing to advance her career at the studio.

42nd STREET, 1933

The granddaddy of all film musicals, *42nd Street* put more clichés into the movies' vernacular than any other. The film is also still impossible to resist, thanks in part to the person who has always received the kudos for making it click, choreographer/madman Busby Berkeley, but also because of all those who haven't received the back pats they deserve—Una Merkel, Guy Kibbee, Dick Powell, Warner Baxter, George Brent, Ruby Keeler (doing some strange gyrating that was labeled tap dancing), and Ginger Rogers as "Anytime Annie," described as a gal who said "'no' only once, and that time she didn't understand the question."

ALEXANDER'S RAGTIME BAND, 1938

Yes, yes, the story of *Alexander's Ragtime Band* is corny, pure kitsch, and no one ages an iota over a twenty-two year period (1915–1938). But few musicals contain such pure joy: Ethel Merman, young and zesty, belting out Irving Berlin's "Heat Wave," Don Ameche singing "Easter Parade," Jack Haley doing "Oh, How I Hate to Get up in the Morning," Alice Faye croon-

ing "Now It Can Be Told," plus dozens of other Berlin songs. None of the tunes, however, set the toes tapping faster than when Tyrone Power, with baton in hand, leads a Carnegie Hall orchestra through the title song—which remains a classic, despite a lyric by Mr. Berlin that is very hard to embrace today: "He can play a bugle call like you never heard before, so natural that you want to go to war." Yeah, sure.

GIGI, 1958

Gigi may be the best musical ever specifically created for the movies, and it is all the more amazing because it was basically a paint-by-numbers job, an attempt to re-create something that had already been done with great success. The picture came about because MGM producer Arthur Freed had been unable to buy the movie rights to *My Fair Lady*. It was such an enormous Broadway success at the time, that its producers said, in essence, "Not for sale—not for many years." Freed decided to create his own *Fair Lady* by buying a story with the same basic premise. He hired the two *Fair Lady* composers, Alan Jay Lerner and Frederick Loewe, as well as that play's costume designer, Cecil Beaton. But out of this re-creation came a movie that not only won more Oscars than any film had received up to that point (ten) but it would remain one of the great jewels of the moviemaking process.

GOOD NEWS, 1947

Betty Comden, who wrote the screenplay for *Good News* with her longtime partner Adolph Green, has often said that the three greatest American films ever made are *The Birth of a Nation* (1915), *Greed* (1925), and *Good News* (1947). The witty Betty was kidding about her film's stature, but count me in as one who'd always prefer watching June Allyson doing "the Varsity Drag" to Lillian Gish fighting the Civil War for Mr. Griffith, ZaSu Pitts suffering, suffering, suffering for Erich von Stroheim, or even Orson Welles mumbling about Rosebud.

Opposite: Joan McCracken and Ray McDonald as the lead dancers in the "Pass That Peace Pipe" number, *Good News*

Left: Louis Jordan (center) raises his glass as Eva Gabor and Maurice Chevalier share a toast in *Gigi*.

THE TEN BEST CASTING IDEAS THAT NEVER HAPPENED

It happens to all of us at least once: we watch an otherwise terrific film and recast the leads in our minds, confident that our choices would have made a great movie even greater. When you're Robert Osborne, it happens all the time. He watches movies with a critic's eye and the perspective of a historian who's seen more films in his lifetime than most of us knew existed. In the following pages, he takes a shot at being the casting director, the expert who decides exactly which actors and actresses should play each role in a film. Although some readers may cringe when Osborne starts fiddling with their favorite movies (replace Tom Ewell in *The Seven Year Itch?*), once they're over the initial shock, his reasoning will give them pause. After all, he's the critic.
—The Editors

CARY GRANT in
SABRINA, 1954

The one thing that doesn't work about Billy Wilder's classy-looking adaptation of the Broadway success *Sabrina* is Humphrey Bogart as the unbelievably rich scion of old money from the Hamptons. It simply wasn't his milieu. Nor did he make it easy for us to believe that Audrey Hepburn would prefer to run off with him rather than with his better-looking, more charming younger brother, played by William Holden. But Cary Grant—well, that's something else again. Alas, Wilder tried but couldn't get him.

Top: Cary Grant
Bottom: Humphrey Bogart and Audrey Hepburn in *Sabrina*

BETTY GRABLE in
GUYS AND DOLLS, 1955

Would Frank Sinatra really have chased—and bedded—Vivian Blaine for years and years? Very doubtful. Blaine was great on stage as Miss Adelaide and on-screen she always had a lovely presence, but the camera didn't love her like it loved Grable. To the credit of producer Samuel Goldwyn, he wanted Grable for the part, and was on the verge of offering it. But Grable had an ailing pet and wouldn't leave its side to keep an appointment with Goldwyn. Piqued over her lack of courtesy to her old boss (years before, La Grable had been one of the Goldwyn Girls), he gave the role to the woman who'd created it on Broadway. But without Grable, the movie never ignited the way it would have with her on board.

Top: Betty Grable
Bottom: Frank Sinatra and Vivian Blaine in *Guys and Dolls*

GARY COOPER in
THE SEVEN YEAR ITCH, 1955

Tom Ewell ended up doing *The Seven Year Itch* with Marilyn Monroe (re-creating the role he'd first done on Broadway, with Vanessa Brown in MM's part), but consider the possibilities if Coop had played the man downstairs, the bumbling shy guy who tries to be a Romeo while his wife and kids are out of town, but who consistently fouls up his attempts at seduction. It would have been *Ball of Fire* (1941) again, 1950s style.

Top: Gary Cooper
Bottom: Marilyn Monroe and Tom Ewell in *The Seven Year Itch*

MARILYN MONROE in
BREAKFAST AT TIFFANY'S, 1961

MM was always Truman Capote's first choice to play Holly Golightly in *Breakfast at Tiffany's,* and she was certainly much closer than Audrey Hepburn to the zany character in Capote's novel. I mean, can anyone really believe that the beautiful, sensible Audrey would go through life with only an orchid and champagne in her New York fridge?

Above: Marilyn Monroe serenades a friend.
Left: Audrey Hepburn in *Breakfast at Tiffany's*

DORIS DAY in
SOUTH PACIFIC, 1958

The screen version of *South Pacific,* the great all-American musical by Rodgers and Hammerstein, came out looking like a bus-and-truck version, with stars you'd expect to find in a touring production rather than in a Broadway company. The perfect Nellie Forbush for the movie was Doris Day—but someone else got the job and the film that remains is only a hint of what it should have been.

Above: Doris Day
Left: Mitzi Gaynor in *South Pacific*

TYRONE POWER in
A STAR IS BORN, 1954

The first notice that Judy Garland was going to appear in a musical remake of the 1937 drama *A Star Is Born* appeared in a trade paper, *Hollywood Reporter,* which mentioned that Garland and then-husband Sid Luft were hoping to entice Tyrone Power to play the ill-fated movie star Norman Maine, opposite Judy. He would have been ideal, especially in 1954 when his own star was fading, just as Maine's does in the story. At Power's home studio, Twentieth Century-Fox, freelancer Gregory Peck was then getting the studio's choice roles. Power practically defined the term "movie star" and was also an excellent actor who would've been heartbreakingly good with Judy. But James Mason got the part and was great (when wasn't Mason great?).

Top: Tyrone Power
Bottom: James Mason

CHARLES BOYER in
KEY LARGO, 1948

Edward G. Robinson was, of course, the definitive gangster in *Key Largo*—as good as good can be. But playing a guy with a gat was nothing new for EGR at this point. That is one reason director John Huston initially thought the film would work better, and the story would have more of an edge, if the crime boss Rocco was played instead by a smooth, elegant, international type. The actor Huston had in mind for the part was that most continental of Frenchmen, Charles Boyer. It was Warner Bros. that scotched the idea. The studio wanted Huston to go the more conventional route, so he decided if they wanted a more down-to-earth and typical gangster type, he'd get the best. That was—who else—Mr. Robinson. But Boyer's presence would have given *Largo* an extra kicker that would have made it even more intriguing.

Top: Charles Boyer
Bottom: Lauren Bacall and Edward G. Robinson in *Key Largo*

GREER GARSON in
ZIEGFELD FOLLIES, 1946

It was Garson for whom Kay Thompson wrote *Ziegfeld Follies'*
satirical sketch "The Great Lady Gives an Interview," done with
such wit in the film by Judy Garland. But the whole point of the
satire is the fact that it's about a great dramatic star, famous
for appearing in somber biographical stories, wanting to be a
song-and-dance babe ("What's Ginger Rogers got that I haven't
got, and what's Betty Grable that I am not?"). It was ideal for
Garson, who had just been seen in *Madame Curie* (1943), dis-
covering radium, whereas Judy was firmly established as a
song-and-dance star. Whether or not Garson could have pulled
it off as well as Garland is open to question, but Garson was
always known as a delightful lady, much merrier than her image
ever hinted. According to Thompson, she and MGM cohort Roger
Edens went to Garson's house one day to audition the material
for her. Garson's mother, who had always wielded a heavy influence in her daughter's decisions, was also present. When
Thompson and Edens finished, Mama Garson stood up, said, "It's
not for you, dear," and exited. That was the end of that.

Top: Greer Garson
Bottom: Judy Garland in *Ziegfeld Follies*

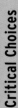

JAMES CAGNEY in
MY FAIR LADY, 1964

No, no, not as Professor Henry Higgins; in *My Fair Lady* even Cagney's giant talent wouldn't have been able to pull that off. He would have been great as Eliza's feisty papa, Alfred Doolittle. He was asked to do it but resoundingly said no—he was officially retired. Cagney's presence, and especially the way he'd sing and dance to "Get Me to the Church on Time," would have added the extra dash of excitement that this uninspired, paint-by-numbers *Lady* could have used.

Top: James Cagney
Bottom: Stanley Holloway in *My Fair Lady*

SUSAN HAYWARD in
THE COUNTRY GIRL, 1954

Jennifer Jones was the star initially signed to do *The Country Girl,* but she had to withdraw because of pregnancy. After that, I don't know if Susan Hayward was ever considered for it—she was under contract to Twentieth Century-Fox whereas this was a Paramount production—and Grace Kelly, who eventually played the part, was Hollywood's golden girl of the moment, so signing her was a coup. The future Princess of Monaco played the part and won an Academy Award for it, and yet, looking at the film years later, she isn't very good in it. Ordinary is the word. The fire, toughness, and cynical edge that Hayward always infused into her work would have been perfect for the role of this "country" girl, but, alas, we never got a chance to see her do it.

Top: Susan Hayward
Bottom: William Holden and Grace Kelly in *The Country Girl*

THE TEN BEST SWORDS-AND-SAND MOVIES

A s "action movies" are to the modern screen, "swords-and-sand movies" were to the Golden Age of Hollywood. Offering swords slashing across the screen and bronzed muscles rippling in fantasy environs, swords-and-sand movies represent an entire genre of Grade A beefcake movies that brought women to the theaters in hopes of seeing the bare chests of their favorite stars. The raucous, fast-paced films filled with contests of strength and derring-do also attracted male audiences, eager for macho heroes to fill their dreams. Whether they were swashbuckling pirates, musketeers, legionnaires, or romantic dons, the men who played these fantasy rogues became some of Hollywood's greatest stars—Douglas Fairbanks (Sr. and Jr.), Errol Flynn, Tyrone Power, Kirk Douglas, Burt Lancaster—and the films became integral parts of their individual legacies. Robert Osborne designates his favorites.

—The Editors

Above: Tyrone Power in *The Mark of Zorro*
Right: Kirk Douglas in *Spartacus*

THE ADVENTURES OF ROBIN HOOD, 1938

The Adventures of Robin Hood won more Oscars in 1938 (four) than any other film that year, yet leading lady Olivia de Havilland has said that neither the film nor its star Errol Flynn was held in particularly high regard by the big brass at their home studio of Warner Bros. Paul Muni and Bette Davis were considered Warners' distinguished players, with Flynn "only" an action star. Never mind that the Flynn films consistently outgrossed those of Muni and Davis. Today, Robin is widely regarded as the high-water mark in adventure tales, the one by which all other such movies are judged. Anyone who's ever seen the climactic swordfight to the finish between Flynn, in green tights, and Basil Rathbone, always the nastiest of villains (except, of course, when Rathbone was playing the brightest of super-sleuths, Sherlock Holmes), will never forget it.

THE PRISONER OF ZENDA, 1937

David O. Selznick's screen adaptation of Anthony Hope's classic adventure tale, The Prisoner of Zenda, has few peers. Even when MGM later used the same script, with the same camera angles, and the same Alfred Newman musical score, it couldn't be duplicated. It wasn't just that the duplicate version in 1952 had Stewart Granger, Deborah Kerr, James Mason, and Jane Greer—not exactly chopped liver—instead of the original's Ronald Colman, Madeleine Carroll, Mary Astor, and Douglas Fairbanks, Jr., but the magic was gone. Seen side by side, the 1937 Prisoner soars and fascinates while the 1952 version, even in Technicolor, is quite colorless.

BEAU GESTE, 1939

Beau Geste, another film with a tie to Ronald Colman, who starred in an earlier silent film version, is a "one for all, all for one" movie. It stars four future Oscar winners (Gary Cooper, Ray Milland, Susan Hayward, Broderick Crawford) and is set in the sands of French North Africa, among the rogues, renegades, and outlaws of the French Foreign Legion. No swordplay in this one but plenty of action, mystery, and strange deaths as three brothers (Cooper, Milland, and Robert Preston) get mixed up in the riddle of who stole a famous diamond from the English estate of their beloved aunt. Rare is the lad who ever sat through this without giving at least a passing thought to running off to Africa and the Legion.

SPARTACUS, 1960

Spartacus has been called the thinking man's swords-and-sand epic. For sure, it was more meticulously made than most, with Stanley Kubrick directing a weighty and distinguished cast (Kirk Douglas, Laurence Olivier, Charles Laughton, Peter Ustinov, Jean Simmons, Tony Curtis, and so on), and with as much derring-do and excitement as any tall tale starring one of the big three—Fairbanks, Flynn, or Lancaster. The swords are out in force in this one, and there's plenty of sand, too, as Spartacus leads the slaves into revolt and manages, at the same time, to pay off all the mortgages for Universal Pictures. It also helped bring screenwriter Dalton Trumbo back from the dead after his career had been seriously derailed when the House Un-American Activities Committee put him on Hollywood's blacklist in the early 1950s.

THE BLACK SWAN, 1942

In the ads for The Black Swan, a drawing of a shirtless Tyrone Power made him look like Arnold Schwarzenegger on steroids. In the movie itself, Ty spent plenty of time shirtless (on the rack, swimming, and, rare for a movie made during the era of the Hays office, in bed with the leading lady)—always looking exceedingly lean and trim. He was, nevertheless, a worthy pirate, ready and able to "yo-ho-ho with a bottle of rum" while capturing, then terrorizing, but ultimately wooing and winning the ultimate pirate heroine-hellcat, Maureen O'Hara. The title, for the record, refers to a pirate ship.

THE THREE MUSKETEERS, 1948

Like Robin Hood, The Three Musketeers was another Fairbanks movie that was remade during the sound era. It almost plays like a musical since it stars Gene Kelly, who leaps and jumps during numerous sword fights as if he were in a ballet. Grand stuff it is, and wonderfully entertaining, made by MGM when the studio still had all its burners cooking. Despite Kelly's presence, the film's action and entertainment values, and a handsome cast that included June Allyson, Van Heflin, and Angela Lansbury, the film's primary publicity thrust was that the picture marked the first appearance of Lana Turner in Technicolor.

THE COUNT OF MONTE CRISTO, 1934

The Count of Monte Cristo is the only film the British-born actor Robert Donat actually filmed in Hollywood, although he went on to become an Oscar winner for Goodbye Mr. Chips (1939) and a genuine movie star as far as American moviegoers were concerned. Count was based on another story by Alexandre Dumas—what would Hollywood have done

Top: Ad for *The Black Swan*
Opposite: Burt Lancaster in *The Crimson Pirate*

without him?—and had a lot of competition from other films of the same ilk (*The Scarlet Pimpernel* [1934], *The Man in the Iron Mask* [1939], and so on), but it had a zip and style that put it yards ahead of the pack.

THE MARK OF ZORRO, 1940

Douglas Fairbanks, Sr., had done a silent version of *The Mark of Zorro* in 1920; twenty years later the creative Rouben Mamoulian guided Tyrone Power through this talkie about a Robin Hood of old California who rights wrongs by night, and by day pretends to be a dandyfied fop to cover his identity. (*The Scarlet Pimpernel* in a sombrero.) The film's climactic sword fight with Basil Rathbone is sensational; Rathbone later said that compared to Power's prowess with a sword, Errol Flynn was a piker. The film also had two striking women in its cast: the gorgeous Linda Darnell as the good girl, and Gale Sondergaard as, of course, the dangerous one.

THE FLAME AND THE ARROW, 1950
THE CRIMSON PIRATE, 1952

What Fairbanks was to the silent screen, and Flynn to the talkies of the 1930s and early 1940s, Burt Lancaster was to the 1950s, thanks to his derring-do genre debut in the comic book–type tale *The Flame and the Arrow* (1950) and its spirited follow-up swashbuckler, *The Crimson Pirate*. In the latter, Burt plays an eighteenth-century pirate who constantly leaps, jumps, tumbles, vaults, pirouettes, and swings from rope as he leads a Mediterranean rebellion against bullies. Bully for Burt. Doing most of his own stunts, he was able to fully use many of the athletic tricks he learned in his pre-Hollywood years when he had actually been a circus acrobat.

THE TEN MOST MEMORABLE NAMES IN THE MOVIES

T he studio "machine" of Hollywood's Golden Age was all about creating stars, and the moguls who shaped them attended to every detail. The tales of how stars got their names are legendary (e.g., the gorgeous Hedy LaMarr was named, some say, in honor of silent-screen star Barbara La Marr, who was known as the Girl Who Was Too Beautiful, although Hedy herself claimed her last name was coined during an ocean cruise with L. B. Mayer because of the surrounding "le mer." Whichever, "Hedy Lamarr" was a much catchier handle than Hedwig Eva Maria Kiesler. Many producers, behind her back, chose to refer to her more often as "Headache Lamarr"). Such monikers as Cary Grant, Judy Garland, and Tony Curtis are sophisticated replacements for Archibald Leach, Frances Ethel Gumm, and Bernard Schwartz, respectively. One wonders what went on in the minds of studio execs when they changed Lucille Le Sueur to Joan Crawford, a forgettable name that seemed to make her part of the crowd instead of separating her from it. Robert Osborne looks at the names that definitely deserve a place in Hollywood history, names that no mother ever thought of.   —The Editors

Right: Helen Twelvetrees
Opposite top: Slim Pickens
Opposite middle: Stepin Fetchit
Opposite bottom: Harry Carey

HARRY CAREY
An early action star, Harry Carey later became a revered character actor. The only pity is that he wasn't cast in the 1934 Charles Boyer–Merle Oberon movie *Hari-Kiri*. It seemed such a natural.

HELEN TWELVETREES
As an actress in the 1930s and 1940s, Helen Twelvetrees (aka Helen Jurgens) had to endure endless jokes about being the ideal costar for Rin Tin Tin and, later, Lassie.

PARKYAKARKUS
Comedian Parkyakarkus actually had a real name: Harry Einstein. He was also the father of comedian-director Albert Brooks, perhaps a greater claim to fame than his name.

AMBROSINE PHILPOTTS
British character actress Ambrosine Philpotts was best known for her work in many of the English-made "carry on" comedies.

TWINKLE WATTS
Twinkle Watts was a preteen foisted on the public by Republic Pictures in the 1940s as a combination Shirley Temple and Sonja Henie. Twinkle did her best to sparkle like Shirley and skate like Sonja, but didn't receive much encouragement from moviegoers to continue working once her wattage dimmed with age.

SLIM PICKENS
Character actor Slim Pickens (aka Louis Bent Lindley) was most notable for riding the bomb at the end of Stanley Kubrick's *Dr. Strangelove* (1963).

STEPIN FETCHIT
Character actor Stepin Fetchit (aka Lincoln Perry) was endlessly typecast in the 1930s as a slow, shuffling African American, always two sandwiches short of a picnic.

VIVIAN PICKLES
The juicy character actress Vivian Pickles is best remembered for playing Harold's desensitized mother from hell in 1971's *Harold and Maude*.

DUCKY LOUIE
Ducky Louie was a teenaged Chinese actor in the 1940s who was first introduced in a World War II movie with Paul Kelly called *China's Little Devils* (1945), and then later costarred with Anthony Quinn in the underrated and rarely seen *Black Gold* (1947).

HUNG HUNG
Taiwanese director of the film, *The Love of Three Oranges*.

THE TEN BEST SARONG MOVIES

When Ramon Novarro and Dorothy Janis donned sarongs in The Pagan *(1929), and he was dubbed "Ravishing Ramon" by his awestruck fans, Hollywood moguls took note. The revealing sarong, they reasoned, was a necessary costume for films set in the tropics, and if the costume was essential to the storyline, censors could not rightfully bellyache. So to get around censors, Hollywood execs soon demanded more island settings and the barest of sarongs. Dorothy Lamour became a big star because of her little South Seas wrap (since the barefoot beauty was self-conscious about her ugly feet, however, designer Edith Head created lovely faux rubber feet to ease Lamour's fears). Determined that no one underestimate the box-office power of the sarong, Robert Osborne defines the landmark moments in tropical cinema. —The Editors*

Below: *Typhoon* lobby card.
Opposite: Hedy Lamarr as the seductive Tondelayo in *White Cargo* (1942).

THE HURRICANE, 1937

No one was more identified with a sarong than Dorothy Lamour, and *The Hurricane* was the definitive Lamour island picture. Probably the reason it was so good is that it was made by the distinguished Samuel Goldwyn rather than at Dotti's home studio of Paramount. Paramount, alas, would wrap a sarong around Lamour and then let her sink or swim pretty much on her own. But this Lamour/sarong movie had great credentials: direction by John Ford, no less, and a story by the authors of *Mutiny on the Bounty* (1935), Charles Nordhoff and James Norman Hall. No doubt the sarongs were also made of better material.

WHITE CARGO, 1942

White Cargo had one major plus: Hedy Lamarr, from Vienna, covered with cocoa butter, running around a sound stage jungle as a wild African savage known as Tondelayo. She looked great in her sarong, although thanks to MGM's creative publicity department, the garment was called something else. The film's ads declared "Hedy rings the gong in her larong," explaining with an asterisk that "larong" meant "Lamarr in a sarong."

SON OF FURY, 1942

In *Son of Fury,* it was the man, Tyrone Power, who spent much of his time wearing a variation on the sarong, cut down considerably from Dorothy Lamour's usual attire. Twentieth Century–Fox's policy was to show Ty shirtless as often as possible in his pictures. The only rule at that studio was that Ty and, indeed, any actor showing skin in a Fox film, had to have a clean-shaven chest. The big boss Darryl F. Zanuck hated hairy chests. Many actors balked (Power, John Payne, Victor Mature, William Holden), but Zanuck was adamant and out came the razors.

ANNA AND THE KING OF SIAM, 1946

One of the gorgeous sights at the movies in the 1940s was Linda Darnell in her Siamese version of a sarong, playing Tuptim in *Anna and the King of Siam*. This was a very classy, upscale version of the famous book that later became the inspiration for all those movie and stage adaptations (straight, musical, animated) that have inundated us since. Darnell didn't have much footage in this version, but was present long enough to be established as one of the many wives of the King (Rex Harrison) to have an extramarital affair, and long enough to get burned at the stake, sarong and all. The cruel irony is that Darnell herself died after being engulfed by a fire nineteen years later. It's worth noting that the director was John Cromwell, the father of actor James Cromwell, who first found fame in the 1990s playing the farmer who owned *Babe* (1995).

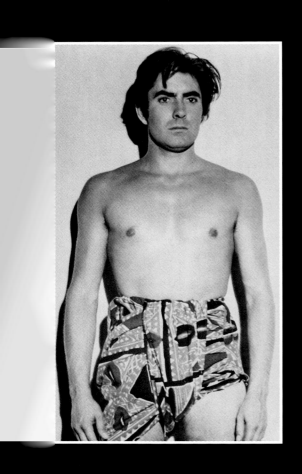

Above: Tyrone Power in *Son of Fury*.
Bottom right: Dorothy Lamour in her trade-
mark sarong, designed by Edith Head
Top right: Maria Montez in a publicity still for
White Savage

TYPHOON, 1940

Nobody filled a sarong better than Lamour, whether her name was Ulah (as in *The Jungle Princess*, 1936), Tura (*Her Jungle Love*, 1938), Aloma (*Aloma of the South Seas*, 1941), Tama (*Beyond the Blue Horizon*, 1942), Lona (*Rainbow Island*, 1944), Lalah (*Road to Bali*, 1952), or any of the other one-named island lassies. It was Lamour for whom the *Typhoon* sarong was invented; the designer was always Paramount's head lady of the needle and thread, Edith Head. Any one of those Paramount island movies could easily be mistaken for any other, except that when Lamour was in her sarong as Dea in *Typhoon,* she got to cavort not only with that most underrated of actors, Robert Preston, but also with a chimpanzee named Koko, all while trying to hold onto her life in that handkerchief-sized outfit as a Technicolored typhoon raged around her.

SOUTH OF PAGO PAGO, 1940

South of Pago Pago was one of the many island movies with Jon Hall, who spent as much time among sand and coral as did Dorothy Lamour, and they were often together. This time he appears as the son of a South Seas native chief, running up against a greedy, ambitious skipper (Victor McLaglen) who's out to get pearls, pearls, and more pearls from the waters surrounding Hall's isle. What sets this sarong picture apart from any other is that one of the women in one of the sarongs is no less than the great, ill-fated Frances Farmer—who seemed to spend an amazing amount of time in films like this when she should have been working in much weightier movie projects, or on Broadway with her pals Clurman, Garfield, Kazan, Odets, and the others at the Group Theatre. Nothing wrong with the way Ms. Farmer looked in her beach attire, but she does give the impression she'd love to crown someone—probably her agent—with a coconut.

THE TUTTLES OF TAHITI, 1942

The Tuttles of Tahiti is another movie with Jon Hall (here clothed for a change) and another island story by Nordhoff and Hall, the authors of *Mutiny on the Bounty* and *The Hurricane. The Tuttles* is about a shift-less, irresponsible head of a lazy family who bets all the family's earthly possessions on a cockfight. With a cast including Charles Laughton, the film deserves a special place on any ten-best list just for the sight of ample character actress Florence Bates in a sarong, serving up the mai-tais and guava juice and obviously having the time of her life as a rather large edition of Dorothy Lamour.

WHITE SAVAGE, 1943

Maria Montez filling a sarong her way—that's what *White Savage* is about. Playing a South Seas babe was particularly good casting for Montez since her English was usually impossible to decipher. (She was the English-speaking actress most in need of subtitles.) Lacking the ability to be understood worked to her distinct disadvantage during those few times she played a sophisticate or a modern-day vixen, but in this movie—as an island girl accustomed to spending most of her time being a pal to Jon Hall, Sabu, and a pet monkey—nobody expected her to have a grasp of "da Englass" or, for that matter, to make any sense at all. And beautiful Maria rarely made much sense anyway. Bless her.

ROAD TO UTOPIA, 1945

Not a foot of *Road to Utopia* took place in a jungle setting, but because Dorothy Lamour was in it (with Bing Crosby and Bob Hope), Paramount figured it couldn't disappoint the fans. There was a brief flash of Dotti in her familiar sarong. That sarong also came in handy when they needed a provocative image of Ms. Lamour for the film's advertising, although this time, since the film was set in the frozen north, she was also carrying a fur muff.

A MIRACLE CAN HAPPEN (a. k. a. ON OUR MERRY WAY), 1948

A Miracle Can Happen is an episodic film with a multitude of stars (Jimmy Stewart, Henry Fonda, Paulette Goddard, Fred MacMurray, Burgess Meredith, and others) about a newspaper reporter, soon to become a father, who asks a series of people how a baby has affected their lives. In the best sequence in the film, Dorothy Lamour sings a funny, self-effacing parody of her own career called "I'm the Queen of the Hollywood Islands." She's wearing—of course—that trademark sarong she'd made so famous. Lamour didn't know it at the time, but this film was also bringing the curtain down on her reign as the movies' Sarong Queen—the end was in sight for sarongs, and sarong movies, in general.

THE TEN MOST PRICELESS CARY GRANT MOVIES

When he was barely a teenager and snuck away to become a song-and-dance man with a troupe of side-show entertainers, Archie Leach never expected to be the world's heartthrob. But a beautiful face and a charm that never quit couldn't go unnoticed. His earliest leading ladies, Marlene Dietrich and Mae West, knew a hunk when they saw one. So Cary Grant's career was born. A survivor of four decades of Hollywood's Golden Age, Grant lived openly with Randolph Scott in a Santa Monica beach house in the 1930s yet wasn't publicly decried as homosexual (although much later, in the more sexually-liberated 1970s, rumors surfaced that the actor, if he was not gay, at least double-gaited); experimented with LSD in the 1960s, yet never was shunned as a drug user; married five times and his fans still swooned. Relentlessly lovable and endlessly adored, he was the screen's most debonair romantic lead. Here Robert Osborne celebrates the best of Cary, and demonstrates the diverse and dynamic roles for which he was heralded.
—The Editors

Right: Cary Grant and Ingrid Bergman in *Indiscreet*.
Opposite: Cary Grant and Rosalind Russell in *His Girl Friday*.

NOTORIOUS, 1946
Cary and Ingrid Bergman in South America, among Nazis. *Notorious* is, arguably, also the best of all the Hitchcock films.

GUNGA DIN, 1939
Cary with Doug Fairbanks, Jr., and Victor McLaglen in India, outwitting a Thuggee cult. *Gunga Din* may be the best of all the adventure films.

BRINGING UP BABY, 1938
Cary and Katharine Hepburn with a leopard, hunting for a brontosaurus bone. Has there ever been a better screwball comedy than *Bringing Up Baby*?

THE AWFUL TRUTH, 1937
Cary and Irene Dunne romping through a comedy about divorce. If *Bringing Up Baby* isn't the best screwball comedy, then surely *The Awful Truth* is.

HIS GIRL FRIDAY, 1940
Cary and Rosalind Russell as headline hunters. In *His Girl Friday* the irresistible pair speak faster than lips are supposed to move.

NORTH BY NORTHWEST, 1959
Cary and Eva Marie Saint being chased around Lincoln's nose at Mt. Rushmore. Courtesy of Mr. Hitchcock, *North by Northwest* combines romance and adventure with cliff-hanging intrigue.

Top: Tony Curtis and Cary Grant
Above: Cary Grant and Katharine Hepburn in
Bringing up Baby
Top right: Cary Grant and Audrey Hepburn in
Charade
Right: Cary Grant and Irene Dunne in
The Awful Truth
Opposite top: Cary Grant and Eva Marie Saint
in *North by Northwest*
Opposite bottom: Cary Grant and Sam Jaffe
in *Gunga Din*

CHARADE, 1963
Cary and Audrey Hepburn are merrily chased through the streets of Paris by some nasty *hommes*. *Charade* is the best Hitchcock thriller that Hitchcock never made.

INDISCREET, 1958
Cary and Ingrid Bergman in a gem that was by far the most underrated comedy of the 1950s. *Indiscreet* didn't work on stage with Mary Martin and Charles Boyer, where it had been called *Kind Sir*, but on screen, under the direction of Stanley Donen, it glows, tickles, charms, and delights.

NONE BUT THE LONELY HEART, 1944
Cary in one of his few starkly dramatic roles. Despite the fact that *None but the Lonely Heart* brought him one of his few Oscar nominations (he received only two during his whole career), it's a Grant film few people know today. Some, however, are unconvinced that this is good Grant. Critic Manny Faber, in the *New Republic*, felt Cary was overly self-conscious throughout and dismissed the film as "one of the biggest hodgepodges Hollywood ever constructed."

SOME LIKE IT HOT, 1959
No, of course Cary wasn't in *Some Like It Hot*. But one thing that turned this Billy Wilder farce into the funniest comedy of the 1950s—and certainly one of the four or five funniest ever made—was Tony Curtis doing such a dead-on impersonation of Grant throughout the film that Cary became an integral part of the project. Wilder never worked with Grant but admits that Cary was his first choice for almost every film he was directing. That dates as far back as 1939, when he attempted to get Cary to be Garbo's leading man in the comedy *Ninotchka*, which Wilder cowrote. *Hot* was living proof that Cary Grant didn't even have to be in the show to steal it.

THE LEAST NECESSARY CARY GRANT MOVIES

A journalist to the core, Osborne can't talk about the best of Cary without pointing out the worst of Cary's films. And, indeed, there were dogs. Almost every actor occasionally picks the wrong script, and for some, that single bad choice can ruin a career. But for the unflappable Cary Grant, not even a few disasters could break his stride. Still, did the world really need to see him play a turtle? Grant admitted that he could "play myself to perfection" So, Osborne asks, why—oh why—did he stray so often?

—The Editors

Cary Grant in *Alice in Wonderland*

NIGHT AND DAY, 1946

Was there ever a really bad Cary Grant movie? Well, frankly my dear, yes. But that's something he never had to be ashamed of, considering he made seventy-two movies in all, most of them dazzlers. Even Cary had his stinkers. That brings up this hypothesis: should the world ever be faced with a plague that could only be halted by burning ten Cary Grant films, the first to be tossed on the flame should be *Night and Day*. Cary plays real-life composer Cole Porter, a man he resembled about as closely as Daniel Day-Lewis resembles S. Z. "Cuddles" Sakall. Said casting disaster was further compounded by Grant delivering what has to be the most lethargic, least interesting performance of his career. Was he ill? Was he a masochist? Are we masochists for sitting through it? Since Grant was a freelance actor at the time, with first pick of all the best scripts in Hollywood, one wonders why in the world he chose to do this one. He was being offered films like *The Lost Weekend* (1945) for Paramount and Billy Wilder, a non-musical, *The Pirate* (1948), at MGM with Greer Garson and Charles Laughton, even a modern version of *Hamlet* that Hitchcock asked him to do (and which, indeed, was announced in the trades on December 20, 1945, as a "go"). Instead we got Cary, sitting at a piano very late one night after a downpour has ebbed and, in all seriousness, listening to the sounds around him. He suddenly gets the divine inspiration to write, "Like the tick, tick, tick of the stately clock as it stands against the wall . . . like the drip, drip, drip of raindrops when the sum'r show'r is through. . . ." Done, mind you, without ever cracking a smile.

THE PRIDE AND THE PASSION, 1957

That cannon! Those clothes! Those stars! That story! *The Pride and the Passion* has Cary as a British officer in Spain during the Napoleonic Wars, plus Frank Sinatra as a guerilla leader named Manuel sporting a Spanish accent with New Jersey overtones, both of them looking quite thin next to the ample Sophia Loren. In 1957, the casting of Grant, Loren, and Sinatra in the same movie promised so much, but as things turned out, it was quite resistible, impossibly long (130 minutes), and unworthy of them all.

THE GRASS IS GREENER, 1960

The Grass Is Greener is another Cary caper with a super cast. It also marked all sorts of on-film reunions: Cary reunited with Deborah Kerr, plus Deborah reunited with Robert Mitchum, plus Mitchum reunited with Jean Simmons, plus Deborah and Jean together again after films like *Black Narcissus* (1946) and *Young Bess* (1953). Plus Stanley Donen (*Indiscreet*, 1958) directing. Who could ask for more? All of us could, actually, because no matter how hard one tries to enjoy this movie, sitting through it, even with that fourteen-karat cast in the spotlight, is like trying to run through mud in snowshoes.

ONCE UPON A HONEYMOON, 1942

Even reunited with director Leo McCarey, with whom he'd worked so successfully before (notably in 1937's *The Awful Truth* and 1940's *My Favorite Wife*), even Cary couldn't save *Once upon a Honeymoon*. He and costar Ginger Rogers entered the same kind of dangerous terrain that Chaplin had entered in 1941 with *The Great Dictator* and Jack Benny and Carole Lombard had pulled off earlier in 1942 in *To Be or Not to Be*—namely, using the Nazis as a background for a comedy at the very time the Nazis were creating such havoc throughout Europe. Those earlier serio-comedies had succeeded; this one was deadly by comparison and even worse when judged on its own.

ARSENIC AND OLD LACE, 1944

By comparison to most of the comedies made these days, Capra's *Arsenic and Old Lace* is funny, basically because it's based on a wittily written and expertly polished play by Joseph Kesselring. But Cary's pretty bad in this movie version, overacting to the point of embarrassing silliness, doing "takes" large enough to be read at a distance of three thousand miles. To his credit, he later said his performance was awful, and that *Arsenic* would have been so much better if Capra's first choice, Bob Hope, had been available to do it. The pity is that this was the only collaboration of the great Capra and the great Grant—and, although it was an enormous financial winner for Warner Bros., it does remain one of the few times Grant's judgment as an actor was totally off base.

DREAM WIFE, 1953

The only film Sidney Sheldon ever directed, *Dream Wife* is something that probably looked good on paper (Sheldon cowrote the screenplay with two others). However, it was played (to borrow a phrase from a *Time* magazine critique of Susan Hayward in a comedy) with a light touch that could knock a horse dead.

THE HOWARDS OF VIRGINIA, 1940

A 985-page historical novel whittled down to a 117-minute movie, *The Howards of Virginia* features Mr. Grant woefully miscast as a man caught up in the politics and hostilities between the colonists and England in the days leading up to the Revolutionary War. D-r-e-a-r-y, a word that can rarely be used in connection with a Cary Grant movie.

KISS THEM FOR ME, 1957

There's nothing really wrong with *Kiss Them for Me*, except that it was a gigantic waste of Cary Grant's time. Like hearing Placido Domingo sing "Mairzy Doates" for 103 minutes.

ALICE IN WONDERLAND, 1933

What a great idea: a big-budget telling of Lewis Carroll's classic story, *Alice in Wonderland,* done with live actors of the caliber of Grant, Gary Cooper, W. C. Fields, Jack Oakie, Leon Errol, Polly Moran, Edna May Oliver, Ned Sparks, and Charlie Ruggles. The problem was that the film could have easily been made, instead, with Wally Wastebasket, Sam Shoebrush, and Betsy Bullfrog because all the players, save Alice, were virtually unidentifiable, each of them hidden under heavy makeup, turtle shells, teddy-bear skins, and other Wonderland costumes. Is that really Cary playing the Mock Turtle? The voice sounds like his, but otherwise one has to take Paramount's word for it, making this thoroughly disposable as a Cary Grant movie. Walt Disney came up with the great idea for this *Alice.* He proposed doing it with a live Alice, to be played by Mary Pickford, entering a Wonderland peopled entirely by animated characters, which his studio animators would draw. But no one had ever done a combination live-and-animated film before (it would be a decade before Disney did just that in a musical comedy called *The Three Caballeros* [1945]). In 1932 he suggested *Alice* for that sort of treatment in a joint project with Pickford, Paramount, and the Disney Company, but Paramount decided to do their hide-the-stars version instead. The decision was made partially because no Hollywood studio in those days would seriously consider a joint effort with another studio, something that started becoming commonplace in the movie business at the tail end of the twentieth century.

The simple rule of behavior in Hollywood was live for the public, work for the public, play for the public. For many stars, those playtime hours—the private moments—were the most difficult to relinquish to their fans. Cameras were always snapping, smiles were always assumed, and glamour was *de rigueur*. Fun and games merged with work on the set, too, as neighborhood-sports such as boxing or ice skating became subjects for films—was anything not the camera's domain? And even the most treasured private moments—at home, "alone" with the kids, or, perhaps, secluded with a clandestine lover—became fodder for the press. Ah, how times haven't changed.

Errol Flynn, left, and Orson Welles help Rita Hayworth celebrate her birthday with Flynn's second wife, the former Nora Eddington. Welles baked the cake.

HAVING FUN

Below: While Charles Boyer and Lauren Bacall were filming *Confidential Agent* (1945), Humphrey Bogart frequently visited the set at lunchtime to challenge the Frenchman to a game of chess.
Bottom: Charlie Chaplin dresses up for a game of doubles ping-pong with partner Bebe Daniels in the backyard of her Santa Monica beach abode.
Opposite: Burt Lancaster gets a piggyback ride from Ava Gardner on the sands of Santa Monica Beach.

Hollywood's studio system didn't leave stars with much time for real fun. The publicity machine was always at work, cameras clicking, smiles demanded. Life as a star was supposed to be glamorous, luxurious, and filled with leisure time. Photographs were taken of stars on the golf course, lounging by their pools, sailing, riding horses—living the proverbial good life. The stories concocted to accompany the photos emphasized every detail of the posh existence of Hollywood's glitterati. Naturally the real stories behind the smiles were often less than happy. No matter how happy they looked, the celebrities were caught in a world filled with the pressure to perform both on the set, at the box office, and offscreen.

Those offscreen performances were perhaps the worst of all for the stars. Even days off became days "on." For many actors and actresses, like Doris Day or Bogart and Bacall, privacy was all they craved. Yet they were forced to put on a happy face at every moment.

The public image was artfully and purposefully crafted by the public relations professionals who worked for the studios, providing visual material to movie magazines. They used journals such as *Photoplay,* founded in 1911, and *Movie Mirror* (which was founded in 1931 and merged with *Photoplay* in 1940 to become *Photoplay–Movie Mirror*), as the unofficial voices of the industry, feeding the public "intimate" looks at the stars as they lived their lives. Studios made certain that few

photos were published showing celebrities smoking, drinking, or cavorting with lovers. To ensure that as many photos as possible would be used, the studios hired top photographers to take pictures that would be irresistible to the magazines.

Above: Virginia Bruce was raised in Fargo, North Dakota, so riding horses was one of the easier aspects of the Hollywood life. A star first at Paramount in 1929 and then at MGM in the 1930s, she made her last picture in 1960, playing Kim Novak's mother in *Strangers When We Meet*.

Right: Cary Grant cavorts on the sand behind his Santa Monica beach house where he lived in the 1930s.

Opposite: Janet Blair, who played the title role in *My Sister Eileen* (1942), was one of Columbia's most prolific performers in the 1940s. The singer's girl-next-door image was promoted by the studio, so it was a natural to find her on a dock fishing, her piano close by.

SHOOTING POOLS

What would the Golden Age of Hollywood have been without swimming pools? The pool—taking whatever shape, color, and depth its environs would allow—became an icon of the rich and famous, a symbol of huge amounts of money and dramatic amounts of glamour. The pool was a place to expose the body in a way that could be sanctioned by even the most conservative critics and censors, yet it was also a spot for blatant sex appeal: nearly nude male bodies in dangerously close proximity to nearly nude female bodies. When studios realized the publicity potential of stars photographed by the pool, almost every star was required to don a suit and "lounge" by the water (typically in full makeup, and often, for the women, wearing sexy high-heeled shoes and jewelry). While pools were grand in the early years (some were replete with artificial waterfalls; others were more athletic, with dramatic high-diving boards), by the 1950s pools became more humorous—the most notable being Jayne Mansfield's heart-shaped pool and Liberace's piano-pool.

Movie magazines of the 1930s, 1940s, and 1950s published the pictures year round. And fans ate it up. They loved the pizzazz of the pool and longed for pools of their own. By the early 1960s, ordinary Americans eager to buy a piece of the good life began finding the funds to install their

Jayne Mansfield's heart-shaped pool was a gift from her husband, Hollywood muscleman Mickey Hargitay.

own backyard swimming pools. As this aspect of a glamorous life became attainable, the pool lost some of its status. Coincidentally, that's also when the studio system began to fall apart and stars took charge of their own image making—typically sans pool.

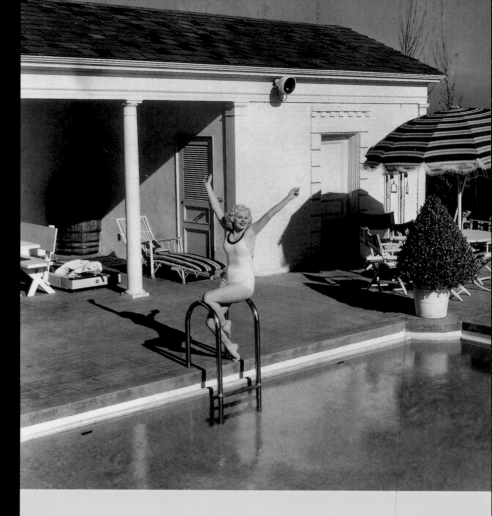

Above: Jean Harlow welcomes visitors to her backyard pool circa 1934.
Below: Ronald Reagan and first wife Jane Wyman tease each other at the pool in 1941.
Opposite left: Sonny and Cher frolic in their pool at their Los Angeles home, around 1965.
Opposite right: Barbra Streisand makes certain that she's in control as then-husband Elliott Gould carries her around the pool at the Beverly Hills Hotel in 1963.
Opposite below: Young stars and starlets never knew when they would be called upon to perform. An invitation to Paramount executive Melville Shaver's party might have been an invitation for publicity, so guests were always ready. From left to right: Howard Wilson, Frank Lose, Alberta Vaughn, Eldred Tidbury, Mrs. Tom Baily, Joe Egli, Mrs. Julian Madison, Julian Madison, Dudley James, Katherine DeMille, Colin Tapley, Phyllis Laughton, Richard Blumenthal, Clara Lou Sheridan (soon to be Ann Sheridan), Alfred Delcambre, Gail Patrick, Ida Lupino, Mrs. Stanley Lupino, and Toby Wing

UNLICENSED LOVE

BY BETTY GOODWIN

William Randolph Hearst and Marion Davies were renowned for the parties they hosted at her houses in Beverly Hills and Santa Monica and at his castle in San Simeon. At this Western party, the newspaper czar dressed like a rancher, the life he loved best.

In early Hollywood, certain celebrities didn't give a hoot for societal rules. In fact, some "brazen" women thought it was challenging to thumb their noses at society and live in sin, if that's what it took to be with their lovers. Typically, married men left their wives and family at home to live with their ladies fair, and because their wives wouldn't grant divorces, the illicit liaisons that started out as clandestine affairs left the wives rich but humiliated. In the cases of Spencer Tracy and William Randolph Hearst, the women they left at home simply read about their husbands' carryings-on in the newspaper, or worse yet, heard about the romances through the Hollywood grapevine. Although both had legendary fun with their young, beautiful partners, the two men's unlicensed love affairs were dramatically different from each other, and, in turn, quite different from modern live-in relationships.   —The Editors

Times have changed where Hollywood's famous unmarried couples are concerned. In the Golden Age of Hollywood, a career could be ruined if a star was found cheating on a spouse. Of course, those were the days when marriages were meant to stick—just like bad reputations. If a couple was caught living together on the sly, studio chiefs intervened. Perfect examples were Vivien Leigh and Laurence Olivier and Clark Gable and Carole Lombard—both couples were ordered to get the necessary divorces and marry each other.

In modern-day Hollywood, few blink when two unmarried celebrities bold-facedly cohabit and even produce offspring. Their lives are open books in the contemporary press. Some well-known unmarried couples are even blasé about their arrangements, an attitude that would have been unthinkable in the first half of the twentieth century. Goldie Hawn and Kurt Russell, both previously married and divorced (twice for Hawn), began living together after costarring in *Swing Shift* (1984) and had one child together. The two bantered publicly about their unmarried status—joking about Russell possibly popping the question in front of millions when they were copresenters at the Academy Awards.

Other stars seem almost defiant about remaining unmarried. Susan Sarandon, who had one daughter out of wedlock with Italian director Franco Amurri, began living with actor-director Tim Robbins after they worked together in *Bull Durham* (1988). Sarandon, who has two children with Robbins, once said of marriage: "The only other thing that I can think of that is as homicidal to a relationship [as marriage] is appearing in the 'Couples' pages of *People* magazine." Likewise, Jessica Lange already had one child with a lover, dancer Mikhail Baryshnikov, before moving in with actor-playwright Sam Shepard, whom she met while working on the movie *Frances* (1982). The couple has two children together. Her analysis in *Vanity Fair*: "I have always followed the most passionate course."

Fifty years earlier, Katharine Hepburn also followed her passions. But her nearly thirty-year relationship with Spencer Tracy had to be conducted in private. As a result, their careers continued to flourish. Together, they set a record in movie history, making nine films as on-screen lovers, including

Adam's Rib (1949), *Pat and Mike* (1952), and *The Desk Set* (1957). Hepburn found scripts for them, many by Ruth Gordon and Garson Kanin, and Tracy insisted on top billing. Other than professionally, the two never appeared in public. The voracious Hollywood press laid off their love affair, perhaps out of ignorance or, perhaps, out of respect. Some observers contended the press didn't want to embarrass Louise Tracy, who was untouchable because of her work in establishing the John Tracy Clinic, which she founded to help the couple's deaf son. Nevertheless, among Hollywood insiders, Tracy and Hepburn were "the most discussed couple in filmdom," according to Anne Edwards in *A Remarkable Woman: A Biography of Katharine Hepburn*. In 1960, Tracy's and Hepburn's names appeared together in columns for the first time, but they were always referred to as "longtime friends," Edwards reports.

Both Spencer and Katharine were married when they met and fell in love on the set of *Woman of the Year* in 1941, though neither was living with his or her spouse. Tracy, forty-one, also was the father of two children. Both stars were Academy Award winners (she for *Morning Glory* [1933], he for *Captains Courageous* [1937] and *Boys Town* [1938]), and the two were infamous high-maintenance individuals with a long string of love affairs to each of their credits. During his marriage, Tracy's lovers included Myrna Loy, Joan Bennett, Joan Crawford, Ingrid Bergman, and Loretta Young, for whom he left his first wife. Young, a devout Catholic, refused to marry the womanizing actor. Hepburn, thirty-four, was involved with her agent Leland Hayward (another famous womanizer) when she obtained a quickie Mexican divorce from Ogden Ludlow Smith, a Philadelphian who had pursued her when she was a student at Bryn Mawr, and then had a live-in arrangement with Howard Hughes. Even though they hadn't been together for years, "Luddy" filed for a legit divorce on grounds of desertion in 1942.

Until the end, Hepburn and Tracy maintained separate houses. As time passed, she acted more like a wife, cooking his meals and caring for him whenever one of them wasn't away on location. As Tracy's health deteriorated in the 1950s—partly brought on by his alcoholism—Hepburn adjusted her professional commitments to work near him and passed on movies that would take her far away. Tracy died of a coronary weeks after they completed work on *Guess Who's Coming to Dinner* (1967). Looking back in her autobiography, *Me: Stories of My Life,* Hepburn conceded that she never fought for marriage, a fact she regretted. "I was complacent. I didn't push for action. I just left it up to him. And he was paralyzed."

The legendary love affair of notorious press lord William Randolph Hearst and actress Marion Davies followed a different course. Because Hearst was a man who wrote his own rules, marriage and societal conventions came to matter very little throughout their three-decade relationship. Hearst was married to Millicent Wilson, a former dancer eighteen years his junior and the mother of his five sons, when he fell for Davies. They met in 1917, Davies a twenty-year-old showgirl with the *Ziegfeld Follies* with a promising future and one film to her credit. Among the fifty-four-year-old Hearst's many corporate interests—which included mines, paper mills, ranches, and magazines—was a film studio he had established in New York.

Davies was already an established beauty (with an obvious stammer) with a gift of talent when Hearst decided he would personally transform her into a major movie star and himself into a movie mogul. He hired coaches and spared no expense backing and supervising most of the forty-five films she made. When Hearst moved his production company to MGM (Louis B. Mayer was lured by the Hearst newspaper editorial and advertising exposure), everyone on the lot wanted to work on her films because of the dollars poured into them. Davies's friends also were granted invitations to San Simeon (Hearst's fabulous castle and 40,000-acre ranch located halfway between Los Angeles and San Francisco) for weekends of tennis, horseback riding, and swimming.

Though Davies made a few hit movies, most were money losers. Hearst's own papers gushed over Davies and her films at a time when movie coverage was given short shrift in most newspapers. However, when reviews did appear, Davies also received positive notice in non-Hearst papers. Hearst hired the legendary gossip columnist Louella Parsons on the basis of a single glowing commentary she wrote about Davies in a rival paper. Hearst also was kind to Davies's family members. Her father was appointed a New York City magistrate by Mayor John F. Hyland, who was a Hearst crony; her brother-in-law was an executive at Hearst's Cosmopolitan Pictures; and her sister, Reine Douras, was a supporting actress on the lot. At one point in their relationship, Davies had become so wealthy that she loaned Hearst $1 million when he was faced with financial problems due to lavish spending and heavy tax burdens.

Early on, Hearst wanted to marry Davies, but his wife would not grant him a divorce. Millicent reportedly reacted to his request by storming off to Tiffany's to buy herself a pearl necklace with a six-figure price tag. For a while, Hearst agreed to stay with Millicent in their thirty-room apartment, the biggest on New York's Upper West Side, and to appear with her socially. In those days, Hearst assigned an operator at his offices to keep tabs on Davies's whereabouts so that they could be in constant touch.

Hearst and Davies kept their affair quiet because of Hearst's political aspirations. When the presidency was no longer in his future, their life together became more open, and "the frankness of their attachment amazed even the blasé film community," wrote W. A. Swanberg in *Citizen Hearst.* Hearst built Davies a palace of her own on the beach in Santa Monica. The two were living together at the time of Hearst's death at age eighty-eight in 1951.

Orson Welles speculated that Davies's association with Hearst might have actually hurt her chances for great success. "Could the star have existed without the machine? The question darkened an otherwise brilliant career," he wrote. Others presumed that Hearst, with all his power, could have found a way out of his marriage, but that Davies herself opposed it. "She was now a millionaire in her own right and could have married many times. She was the free agent, held the whip hand, but chose voluntarily to remain loyal," wrote Swanberg.

Davies was not invited to Hearst's funeral and there was no mention of her in his will. However, the year before his death, Hearst gave her a trust fund with income from 30,000 shares of Hearst Corporation preferred stock. After his death, her attorneys came forward with an agreement showing that Hearst had pooled her 30,000 shares with his $170,000 and gave her sole voting power in the corporation. Once again the free agent, Davies agreed to relinquish her voting rights and serve as an advisor for one dollar per year.

Strong women both, Davies and Hepburn were willing to make love without a license in an era when few females had the courage to fight social mores.

Spencer Tracy and Katharine Hepburn have become the most famous of legendary couples who never married. Their love survived the trials of and his constant drinking.

STARS AND THEIR PETS

Psychologists offer that Hollywood celebrities have a special fondness for their pets because the animals love them no matter what: hit film or no hit film, five pounds up or five pounds down, breast augmentation or flat chest, balding pate or full pompadour. It may be simplistic, but who are we to argue? Pickford and Fairbanks, the ubiquitous pair of the early cinematic 1920s, were famed for their love of dogs, and at one time, the couple had as many as ten canines romping the grounds of their huge estate, all of varying breeds and sizes. Doris Day, a devoted friend of four-legged creatures, went so far as to finance a hotel, the Cypress Inn, in her hometown of Carmel, California, to which pet lovers even today can bring their furry friends for a few additional dollars a day. While many pets have become stars themselves, the animals pictured here are those who stayed out of the limelight and stayed faithful to masters and mistresses. For most, their only time in front of the camera was when the star wanted a little attention for their hairy best friends.

Cat-lover Kim Novak, who starred in several prestigious 1950s movies including *The Man with the Golden Arm* (1955), *Picnic* (1956), and *Vertigo* (1958), first came to Hollywood after winning a beauty contest sponsored by a refrigerator manufacturer. "Miss Deepfreeze's" career tumbled in the 1960s, but she never lost her love of animals. She married a veterinarian in 1976 and saw the century out raising horses and llamas.

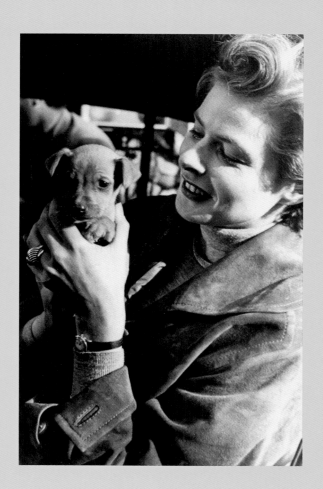

Above: Jean Harlow poses in her backyard
with her two best friends, circa 1935.
Right: Ingrid Bergman was making films in
Europe in 1953 having been barred from making films in America because of her notorious
affair with director Roberto Rossellini.
Slandered as a "free love cultist" and
"Hollywood's apostle of degradation" on the
floor of the U.S. Senate, she adopted her tiny
puppy in Paris. She made a remarkable come-
back in 1956 when she won an Academy Award
for her acting in *Anastasia*.
Opposite: Lucille Ball and her cockapoo Tinker
shared some fun on an RKO set in 1943.
Married less than two years to Desi Arnaz,
Lucy was always dressed for photos, even
when she wasn't working on a film.

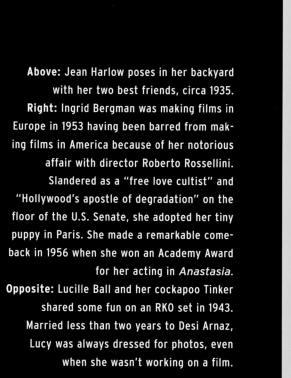

Right: Douglas Fairbanks and Mary Pickford had a separate kennel for their pet dogs, but Rex, shown here, starred in five films and became a star in his own right.
Below: Just after signing with MGM in 1931, an almost thirty-year-old Clark Gable poses with his favorite mutt for one of his first studio publicity shots, on the bank of the L.A. River.
Opposite: Esther Williams and her cocker spaniel pose on the rocks near Malibu Beach.

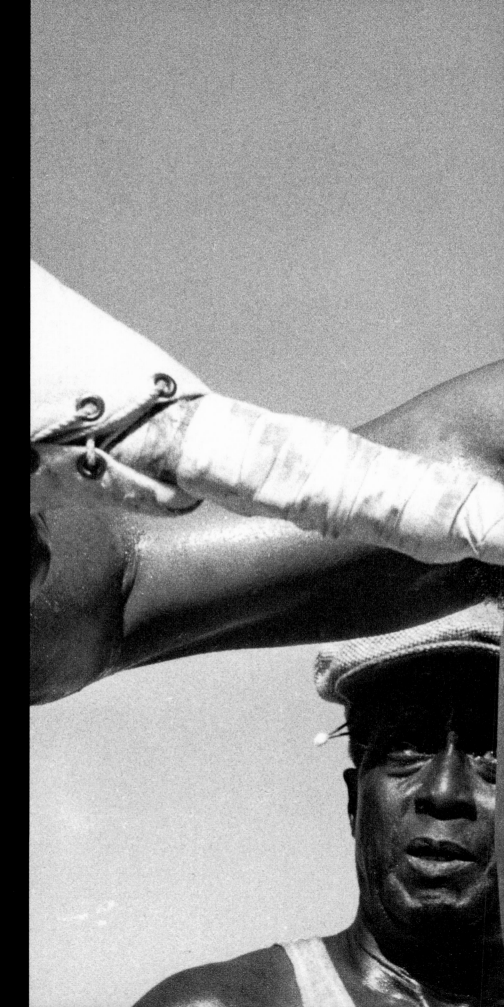

ON THE ROPES

O f all the popular sports that have made it to the screen as subjects for feature films, boxing has been the knockout favorite. Forget football, base-ball, basketball, soccer, ice hockey, volley-ball, or any other team sport. And while it has been said that it is easier for audiences to pull for an individual than an entire team—in films, that is—there have been very few movies about competitions involving track, golf, auto racing, horse racing, wrestling, ice skating, or swimming. Sonja Henie and Esther Williams were box-office champions because of glossy production numbers, not challenging opponents.

More than any on-screen sport, cine-matic boxing relates to the American dream, where good guys who work hard win. Plus, those stripped-to-the-waist bodies bring in box-office dollars. There has seldom been a shortage of actors anxious to be contenders, or new heroes waiting to step into the movie ring.

Once audiences heard the first clang of the ringside bell in early sound movies, they could relate to the fun they had personally experienced in the ring or around it. Boxing was America's neighborhood sport—fun for the gang. To see prizefighting on the screen was bigger-than-life entertainment. So box-ing was on its way to decades of screen popularity. It probably didn't hurt that Wallace Beery won an Academy Award in one of the earliest boxing films of the new

James Earl Jones as boxing champ Jack Jefferson in *The Great White Hope* (1970)

sound era, playing a washed-up prizefighter in 1931's *The Champ*. (Fredric March was first announced as best actor for his dual role in *Dr. Jekyll and Mr. Hyde* [1931], but Beery had received only one vote fewer than March, so both were given the award for 1931–32.) Nor did the presence of such studly stars as John Garfield, Clark Gable, William Holden, Elvis Presley, James Earl Jones, Paul Newman, Sylvester Stallone, Kirk Douglas, Robert DeNiro, Denzel Washington, and Brad Pitt, cast as fighting leads, hurt the continuing popularity of these films in the years that followed.

It has been estimated that a few hundred fight-themed films have been released since Thomas Edison put boxer "Gentleman Jim" Corbett (who was the subject of a highly successful movie biography, *Gentleman Jim*, in 1942, starring Errol Flynn) before his camera in 1894. While a number of films have been based on real-life ring favorites, an even greater number have been pure fiction—and pure gold at the box office.

From the 1930s onward, Hollywood has loved boxing. The sport has all the elements to keep audiences jumping in their seats. There's the underdog, believing in himself, working, training, and sacrificing to make his dream come true. It's David and Goliath, good versus evil, fighting for survival. It's everyman, standing alone before the world, bare chested in his quest for success. It's action, blood, sweat, and tears, and being saved by the bell. The hero may not always win, but he can still come out a winner. Win or lose, he usually gets the girl in the final reel.

Right: Elvis Presley in *Kid Galahad* (1962)
Below: Wallace Beery and Jackie Cooper in *The Champ* (1931)

Right: John Garfield gets patched up between rounds in *Body and Soul* (1947). Garfield was nominated for an Academy Award for best actor.
Below: Lee J. Cobb, Adolphe Menjou, Edward Brophy, Don Beddoe, and William Holden in *Golden Boy* (1939)
Bottom: Giant boxer gets a bad beating from Max Baer in *The Harder They Fall* (1956).

SECRETS OF THE HOLLYWOOD HOTELS

Hollywood hotels. They are often referred to as the "play-grounds of the stars," but they have always been more than that. For many, they have been safe havens in a frenzied world—"home," as Warren Beatty called the Beverly Wilshire Hotel for years before settling down with Annette Bening. For others, they were the sites of trysts, dangerous liaisons in a land rife with gossip. And for a very select few, they became their final stop in Hollywood.

—The Editors

Hollywood Knickerbocker Hotel
(1714 N. Ivar Avenue)

When it opened in 1925, the Hollywood Knickerbocker attracted numerous celebrity guests because of its studio-friendly location. Such stars as Gloria Swanson, Rudy Vallee, Cary Grant, and Dick Powell couldn't resist being smack in the middle of Hollywood, so the Knickerbocker quickly became the place to be and remained so for decades. It was Errol Flynn's first home when he arrived in Hollywood in 1935. Before moving to California for movie roles in 1944, Frank Sinatra stayed at the Knickerbocker. So did Elvis Presley in the mid-1950s.

The Knickerbocker had its share of scandals and tragedies. In 1943, the police forcibly escorted mentally troubled Frances Farmer through the lobby to a waiting car. She was wrapped in a shower curtain. An alcoholic, she had failed to report to her parole officer after being convicted of drunk driving and disorderly conduct. Five years later, while standing under the lobby chandelier, pioneer silent-film director and producer D. W. Griffith dropped dead from a cerebral hemorrhage. Alone and bitter, the man who brought America its first four-reel film, *Judith of Bethulia* (1914), *The Birth of a Nation* (1915), and *Intolerance* (1916) died nearly forgotten by the industry he helped create and develop.

In 1962, noted costume designer Irene lived her final moments at the Knickerbocker. The heir to Adrian's throne at MGM, Irene had designed for the studio's top stars of the 1940s and 1950s, including Lana Turner, Grace Kelly, Judy Garland, Greer Garson, Ginger Rogers, Irene Dunne, and Elizabeth Taylor. With MGM's approval, she started a couture business, selling her own custom-designed gowns in her own posh Beverly Hills boutique and in expensive speciality shops nationwide. Despite her success, her life soured. Her first husband died. She remarried but that union ended when he too passed away. Her depression unbearable, Irene rented a room on the Knickerbocker's highest floor, where she drank herself into a near-stupor, slashed her wrists, opened a window, and jumped. Four years later, William Frawley, who played Lucille Ball's neighbor Fred Mertz on TV's *I Love Lucy,* walked out of the hotel's bar and dropped dead on the sidewalk. (The following year, 1967, that lounge area was used as the hotel bar where Dustin Hoffman and Anne Bancroft, as Mrs. Robinson, rendezvoused in *The Graduate* [1967].)

The Hollywood Knickerbocker is today an apartment building.

Entry to the Hollywood Knickerbocker, 1932

Lobby, Hollywood Knickerbocker

Entry of the Garden of Allah

The Garden of Allah
(8100 Sunset Boulevard)

Before it became the playground of Hollywood literati and the party crowd, the Garden of Allah was the home of Russian actress Alla Nazimova. For nine years, from 1918 to 1927, the three-and-a-half-acre estate along Sunset Boulevard was a showplace with exotic plantings and the biggest swimming pool in Hollywood. (It was shaped like the Black Sea to remind Nazimova of Mother Russia.)

By 1926, however, Nazimova's career had hit the skids and she decided to turn her home into a hotel. After a rather shaky start, the newly named Garden of Allah became an oasis of creativity, attracting out-of-towners, particularly New Yorkers, to its lush setting, twenty-five private bungalow villas, bar, and restaurant. "It became a sort of West Coast Algonquin," said swinging bandleader Artie Shaw, who lived at the Garden with his then-wife, Ava Gardner.

The Garden's reputation for fast and fun times drew actors, writers, directors, and deal makers who checked in for months at a time, not the usual one-nighters. Over the next thirty years or so, until 1959, it played host to Hollywood's A-list crowd. Robert Benchley was one of the first to discover the Garden. He was followed by Dorothy Parker, F. Scott Fitzgerald, Dashiell Hammett, and Somerset Maugham. George S. Kaufman hid out at the Garden when Mary Astor's scandalous love diary was published. A married man, Kaufman was named as her most experienced paramour.

The Garden's pool was the gathering spot for guests. It was there that Benchley, in evening dress, fell in, then remarked, "I must get out of these wet clothes and into a dry martini." Tallulah Bankhead also fell in one evening. She was wearing an evening gown and loaded with jewels, causing her to sink to the bottom. Johnny Weissmuller dove in and pulled her out, but she was then stark naked. "You've all wanted to see my body," she told the onlookers. "Well, here you are!"

Marlene Dietrich regularly swam nude in the Garden pool at five in the morning. Greta Garbo regularly swam laps fully clothed.

Before Norma Jean Baker changed her name to Marilyn Monroe, she sipped soft drinks at the pool hoping to catch the eye of a producer. Clark Gable was after more than Carole Lombard's eye as he romanced her secretly in a poolside villa. Next door, Humphrey Bogart and Mayo Methot, known as "the battling Bogarts," wrangled over his new love interest, starlet Lauren Bacall. Ramon Novarro, W. C. Fields, Gary Cooper, William Powell, Cesar Romero, Glenn Ford, John Barrymore, Laurence Olivier, and Orson Welles all checked in from time to time. According to Anthony Quinn, "We called it 'the riding academy' because of all the love affairs that went on there."

In the 1950s the Garden turned seedy, but the stars still came to hang out in the bar or around the pool: Peter Lawford, Sammy Davis, Jr., Tony Curtis, even Mickey Cohen, the West Coast gangster. Singer Johnny Ray was one of the last "name" visitors. He was usually drunk, sickly in appearance, and looking for some action. Somehow, he fit right in.

The Garden of Allah was sold in 1959 and demolished to make way for a bank.

The Hollywood Roosevelt Hotel
(7000 Hollywood Boulevard)

The grand opening of the Hollywood Roosevelt in 1927 attracted the greatest number of stage and screen stars ever assembled. Part of the attraction was the new twelve-story hotel itself, the first luxurious hotel in the Hollywood area that had film-industry money behind it. The Roosevelt was situated on the west end of Hollywood Boulevard where important—and majestic—theaters like Grauman's Chinese and the El Capitan were opening their doors. But its biggest draw for the Hollywood set was the Roosevelt's mogul connection. The syndicate responsible for building the hotel included such screenland heavyweights as actors Douglas Fairbanks and Mary Pickford, and executives Louis B. Mayer, Marcus Loew, and Joseph Schenck.

The first public presentation of the Academy Awards was held on the second anniversary of the Academy's founding on May 16, 1929, in the Roosevelt's Blossom Room. With virtually a who's who of Hollywood in attendance—Janet Gaynor and Emil Jannings took home acting awards that night—the hotel soon became known as the "Home of the Stars."

Over the years, the Hollywood Roosevelt has welcomed many of the biggest names in movies to the Blossom Room, the poolside Tropicana Bar, and the famed Cinegrill lounge: both entertainers and celebrity guests such as Betty Grable, Errol Flynn (who seemed to have checked into every Hollywood hotel at one time or another—for one reason or another), Carmen Miranda, Humphrey Bogart, and Charles Laughton. But it was Marilyn Monroe and Montgomery Clift who left the most lasting impressions. Their spirits reportedly haunt the Roosevelt to this day. For Monroe, it is a ghostly image in a lobby mirror. For Clift, it is a cool wind that lingers in the hallway outside Room 928, where he lived for three months in 1952.

The twelve-story Hollywood Roosevelt Hotel

The Château Marmont on the Sunset Strip, 1951

Festive entry to the Ambassador Hotel, 1980s

Rehearsing *Rebel without a Cause* in Nicholas Ray's bungalow at the Château Marmont with James Dean, Jim Backus, Natalie Wood, Nick Adams, and other cast members

The Ambassador Hotel
(3400 Wilshire Boulevard)

From its opening in 1921, the Ambassador was Los Angeles's grandest hotel. A few miles away from the glitz of Hollywood, the Ambassador rose up from rambling acres of lawn and swimming pools, an elegant showplace for local society to dine, be seen, or be entertained. The blue blood of Los Angeles frequented the Ambassador: lavish weddings took place at the Ambassador. Debutantes were hailed in the social events of the season. So Hollywood wanted in.

It didn't take long before the elite of the booming film industry were Ambassador regulars. And why not? It had everything anyone could possibly want or need: fashionable bungalows, a huge pool with a sandy "beach," tennis courts, a miniature golf course (a favorite of Howard Hughes and Katharine Hepburn). And, of course, there was the glamorous nightclub, the Cocoanut Grove, with its grand staircase, waterfall, stars twinkling in a blue ceiling sky, and stuffed monkeys looking down on the partygoers with blinking eyes from faux coconut palms. (John Barrymore kept a real pet monkey in his Ambassador bungalow as a roommate.) Much of the exotic decor at the Grove was either inspired by or provided by Rudolph Valentino from his film *The Sheik* (1921).

Valentino was a longtime guest at the Ambassador, as were other stars of his day. Marion Davies and William Randolph Hearst had a wing at the Ambassador for close to a year during the early 1920s. For one of their extravagant costume parties, they rode a horse through the lobby and into the Cocoanut Grove.

Tallulah Bankhead, after a night of partying and prompting by friends, once sneaked into John Barrymore's bungalow and bed, and hid under his sheets. When Barrymore found her, he was unmoved. "Another time, Tallu," he sighed. "I'm too drunk and you're too awkward."

During the production of *Hell's Angels* (1930), Howard Hughes also lived in a bungalow at the Ambassador. He was much more receptive to his late-hour visitors.

Numerous scenes for motion pictures and television were filmed at the Ambassador. Among the most memorable were the 1936 and 1954 versions of *A Star Is Born,* which featured the Cocoanut Grove in location shots.

The stars who came to the Ambassador, to work, to live, or to play, made fewer headlines than many of the politicians. One event in particular stands out and will be forever linked with the hotel: the assassination of Democratic presidential primary candidate Robert F. Kennedy. Kennedy was at the Ambassador for the 1968 California primary, and on the evening of June 5, he stepped to the podium in the hotel ballroom to accept victory cheers from the crowd. Then, with "On to Chicago," he exited through the kitchen/pantry area, where Sirhan Sirhan was waiting. Kennedy was shot from point-blank range. The Ambassador Hotel was closed in 1988.

Although numerous plans for the property have been announced since then, its future remains uncertain and the original building stands decaying in the heart of Los Angeles.

The Château Marmont
(8221 Sunset Boulevard)

The castle-like Château Marmont has stood on a hillside above the fabled Sunset Strip since 1929, when it opened as "the newest and most luxurious apartment house in Los Angeles." But its show-business connections were not established until 1931, when Albert E. Smith, cofounder of Vitagraph, one of the pioneer production companies, bought the property and turned it into a hotel.

In the early days, the Château Marmont was located in "the faraway part of town," on the edge of the as yet undeveloped Sunset Strip. Still, as the new owner boasted, it was "fifteen minutes from everywhere," close enough but still remote. It was a good selling point, and the hotel became a hideaway for artists, writers, musicians, and the stars of stage, screen, and, later, television. New Yorkers and Londoners, in particular, loved its Old World charm—and privacy. Guests could enter and leave the hotel without having to go through the lobby.

It was Harry Cohn, head of Columbia Pictures, who rented the small penthouse at the hotel for his two hot-blooded young stars, William Holden and Glenn Ford. "If you must get in trouble," he proclaimed, "go to the Marmont."

Jean Harlow went to the Marmont with her third husband, cameraman Hal Rosson, for their honeymoon. But her nightly visits with fellow costar Clark Gable had the staff talking. Since she and Rosson had rooms with separate entrances, it was relatively easy for Gable to come and go without having Rosson notice.

Grace Kelly, in the early days of her film career, started rumors at the Marmont when she roamed the corridors in the late evening hours "looking for love" as the hotel staff referred to her habit of knocking on strangers' doors and then staying for a long visit.

In a Marmont bungalow, Natalie Wood began a relationship with director Nicholas Ray that nearly ended in tragedy. One of her smitten costars in Rebel without a Cause (1955) was so jealous of their affair that he wielded a gun on the set threatening to kill Ray. The gun was wrested, and filming continued. So did Ray and Wood's affair.

Bette Davis and Gary Merrill fought wildly at the Marmont. So did Shelley Winters and Anthony Franciosa, who had eyes for Anna Magnani—Shelley chased him with a knife to Magnani's suite.

It was at the Marmont that newcomer-to-America Billy Wilder willingly slept in the foyer of a women's restroom while awaiting a vacant room.

Howard Hughes spied on young ladies at the pool from his penthouse suite, and playwright Clifford Odets pined for Marilyn Monroe.

Virtually every star came to the Château Marmont during his or her career. Many of them were on the way up, such as Barbra Streisand, Hedy Lamarr, and Warren Beatty, or on their way down and out, such as John Belushi, who died there.

STARS AND THEIR KIDS

No matter how diligently stars tried to separate their family lives from their public lives, it was not always possible. Photographs of celebrated people and their children were often more sought after than pictures of the stars alone. In the 1930s and 1940s, when actors or actresses expanded their families, studio photographers stopped just short of the delivery room to provide on-the-spot coverage of America's big-name births. Some stars put up a fight and would only allow portrait studio photographers to capture their kids on film, but others allowed the cameras into their homes. When stars regained control of their private lives and told the studios to nix the mandatory photo sessions, celebrity-name children became off-limits. For months after she was born, a picture of Madonna's baby Lourdes was a hot item among the paparazzi. Arnold Schwarzenegger's children have rarely been photographed; ditto for the kids of Annette Bening and Warren Beatty. But in the Golden Age of Hollywood, photos like these helped to expand the meaning of Hollywood history.

Below: Humphrey Bogart and Lauren Bacall show off their first-born son, Stephen, to anxious photographers.
Opposite left: John Barrymore and his wife Dolores present John Barrymore, Jr., in June 1932.
Opposite right: Edward G. Robinson even dressed like a gangster to greet his new baby son.
Opposite below: May Britt and Sammy Davis, Jr., with new baby Tracey in July 1961

Right: Daddy Steve McQueen admires his diapering job on daughter Terry at home in the Hollywood Hills, 1960.
Below: Rita Hayworth played with her baby Rebecca, while husband and dad Orson Welles snapped the shot.
Bottom: Marlene Dietrich's daughter Maria would grow up to be actress Maria Riva and pen a detailed biography of her mother. Born in 1925, she was the daughter of Rudolf Sieber, the Czech production assistant Dietrich met when he hired Dietrich to appear in one of her earliest German films, *The Tragedy of Love* (1924).

Above: Edgar Bergen had three kids in this picture, it seems, but only one of them was living and breathing: beautiful little Candice, who grew up to be a star despite her wooden-headed "brothers."

Below: Melvyn Douglas and his wife, actress Helen Gahagan, traveled frequently. She snapped this photo of her two favorite males in 1943. She went into politics, and Californians elected her to two terms in the House of Representatives, but she lost a bid for the Senate to Richard Nixon in 1950.
Opposite: Mickey Rooney allowed studio photographers to follow him to the father's viewing window, the day after the birth of his second son.

A STAR IS BORN TO A STAR

"Hello, Liza. Hey, hello Liza. It's so nice to see you here where you belong." So sang Judy Garland to the tune of "Hello, Dolly" on a November night in 1964 when she and her eighteen-year-old daughter Liza Minnelli appeared together at the London Palladium. The crowd roared, Judy quipped, Liza giggled, and the momentous joint concert made history. Mother and daughter embraced throughout, their love and admiration for each other apparent. But an underlying power, some would call it competition, emerged on stage. Liza remembers that "Immediately after the Palladium show, Mama's competitiveness disappeared. She then fell into a period of unparalleled motherhood." Reviewers succumbed to the ease of comparing mother and daughter, but no one could deny that Liza Minnelli was proving to be a talent in her own right. In later years, even after Judy died and Liza began earning the critical and award-winning success that Judy had only dreamed of, the famous daughter's career was still beset by motherly comparisons. Fans alternately longed to hear Judy in Liza, but admonished her for being too much like her celebrated mother. As Liza asserted in 1975, "It never crossed my mind that I would grow up to 'be' my mother till people told me so and made me afraid of it. I'm me. I've made it on my own." This pervasive need to make a name for herself has been Liza Minnelli's driving force. Yet no matter how independent Liza may wish to be, that evening when mother and daughter clung to each other crooning "Can't you see we're really here to stay? Hey, we're never gonna go away again" has left audiences believing that they were meant to perform together.

Liza May Minnelli was born to screen legend Judy Garland and visionary director Vincente Minnelli on March 12, 1946. As an adult, Liza told interviewers that she got her drive from her mother, and her dreams from her father.

Toddler Liza Minnelli gives Mama Judy Garland a backstage kiss. Liza made her movie debut at the tender age of three as Judy's on-screen daughter in *In the Good Old Summertime* (1949). Years later, she earned an Academy Award as best actress for her mesmerizing performance in 1972's *Cabaret*.

In 1963, Judy Garland proudly escorted seventeen-year-old Liza Minnelli during her smash off-Broadway hit *Best Foot Forward*. Judy intentionally stayed away on opening night so as not to distract attention from her avant-garde daughter. As Judy proudly gloated, "Liza's the first one of us to do this. I never had a Broadway show." The successful revival was Liza's first performance in which her talent played a stronger role than her name.

9

Hollywood glistened after dark in its Golden Age, on-screen and off. Suave vampires emerged seductively from their coffins, sexy sirens donned revealing evening gowns and luscious lingerie, and bathtubs became the ultimate setting for sensuality on the screen. Nightclubs that would become legendary showcased the most beautiful people in the world. Hollywood's after-hours image was all about sex and romance, glitz and glamour. Everything America craved went on in the dark of Hollywood nights.

In what fit like a second skin, Mae West tantalized the audiences of *It Ain't No Sin* (1934).

IN THE DARK

WHERE THE STARS CAME OUT TO PLAY

BY JIM HEIMANN

What happened after the sun set was not big news in Hollywood at the beginning of the twentieth century. Southern California was about sunshine, oranges, and beaches, all things to be appreciated by day. There were no fancy nightclubs, no elegant restaurants, no entertainment palaces that catered to film folk. So when the first movie studios opened up shop in 1909, something had to change. There were few places where movie stars could go to be seen, no place to unwind after a hard day's work. As one oft-quoted line asserted, "After nine o'clock, you could shoot a cannon down Hollywood Boulevard and never hit anybody."

About the only spot that attracted celebrities was the Hollywood Hotel, a Mission-Moorish-style building at the corner of Hollywood and Highland, where new-to-town actors and actresses set up temporary housekeeping. Within a short time, in need of some fun, the young celebrities instituted dances in the lobby every Thursday night, while proprietress Mira Hershey, of chocolate bar fame, kept a watchful eye to make sure there was no drinking or smoking. But the Hollywood set needed more excitement.

Venturing to downtown Los Angeles, they headed for the Alexandria Hotel. A magnet for stars and deal makers, with an elegant lobby rug that was called the "million-dollar carpet," the Alexandria was where Herbert Somborn, who would later found the Brown Derby restaurant, met his soon-to-be wife Gloria Swanson. Fight promoter Baron Long soon opened three nightclubs. One, the Vernon Club, in the bean fields near downtown, became Hollywood's first bona fide nightspot. It offered the glitterati a place to go, sign autographs, and hold their own private parties. Long was the first to notice the talent and good looks of a swarthy young man named Rudolph Valentino, and hired him as a tango dancer for thirty-five dollars a week. Long also initiated floor shows, dancing, chorus girls, and a full orchestra on stage every night, a combination that would be *de rigueur* at nightclubs for decades to follow.

Restaurants caught on to the allure of Hollywood and came up with dishes honoring stars: "Shrimp à la Buster Keaton" and "Chicken à la Fanny Ward" were celebrated fare at the Sunset Inn in Pacific Palisades. Dance clubs emerged with celebrities as judges, and often those dancers would soon be bigger stars than anyone could imagine. In 1921, at the Ambassador Hotel's new Coconut Grove, where imitation palm trees swayed with fake monkeys climbing the trunks, winning a dance trophy was the most prestigious accomplishment. Here Charleston queen Lucille Le Sueur fought hard to beat Jean Peters, another shimmying fanatic. When Lucille became Joan Crawford and Jean turned into Carole Lombard, the competition continued—but the prize was bigger (Carole finally got the man, Clark Gable).

Not far away, the Montmartre Cafe in Hollywood gave the Grove some competition when it opened in 1922. With its elegant Czech chandeliers and Belgian carpets, the Montmartre taught Hollywood ladies how to "lunch" in style. Each afternoon its silver-laden tables were filled with celebs, and by night, tourists were kept away by a red velvet rope. So well known was the Montmartre that the king of Sweden, Britain's Prince George, and Winston Churchill rubbed elbows there with the likes of John Barrymore, Joan

Opposite: Cafe Trocadero was *Hollywood Reporter* publisher Billy Wilkerson's big foray into the nightclub business and it was the place to be seen for anyone who wanted to be a star in Hollywood. Robert Cummings and Marsha Hunt frequented the Troc.
Below: Mocambo became the major competition to Ciro's—stars headed there, but it didn't have the staying power and closed its doors in 1958.

Right: Writer-director Preston Sturges opened the Players across from the Château Marmont and named it after a New York theatrical club, so he attracted an East Coast crowd as well as the Hollywood set. Sturges was on hand every night, as if hosting a party for the likes of Bogart, Chaplin, Stanwyck, and his buddies Howard Hughes and William Faulkner.

Below: Chasen's restaurant, shown here in 1938, remained in this same Beverly Boulevard location until it closed its doors in 1995. A favorite of Ronald Reagan's, he proposed to Nancy Davis there, and many years later, feasted on "Boiled Beef Belmont" and held "kitchen cabinet" meetings in his favorite booth while he was president of the United States. Chasen's was also the birthplace of the Shirley Temple, the liquor-free cocktail Dave Chasen created for the little girl with curls who demanded a drink when she dined there.

Crawford, Marion Davies, and the Marquise de la Falaise de la Coudray, aka Gloria Swanson.

Meanwhile, Swanson's ex-husband Somborn opened what was to be the most famous restaurant in Hollywood's long history, the Brown Derby. Shaped like the ubiquitous hat of the day, filled with waitresses who were ex-*Ziegfeld Follies* girls, and catering to the late-night crowd, the Derby became the place to be seen. Everyone in Hollywood made the scene at the Derby. No wonder gossip columnist Louella Parsons made the second Derby—the one on Vine Street in Hollywood—her satellite office.

By the 1930s the Coconut Grove and the Derby were still the hot spots. But new nightspots, like the Embassy Club, began offering stiff competition. Many of Hollywood's elite sat on the board of directors of this membership-only establishment, including Marion Davies, the omnipresent Gloria Swanson, Norma and Constance Talmadge, Sid Grauman, who owned the Chinese Theater, and King Vidor. On opening night Swanson showed up in a satin gown with rhinestone straps, dragging her ermine, and Corinne Griffith matched her for elegance in gold chiffon.

Club La Boheme was among the first to burgeon after the stars deserted the Embassy. On a yet-to-be-glitzy Sunset Strip, La Boheme had a perfect location overlooking the city. The site was so good that businessman Billy Wilkerson took over the spot and opened his famed Cafe Trocadero in 1934, the year after Prohibition was repealed. His first club, the Vendome, was the very spot where Louella Parsons got the scoop that Pickford was divorcing Fairbanks, a story she couldn't keep secret. Since he owned the *Hollywood Reporter,* Wilkerson's name was gold—the stars wanted to keep him happy, so they kept his clubs busy. Agent Myron Selznick hosted the opening night private bash, with a guest list that sounded like studio roll call—Gilbert Roland, Myrna Loy, Jean Harlow and companion William Powell, Dorothy Parker, the Bing Crosbys, the Sam Goldwyns. The Golden Age of Hollywood Glamour had begun.

The Derby, the Grove, the Vendome, the Troc—they were an unbeatable foursome throughout the Depression. With spots like those, the public could forget about the sorrow for a while. They could read about the glamour and the pâté in movie mags. And if they were lucky enough to live near Hollywood, fans could wait outside for autographs and glimpses of their favorite stars.

Many eateries flourished in the 1930s, but one newcomer matched the popularity of the powerhouse four, a little dive that specialized in barbecued ribs and chili. Owned by a former vaudevillian named Dave Chasen, the Southern Pit Barbecue on Beverly Boulevard near Doheny attracted a stellar crowd because of Chasen's entertainment connections and because the food was so damn good. Before long, Chasen's had grown into a first-class restaurant catering to the tastes of W. C. Fields, Jimmy Cagney, and Jimmy Stewart. Its popular reputation held on throughout the 1950s and 1960s.

In 1940, the enterprising Wilkerson opened Ciro's on the Sunset Strip, having sold the Troc a few years before. For the next two decades Ciro's was the sine qua non of Hollywood nightclubs. It met its match a year later when Mocambo opened, outraging the public with a ten-dollar cover charge. The well-heeled traipsed between Mocambo and Ciro's on alternate nights, making both clubs the talk of the town. Preston Sturges opened the Players the same year. Prince Michael Romanoff's eponymous restaurant in Beverly Hills became the chic eatery, despite the fact that his royalty was as much a figment of imagination—his—as any Hollywood film. Before long the names of these hot spots were as internationally famous as the filmland gods and goddesses who frequented them.

The 1920s, 1930s, and 1940s were Hollywood's nocturnal glory days. The dripping-with-diamonds, tuxedoed, star-filled nights of the Golden Age of Hollywood are gone. The Coconut Grove, Chasen's, Romanoff's, the Trocadero, Mocambo, and, yes, even the hat that was the Brown Derby have disappeared, left to be remembered in history books. But thanks to those photographers who captured the history on film, the magic of the day remains.

VA-VA-VOOM BAZOOMS

When Audrey Hepburn came on the Hollywood scene, she had two problems: her breasts. She didn't spill out of gowns the way the glamorous stars of Hollywood did. But, as Billy Wilder predicted, she "singlehandedly made bazooms a thing of the past."

Until Hepburn transformed Hollywood's image of glamour, however, voluptuousness was essential. Marilyn and Liz had seen to that, and Ava, Rita, and Mae before them. Every star had to find a way to look seductive. The curvier the better. The tighter the dress, the more to reveal. Hollywood wanted evening gowns that spoke messages so loudly that sometimes it hurt. Mae West, for instance, wore dresses that were so tight that she couldn't sit in them. The "leaning board" was invented just to enable West to rest between takes. Adrian, unquestionably the most gifted costume designer in Hollywood history, resigned when he was forced to flaunt his muse Garbo's body by lowering the necklines and tightening seams for her role in *Two-Faced Woman* (1941). After seeing herself so exposed, she too left Hollywood, never to make another film.

Looking back, there is something so very "Hollywood" about voluptuous women in revealing dresses—perhaps Garbo was right to want to be alone, away from it all. She could leave it to the gals who had it and wanted to flaunt it.

Above: Sophia Loren couldn't minimize her assets, even in a conservative sheath. Here, paparazzi snap her and her sister.
Right: In a photo by renowned Hollywood photographer Ray Jones, Mamie Van Doren poses for one of her first publicity shots at Universal International Pictures. The X design of her gown marked the focus of her career.

OF SEX AND VAMPIRES

BY PHILLIP DYE

O f all the shadowy, mythic creatures of European folklore that have appeared in movies, none has been so successfully creepy to audiences as the loathsome vampire and the menacing werewolf, but, of the two, vampires reign supreme.

Movies show rampant inconsistencies about vampire lore, however. Some vampires cast no reflections in mirrors; others do. Some turn into bats; others can't. Sometimes sunlight kills vampires; sometimes it doesn't. Sometimes stakes do the job; other times beheading is essential. Some vampires survive burning; others don't. Running water could do in some vampires; others just get wet and continue their evil deeds.

The truth is, the Hollywood vampire is far removed from the European myth that spawned it. In movies, vampires are pallid, with a lean and hungry look. But European folklore describes the vampire as looking florid and bloated as if gorged with stolen blood, exactly resembling corpses in early stages of decomposition. Since the dead look has never been appealing to movie audiences, vampires received studio makeovers; they had to look sexy. Hollywood reinvented the vampire legend, and in doing so explore themes of sexuality, mortality, and the nature of evil.

This was achieved by grafting onto the vampire yet another European legend, that of incubi and succubi (male and female demons, respectively, who take human shape and lure people into sexual intercourse). The modern movie vampire may drain victims of blood, but the hinted-at seduction involves willing victims embracing the devouring of their own souls.

Although an occasional figure in literature, a vampire of the undead, blood-sucking variety did not appear in movies until 1922, with director F. W. Murnau's unauthorized adaptation of Bram Stoker's novel *Dracula*. Steeped in traditional lore, this German version followed Stoker's description of a hideous being with pointed ears and rodent teeth. There was nothing sexy about this cadaverous creature, but at the end of the movie, the heroine, being pure of heart, is able to lure the plague-causing Nosferatu to her bed. The woman tricks the vampire into staying with her past daybreak, and Nosferatu disintegrates into a puff of smoke. This concept, that sunlight is fatal to vampires, actually has no place in vampire mythology. Murnau, in fact, misread Stoker's symbolism at the end of his book (Dracula is killed at dawn, not by dawn). However, other creatures of myth reportedly disappear at first daylight, and this lethal dose of sunlight, so compelling a mode of destruction and so powerful a metaphor, was subsequently imitated in countless vampire movies.

Also inspired by European myth, Danish filmmaker Carl Dreyer's *Vampyre* (1931) told an atmospheric tale of slowly building menace. His vampire had the form of an ugly old woman, who turns to bones after the traditional stake is driven through her heart while she is resting in her coffin. This, too, has been widely misconstrued by Hollywood. The purpose of the stake in myth was not to pierce the undead heart but to literally pin the vampire to the earth in its grave, so it could not rise again.

Opposite: Count Dracula (Bela Lugosi) finds he no longer requires the assistance of his mad servant Renfield (Dwight Frye) in *Dracula* (1931).
Below: The classic European vampire, Max Shreck was the plague-spreading Count Orlok in a trick publicity still from *Nosferatu* (1921).

Above: "Man of a Thousand Faces" Lon Chaney played a vampire in *London after Midnight* (1927).
Opposite: In *Mark of the Vampire* (1935), the Hollywood vampire couple, Count Mora (Bela Lugosi) and Luna (Carroll Borland), established the movie-vampire look that would prevail for the next forty years.

The first Hollywood vampire movie, *London after Midnight* (1927), starred the "Man of a Thousand Faces" Lon Chaney as a bizarre-looking vampire with bugged-out eyes and bear-trap teeth. This vampire turns out to be a hoax, an example of how early Hollywood was reluctant to deal with the supernatural. In fact, for many years after *London after Midnight,* the closest Hollywood came to creating a "vampire" was the man-ruining femme fatale of the Theda Bara ilk.

All that changed after Universal studios hired Hungarian actor Bela Lugosi to repeat his stage success as Dracula in a movie. Modern eyes have been jaded by dozens of Lugosi movies and imitations, but 1931 audiences were mesmerized by Lugosi's frightening performance. Having been a romantic leading man, Lugosi presented Dracula as a suave, handsome, and exotic villain, a sort of Rudolph Valentino of the undead. As a stealthy predator with a hypnotic gaze, Lugosi radiated an alluring menace and sexual power, a look that dominated all subsequent vampire movies.

The overt sexuality of the British Hammer Studios vampire movies of the 1950s, starring Christopher Lee as a new, virile vampire villain, resulted in a boon of increasingly adult-oriented fare at America's drive-in theaters in the 1970s. This type of horror provided ample opportunities for nudity and perverse sexuality, and this revealed itself most of all in European B-movies with adult themes, now collectively dubbed "Eurotrash horror."

Lesbianism, which had been hinted early in movies such as *Vampyre* and *Dracula's Daughter* (1936), and more broadly suggested in *Blood and Roses* (1960), became very blatant in Hammer's *The Vampire Lovers* (1970) and *Lust for a Vampire* (1970). Sex, lesbianism, and nudity were the main focus in Eurotrash sleaze with beautiful, nubile girl victims seduced by beautiful predatory females. *The Hunger* (1983) was part of the "new wave" vampire movies of the 1980s, with bigger budgets, stars, and effects than horror movies of this sort had previously been given when regarded as merely B-movie fare. These neo-vampires threw away most of the stale conventions (no more opera capes) to reinvent the genre. Vampires became cool.

Late-twentieth-century movies were tailored to appeal to the music-video generation of moviegoers. Francis Ford Coppola's *Dracula* (1992), for one, with the sound turned off, looks like a rock video. This revisionism was also partly inspired by Anne Rice's popular vampire novels even before her *Interview with the Vampire* (1994) reached the screen. Vampires, such as Frank Langella's Count in *Dracula* (1979), came to be presented as anguished souls, trapped in their nocturnal lifestyle, wanting the pity of their victims before ripping out their throats.

It is a genre that has seen many transitions. It will likely see more as film-makers explore further variations on the restless, hungry undead, which have transformed a morbid myth to a cinematic phenomenon.

THE ELEGANT VILLAIN
BY BETTY GOODWIN

Below: Vincent Price worked in Hollywood as a leading man for almost two decades before being cast in *House of Wax* (1953), which started his horror-film career. In later years, playing on his nasty image, the accomplished actor hawked an array of commercial products including Creamettes Macaroni, Hayward's Pickles, Monster Vitamins, the Agatha Christie Mystery Collection, and Tang.
Bottom: Vincent Price was considered one of Hollywood's most refined actors; in all details of his life, on-screen and off, he was a symbol of elegance.

He was all of them—"The Crown Prince of Terror," "The King of Horror," and "The King of the Grand Guignol." "Whenever a black-draped figure is needed to peer joyfully down upon the last remains, or someone is needed to lurch about at the bottom of an elevator shaft, laughing and groaning, they send for Vincent Price," wrote Hollywood columnist Roderick Mann. So it was. Price was probably the most well-educated villain to hit the Hollywood screen, playing the acting game to make enough money to follow his dream of being an artist and fine art collector. In the early 1950s, he donated sufficient art to establish the Vincent Price Gallery at a Los Angeles college. In the 1960s, he served diverse echelons of the American art-buying community, first on a committee under First Lady Jacqueline Kennedy to restore paintings to the White House, and then as an art buyer for Sears, Roebuck & Co. But America remembers him as its favorite horrormeister.   —The Editors

With his sinister mustache and spooky theatrical delivery, Vincent Price was anointed to horror genre royalty in the 1950s and 1960s, following in the frightening footsteps of Lon Chaney, Boris Karloff, and Bela Lugosi. Some credit Price with keeping the genre breathing during those years. Throughout his fifty-plus-year career, Price's cackle became so familiar that he was hired to tape the voice of the Haunted House at EuroDisney—in French, something he could do with ease, having mastered the language while studying art at the Courtauld Institute in London.

Though Price's filmography lists more than one hundred movies, the stand-outs were *House of Wax* (1953), in which he turns the corpses of his enemies and his lovers into wax figures; *The Fly* (1958), playing the brother of a scientist who becomes part insect after being trapped with a fly in his matter-transmitter machine; and *House of Usher* (1960). The latter was the first of several successful movies Price made based on Edgar Allen Poe stories for director Roger Corman. Yet, for all of Price's classics, the actor made a purposeful mockery of the genre that was his bread and butter. Despite his humorous approach, he took his work seriously. "You must believe some part of them," he said of his films. "Not all of it, but you must be able to believe this could happen. Otherwise, it's not frightening."

Born on May 27, 1911 (sharing a birthday with fellow spook Christopher Lee, who starred in horror films produced by the British Hammer Studios), to a well-to-do St. Louis, Missouri, family with descendants going back to the Mayflower, Price's father owned the National Candy Company and his grandfather made his fortune from the Price Baking Powder Company. After graduating from high school, he traveled solo on a grand tour of the art museums of Europe. He earned a degree in art history and English at Yale and taught school for a few years before studying art in London.

Art was only one of his dreams, however. The other was the stage. He made his theatrical debut in London playing a small part in *Chicago* (1935) starring John Gielgud (later Sir John). That year, he played Prince Albert in *Victoria Regina,* then followed the production to Broadway, where the title role belonged to Helen Hayes. Price joined the Mercury Theater with Orson

Welles and became a major stage presence before embarking on a film career soon after. His first horror picture was *Tower of London* (1939) with Basil Rathbone. Even though early in his career Price played as many straight dramatic roles, including *Laura* (1944) with Gene Tierney, as scary roles, it was his part as Professor Henry Jarrod in the 3-D hit movie *House of Wax* that cemented his position as a horrormeister. His favorite film role was *Dragonwyck* (1940), in which he played a drug-addicted monomaniac who is unkind to his wife.

Never one to sit idle, he played his share of mad scientists and murderous husbands, and appeared frequently on television, starring as a regular on *Pantomime Quiz*. He was also a regular on *Hollywood Squares* and appeared as Egghead on *Batman*. From 1981 to 1989, he hosted the PBS series *Mystery*.

Following divorces from Edith Barrett and Mary Grant, Price was married to actress Coral Browne until her death in 1991. From his previous marriages he had two children, a son Barrett and a daughter Mary Victoria (who published a biography of her father in 1999).

Price concluded his career in *Edward Scissorhands* (1991), playing opposite Johnny Depp, a star young enough to be his grandson. In 1993, the cultivated gentleman who had spent his film career scaring us succumbed to lung cancer in Los Angeles, and his ashes were scattered at sea.

SHEER PLEASURE

Nothing said sex to early Hollywood audiences better than lingerie. Censors allowed sleepwear and chemises to be shown, as long as the garments didn't violate the strict Production Code of 1934 that emanated from the Hays office. That meant no obvious nudity or suggestiveness. Adhering to the former and laughing at the latter, the men who ran Hollywood went about demanding that as much sexy lingerie be incorporated into their movies as possible. Maribou, fur, rhinestones, and lace were all essential elements of the negligees and underwear that Hollywood's actresses donned. Thus designing lingerie was an integral part of any studio costume maven's job if he or she worked

Below: Jimmy Durante flirts with two starlets, Greta Granstedt, left, and Joyce Compton, on the set of Paramount's *Phantom President* (1932).

Above: Playing a Parisian tailor, Maurice Chevalier gave the censors a jolt as he measured the chemise-clad Jeanette MacDonald's bustline in *Love Me Tonight* (1932).

Left: Maria Montez was as loyal to her fans as they were to her. She sent this risqué photo to every fan who sent in fifty cents.

on romantic comedies and dramas in the Golden Age. When Travis Banton designed negligees for Mae West, he used fabric that clung to her curves, and oodles of feathers or fur to advance her "Hollywood's most successful lady of the night" image. In Hal Wallis's terror-filled *Sorry, Wrong Number* (1948), director Anatole Litvak told designer Edith Head to go all out on the bed jacket and gown that a bed-ridden Barbara Stanwyck would wear throughout the film. Head acknowledged that she spent $3,000 just for the French silk satin and lace she used to create the negligee. Four exact copies were made, since Stanwyck wore the same design through most of the film.

Certain bits of underwear have become classics because of the movies, their images etched in our brains like fine art: Scarlett's corset designed by Walter Plunkett for *Gone with the Wind* (1939); Ellie's borrowed pj's in *It Happened One Night* (1934) designed by Robert Kalloch; and Maggie's slip that Helen Rose designed for *Cat on a Hot Tin Roof* (1958). Though those pieces have been pictured from every angle since they first hit the screen, there are thousands more pieces of underwear and nightwear that demonstrate the importance of lingerie in the movies. In the words of Miss Head, "Lingerie is more essential to the bedtime story than the bed."

Left: "The more outrageous the lingerie, the better," was Mae West's motto. She modeled in her own bedroom. Note the "MW" on the telephone dial.

Below: Edith Head designed the peignoir that Barbara Stanwyck wore as she played a bed-ridden socialite destined to be murdered in *Sorry, Wrong Number* (1948).

Opposite: Ann Sheridan was as sexy as 1940s stars could be, so she was draped in satin robes for her publicity shots.

SPLISH SPLASH

I n the first two decades of the twentieth century, the bath was the setting of some of the most provocative and sensuous movie scenes that had ever been filmed. A far cry from the uptight Victorian traditions that were still stymieing women, movies were turning females into blatant objects of desire. While it was still rare that a naked body was completely revealed, the tub itself intimated nudity and aroused the imaginations of audiences everywhere. To an industry that was trying to police itself when it came to morality on the screen, a bath scene was a way to imply nudity without really showing it. However, as time passed, the likes of Cecil B. DeMille began taking nudity in the

Below and right: The 1932 version of *The Sign of the Cross* featured Claudette Colbert as the beautiful Poppaea, seductress of Nero and Marcus Superbus, in one of Cecil B. DeMille's most luxurious bathtub scenes.

Above: No bubbles hide Gloria Swanson's nude body in Cecil B. DeMille's first bathtub scene. Swanson is shown here with Julia Fay in *Male and Female* (1919).

bath to extremes, showing as much of the body as possible.

DeMille was the first to capture a woman bathing on film in *Male and Female* (1919). Of course it was Gloria Swanson, the most liberated woman of the age, who would luxuriate in the Japanese-style sunken tub, rubbing her body with soaps and sponges to excite her fans. The movie was such a success that DeMille became obsessed with filming women who were taking the waters, so each new tub scene in his films became more and more lavish. He fine-tuned the art of making bubbles, learning by trial and error that asses' milk effervesced longer, better, and whiter than cows' and goats' milk, so he demanded that several gallons be available on every set (no easy feat in a Hollywood that was surrounded by a suddenly burgeoning Los Angeles, where farms—especially those with donkeys—were moving farther and farther into the hinterlands). Since these perfect bubbles created a shield for whomever was scheduled to bathe, even his most dramatically endowed stars could be submerged in a heap of the encapsulated air, and fans would be panting in their seats. By the time Claudette Colbert appeared as Cleopatra, DeMille's bubbles met no match. She was sufficiently covered, but sexuality was implied by the overt hedonism of the scene, with female slaves

Above: Even Aesop's fables had bath scenes in early Hollywood. In *Night in Paradise* (1946), Merle Oberon plays the temptress who bathes in a clam shell and tantalizes Turhan Bey, who plays Aesop, helpless under her bubbly spell.

Opposite: This risqué bath scene from *A Man's World* (1918) made audiences drool and censors cringe.

surrounding the bathing queen, meeting her every need.

Greer Garson, Elizabeth Taylor, Marilyn Monroe, Charlie Chaplin, and Harold Lloyd all soaked on screen during the first five decades of film history. The bath tradition in the movies has managed to flourish despite conservative periods, censors' codes, and feminist movements.

Right: Lana Turner luxuriates in a French porcelain tub in the 1952 remake of *The Merry Widow* (1932), based on the Franz Lehar operetta of the same name.
Below: Liz Taylor, as prostitute and mother of a dead daughter, plays rubber ducky with Mia Farrow, as daughter of a dead mother, in *The Secret Ceremony* (1968). Critic Rex Reed called the film "garbage . . . totally ridiculous," but the bath scene was memorable.

10

The world's fascination with Hollywood never dies. Our appetite for Hollywood nostalgia never ends. As long as there are photo archives to be searched, memoirs to be read and reread, celebrated cemeteries to be visited, and oral histories to be recorded, there will be fans to savor the memories. And, of course, as long as there are old movies, the likes of Valentino, Monroe, and everybody else's favorite stars will never die. God save the film preservationists. May big donors provide the money to keep their craft alive so the world's great films will always be with us in the state they were meant to be seen. As far as Hollywood goes, there is no end in sight for its glory. No end, except perhaps for the artfully flaunted rears displayed on the next few pages—the delightful side of Hollywood.

When Rudolph Valentino died, reverent women from all over the country flocked to Hollywood to mourn the passing of the first—and perhaps the greatest—screen lover of all time.

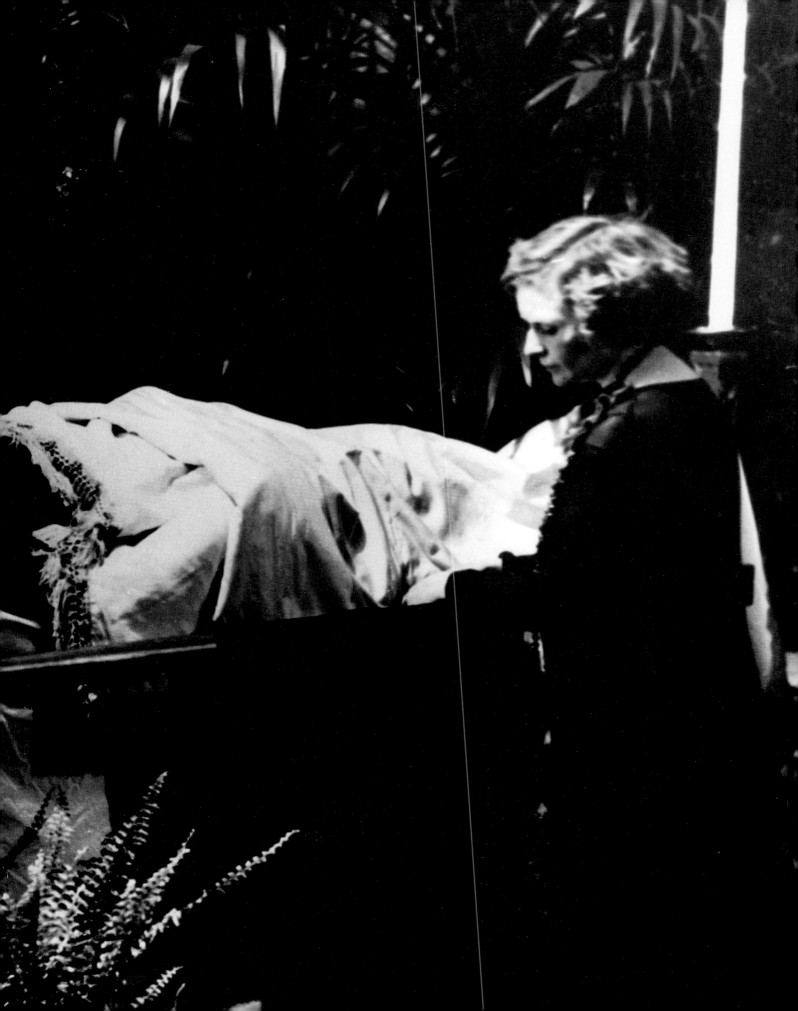

ENDS IN SIGHT

D écolletage may be the most prevalent symbol of sexual energy in the movies, as the camera adoringly zooms in on breasts and costume designers find provocative ways to make the most of even the flattest chests. But there is another erogenous zone that has often been more prominent, frequently more alluring and decidedly more fun to describe. It is the derriere. The ass. The tush. The fanny. Unisex by nature, asses—by any name—have won Hollywood's adoration.

By recognizing that rumps are truly the seat of arousal, filmmakers have learned an important lesson: guys' buns can be as provocative as the female fanny, and that's pretty provocative. In *Tarzan the Ape Man* (1932), Johnny Weissmuller wore loincloths split to the waist on each side, offering just a hint of a muscular butt when he swung through the trees. Likewise, in *Ben-Hur* (1925) and *The Pagan* (1929), Ramon Novarro's costumes revealed the curve of his behind while titillating his fans of both sexes, challenging the censors and helping establish a need for the morality code that eventually emanated from the Hays Office.

On the female front, Mae West and Jean Harlow celebrated the power of the backside, making padded girdles forever a staple at Frederick's of Hollywood. There was no need to call in a "body double" for tush shots (a job necessitated by modern stars who refused to pose nude either for moral reasons or because they judged their bodies to be imperfect); the voluptuous women of the Golden Age posed for their own back-

Above: Shiny satin helps accentuate Mae West's hourglass figure. Proud of her shapely silhouette, West quipped about her body often: "The curve is more powerful than the sword."

Opposite: Draped languidly in a diaphanous gown, Jean Harlow poses for photographer George Hurrell in 1933. He noted that she was a good subject. "I would say, 'change the position of your left hand,' and she would deftly move her palm or fingers a fraction of an inch without altering the whole effect."

side shots, either augmented by padding or perfectly flexed to get the most from their gluteus maximus muscles.

Throughout the 1940s, Betty Grable's famed World War II pinup made female derrieres an important feature to flaunt for women everywhere. However, once Johnny came marching home again and took possession of his woman, the uptight elastic girdle bound Rosie the Riveter's assets and turned her into a restricted housewife. Along came the late 1960s, though: bras burned and girdles lost their garters. Pantyhose brought a smile to cheeks. The derriere was free to jiggle once again. And with that, bikinis, thongs, and even less continued to remind the movie world that a film can make money when there's an end in sight.

Below: MGM studio photographer Frank Powolney's famous World War II pinup of Betty Grable apparently showed off more than her fabled "million-dollar legs." The rumor that Grable was pregnant at the time this photo was taken was apparently disproved by frontal shots taken the same day that revealed a flat tummy. More than three million prints of this photo were distributed to the armed forces.

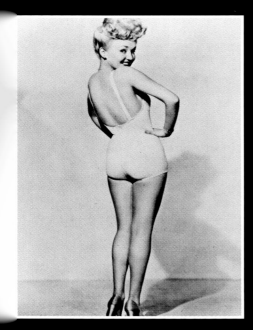

Opposite: Marlene Dietrich paused poolside at her home in Beverly Hills and gave the photographer a raunchy view. Since she was renting the house of Countess di Frasso ("Dorothy" to Marlene), the actress allowed studio photographers to come home with her for the first time, and cheesecake photos such as this one resulted.

Left: Grace Kelly playfully flashes her backside to the cameraman during a barbecue at costume designer Edith Head's Beverly Hills hacienda. Kelly always refused to give out her measurements, but Head often noted that Kelly had "a shapely rear, that sometimes looked too flat in tight clothes."

Below: Sexy Ann-Margret offered a cameraman cleavage front and rear. Discovered by George Burns, screen-tested in 1961, Ann-Margret was called the "female Elvis Presley" for her gyrations while singing and dancing. She admitted that she didn't know much about acting, but by 1964, she simultaneously had a million-dollar contract with MGM, a four-year contract with Twentieth Century–Fox, and a three-picture deal with Columbia.

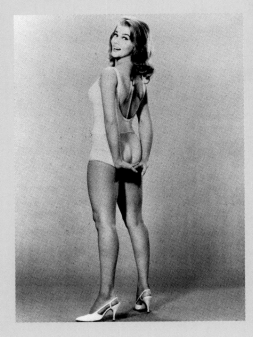

SAVING FILM HERITAGE: FROM THE TRENCHES

BY ROBERT A. HARRIS AND JAMES C. KATZ

Movies have lives of their own and, until recently, those lives have been extremely mortal. Indeed, a movie dies an undignified death, decaying in poorly labeled film cans hidden in old warehouses, colors fading to nothing, sound degenerating, film deteriorating. But because of determined film restoration specialists, such as these authors, and because of grants from institutions that honor the art form, the greatest films are being preserved. It means that films we thought had met their ends now can be saved, immortalized to entertain for generations to come. —The Editors

Authors Harris and Katz restored Alfred Hitchcock's *Rear Window* (1954), a film that was released to high acclaim at the end of the twentieth century.

When Ron Haver completed the restoration of *A Star Is Born* in 1983, he purposefully left out the song "When My Sugar Walks down the Street" from the famed "Born in a Trunk" sequence, since director George Cukor had made that cut after the first preview in 1954. Even though Haver had used stills to substitute for other lost footage in the film, he did not try to re-create this sequence with Judy Garland and Jack Baker, since adding it back would make it differ from Cukor's vision.

Film restoration is a field in its infancy. The new century will watch it mature. So far, films restored have run the gamut from the earliest works of cinema to the films of American director D. W. Griffith, French director Abel Gance, and their contemporaries in the late silent and early sound era, to the Technicolor period of the 1930s through the 1950s and beyond. Each era and type of film carries with it its own set of challenges.

The basics of film restoration involve the gathering of all film elements (rolls of picture and sound) worldwide for the film to be restored or reconstructed, as well as all extant production and post-production paperwork. But from that point on, the differing elements of filmmaking and the era go in many directions, creating a situation in which an archivist might well be advised to specialize in films of a certain period or type of filmmaking.

What we consider "real restorations" or "reconstructions" of note during the period have been Kevin Brownlow's work on Abel Gance's 1927 *Napoleon*; Ronald Haver's reconstruction of George Cukor's 1954 *A Star Is Born*; Robert Gitt's (for UCLA) three-strip reconstruction/restoration of the first three-strip Technicolor feature *Becky Sharp* (1935) as well as his work on John Ford's Technicolor *She Wore a Yellow Ribbon* (1949); and Frank Capra's *Lost Horizon* (1937). Added most recently to the list are Frank Capra's *Matinee Idol* (1928), restored by the Academy of Motion Picture Arts and Sciences (AMPAS) in association with Columbia Pictures, and *In the Heat of the Night* (1967), this time with AMPAS in association with MGM. Our own work on films such as *Lawrence of Arabia* (1962), *Spartacus* (1960), *My Fair Lady* (1964), *Vertigo* (1958), and *Rear Window* (1954) has made us specialists in the 1950s and 1960s.

What is equally detrimental to the future of quality film restoration are the plethora of poorly researched or edited journalistic reports about the current state of film restoration. If one were to believe the press, there have been dozens of brilliant film restorations in the past few years alone. Unfortunately, many of these writers don't understand what's happening—or not happening—to classic films. They can't educate their readers. Add to this various "video" or "restored for video" works, which further muddy the waters.

However, the films listed above don't even make a dent in the problem of film survival. There are thousands of films that should be preserved and prized like rare books, but that isn't happening. What's worse is that the public is being led to believe that it is happening within the private sector, so public funds aren't easy to garner. There's a wonderful line in John Ford's *The Man Who Shot Liberty Valence* (1962) that states something like: "When legend becomes fact, print the legend." Unfortunately, the survival of our film heritage and just how much is being done within the studio system to preserve that heritage is, in some cases, more legend than fact. The public—and many of the people within the film industry—actually believe that the alternate formats equate with restoration and preservation. All of this confusion—much of it industry-bred misinformation designed to sell tickets to supposed restored films or sell videos or DVDs—

does nothing more than stall actual film restoration at best, and lead to destruction of the films at worst.

What the public needs to understand is that films cannot be restored via video. In order to save these films for future generations, the owners must, while working with film archivists and/or archival institutions, actually start from the ground up and create all-new picture and sound elements from the finest surviving materials that will protect the film for years to come. It is from these elements that new duplicate negatives, prints, and high-quality video transfer may be produced.

While some studios do a perfectly professional job of archiving, preserving, and restoring their assets, others—not to be left off the bandwagon—have taken an almost wag-the-dog position. While maintaining that all is well in Mudville, and taking great pride in their work, they point a finger squarely in the direction of the "real" restoration problem: "orphan films." An orphan film is a property without corporate or private ownership. Whether an entertainment-oriented feature film, a documentary, or something as simple as old, small-town home movie footage, these films are in desperate straits. Many times they have lapsed into the public domain and many must be mentored by individuals or archival institutions—all seeking the same public funds—to survive.

While the legitimacy of orphan films needn't be questioned, and while funding to preserve these films is of great importance, the reality of the situation is that, in many cases, important studio films are in worse condition than the orphan films. Within the video-driven film preservation/restoration scenario, major feature films will be left to rot until a video colorist can get an acceptable transfer of an extant fading film element.

If a company has the option of spending from $30,000 to over $1 million to save a 35mm or large format film and can actually create elements that will save the film for centuries to come, too many decisions are being made to go with "adequate" for DVD. The need for immediate financial gratification comes to the fore. Too many times a beautiful video is delivered to the unsuspecting public, or on occasion the original negative is used as a transfer element, thereby resigning the original negative to a worse fate than it would have suffered had it remained locked away—undisturbed, unpreserved, unrestored, and untransferred.

The following films, "restored" for video or the theater while the original film elements may molder, include the non-orphans: *The King and I* (1956), *The Alamo* (1960), *Ben-Hur* (1959), *North by Northwest* (1959), *El Cid* (1961), *The Graduate* (1967), *Gone with the Wind* (1939), *Around the World in 80 Days* (1956), *The Godfather* (1972), and *Dr. Zhivago* (1965).

We have an industry that cannot agree on what "film restoration" actually is. We have bright and generally responsible journalists who can be swayed into belief by well-written studio handouts and the overriding fear of being removed from screening lists. We have a public that innocently views the latest DVD and makes the assumption that the "film" actually still exists as film and is in some way preserved. We are very much in that same position taken a quarter of a century ago when nitrate studio negatives were copied onto unstable stock and then dumped unceremoniously into the Pacific or used as landfill. And who are the executives who make these decisions?

With studios being consumed and traded like coveted baseball cards and with film libraries being broken up, sold, and restructured, it has become virtually impossible for experts to properly conserve, preserve, and restore on any rational basis.

With a large number of titles coming of age in the new century, we are dealing with more faded, shrunken, and decomposing rolls of acetate, containing both picture and sound, than most people can imagine. It is important that the public plays an active role in forcing the preservation of this important art form, or the legacy of a century of filmmaking will be lost. We repeat: some studios are doing a superb job of saving and conserving the film world's heritage (and the studios' film assets). For others, and sadly, for many great films, it is almost after the end.

WHAT A DRAG

In the first half century of Hollywood, smoking was a sign of the times. Sexy, daring, sophisticated, menacing, threatening, deadly—those were the images a simple draw or puff could elicit. What could have been more romantic than when Paul Henreid lit two cigarettes at once in *Now, Voyager* (1942), one for himself and one for Bette Davis. And what 1930s and 1940s celebrity wasn't photographed with a smoke between his or her fingers or lips at least once? Bogie and Bacall, Hayworth and Welles, Gable and Lombard—they all smoked and communicated sex appeal. As the 1950s and 1960s came along, even Misses Clean (but still Sexy) Audrey Hepburn and Grace Kelly were known to take a drag. It was all part of the image.

An easy affectation to mimic, Americans smoked right along with their stars. They may not have had fancy cars, swimming pools, glamourous gowns, sparkling diamonds, or torrid love affairs, but fans could smoke. They could be just like their favorite stars. And on at least one important count they were. Bogart died of throat cancer; Gable died of a heart attack; Bette Davis of lung cancer and Audrey Hepburn of colon cancer; the obese Welles of a heart attack; Gary Cooper, John Wayne, the list goes on.

Dean Martin unfairly had the reputation of a hard-drinking, chain-smoking ladies' man. He was just a smoker, and he died in 1995.

Above: John Wayne smoked throughout his career and had a cancerous tumor in his lung in 1963. He died in 1979.

Top right: Anthony Quinn posed for a publicity shot in 1970 with a cigarette in hand.

Middle right: Actors smoke cigarettes; moguls smoke cigars; it's the Hollywood tradition. In 1956, Alfred Hitchcock showed his moguldom.

Bottom right: His virile physique and carefree manner made Gary Cooper the perfect male lead. A chain-smoker all of his adult years, he died of cancer in 1961, at sixty.

Opposite top left: Sal Mineo cultivated his tough-kid image and smoking was part of it. He was stabbed to death in 1976 at thirty-five.

Opposite middle left: Gregory Peck, "Mr. Clean," was caught with a smoke in 1953.

Opposite bottom left: In the 1950s, Paul Newman's sexy bad-boy image almost required that a cigarette hang out of his mouth whenever he wasn't kissing.

Opposite top right: At recording sessions, even the man with the golden voice had to stop for a smoke, a habit he picked up early singing in smoky nightclubs. Frank Sinatra died in 1998.

Opposite middle right: After Yul Brynner died in 1985 of lung cancer, the American Lung Association released anti-smoking public service announcements he had filmed in his dying days.

Opposite bottom right: On the set of *Giant* (1955), James Dean takes a smoke break.

Above: Lauren Bacall was often photographed smoking, but on the set of *Bright Leaf* (1950) she plays with a very long cigarette. Her beloved Humphrey Bogart died of throat cancer in 1957.

Right: Marlene Dietrich, who had little concern about promoting a feminine image, was often photographed smoking.

Below: In 1932, sultry Mae West posed for a Paramount publicity still, her cigarette just a subtle prop. She died in 1980 after several strokes.

Opposite: A longtime chain-smoker, Bette Davis attributed her raspy voice in her old age to years of puffing. She died of breast cancer in 1989 at eighty-one.

HOLLYWOOD NEVER DIES

As popular as the corner of Hollywood and Vine. As entertaining as a day at Disneyland. The pursuit of celebrity graves by fans from all over the world, for most, is not some macabre preoccupation, but rather a tribute to all who created Hollywood. The stars left their final, and sometimes most lasting, impression in a glamorous manner or with quiet reserve, and their fans want to see it. A trip through the Hollywood Forever Cemetery behind Paramount studios in the heart of old filmland is like a trip through the history this book has traced. Rudolph Valentino; Douglas Fairbanks; Cecil B. DeMille; Tyrone Power—dozens of early Hollywood's biggest names are viewed daily by visitors. It is a remarkable monument to the industry. Nobody dwells on the fact that Valentino died of a perforated ulcer, or on the heart-related deaths of Fairbanks, DeMille, and Power. How they died is not the interest, but rather how they lived.

Forest Lawn Cemeteries in Glendale and the Hollywood Hills hold the graves and tombs of more Hollywood celebrities than any resting place in the world. In Glendale, the original Forest Lawn memorial park, lie Errol Flynn, Humphrey Bogart, Mary Pickford, Walt Disney, Clark Gable and his beloved Carole Lombard, Jean Harlow, Spencer Tracy, and dozens of other noted stars. And, in the Hollywood Hills, where the Forest Lawn memorials are nestled on rambling slopes adjacent to Griffith Park, stars such as Bette Davis, Lucille Ball, Stan Laurel, Gene Autry, and Buster Keaton are remem-

bered as they each requested. Their memorials have become as photographed as any star on Hollywood Boulevard's Walk of Fame.

Visiting the Westwood Village Memorial Park, hidden among West Los Angeles's office buildings and movie theaters, provides another lasting image of Marilyn Monroe, Natalie Wood, Dean Martin, and the other film industry people who rest there with them. It is a tiny cemetery where fans gather, leaving flowers and messages of love and sorrow and thanks. On Monroe's birthday, her fans assemble by the hundreds to salute a tomb that bears simply her name and the years of her birth and death.

These monuments to Hollywood will, for centuries to come, offer the last words on Hollywood celebrity. Some wished only to be remembered by their name, separate from their Hollywood legend. But others reflect the spirit of Hollywood and the gratitude of the deceased for a life lived well. Valentino, for instance, loved his dog Kabar so much that, three years after Valentino's death, his beloved pooch was laid to rest in the Los Angeles Pet Memorial Park as the Sheik had requested.

Some stars approach their epitaphs with a lightheartedness that is consistent with their lives. Consider the gravestone in Hollywood Forever Cemetery that memorializes Mel Blanc, the famous voice of Bugs Bunny and Porky Pig and thousands more characters. It bears a few words that symbolize his career: "That's all folks."

Hollywood history is more than just a fabulous collection of stories and images. It is world history born in the hearts of men and women, experts and not, who are willing to share their knowledge and their passion with almost anyone who asks—but especially with those who promise to pass on the correct message. To these wonderful Hollywood specialists and lovers, we offer our deepest thanks:

Betty Lasky, Richard de Mille, Fay Wray, Cecilia DeMille, Sue Lloyd, Annette D'Agostino Lloyd, Barbara and Margaret Whiting, Linda Jones, Harold and Lillian Michelson, Jon Provost, Billy Barty, Eddie Brandt, Dawn Moore, Tom Kelley, Jr., Roger Corman and Robert A. Harris and James C. Katz, as well as the late Clayton Moore and Tom Kelley for graciously sharing pieces of their personal histories and their firsthand knowledge of a Hollywood that the rest of us can only hope to know through words and pictures.

Marc Wanamaker for taking the time for so many years to collect and disseminate the treasures of this special place called Hollywood. No one strives more diligently to right the wrongs of Hollywood historians who didn't finish their homework. Hollywood history would be incomplete without Marc's body of knowledge and the priceless collection of historic photographs he calls Bison Archives.

Film historian Robert J. Osborne for kindly providing a view of films and stars that can only come from someone who has spent years watching thousands of movies and has found something notable about each of them, be it good, bad, or terribly funny. We are greatly indebted to him.

The staff of the Academy of Motion Picture Arts and Sciences Center for Motion Picture Study Margaret Herrick Library, not just for their tireless help on this volume, but for their continuing service to the world in preserving the history of the motion-picture industry. We extend our special thanks for their knowledge, help, and remarkably kind support to the dedicated and gentle Sue Guldin, the determined Marcelle Angelo, the very thorough Margie Compton, and the smiling Matt Severson, whose tireless help in locating and retrieving historic photographs made this book possible. Frans Offermans's skill of photographic reproduction adds immeasurably to the quality of this book and we offer our thanks for his behind-the-scenes wizardry. Also our gratitude goes to the indefatigable Stacey Behlmer, who continually surprises us with her knowledge of Hollywood history, her attention to the smallest details, and her positive approach to great challenges. Sandra Archer and Carol Cullen made special efforts that turn research library users into fans. And at the helm, Linda Mehr deserves special kudos for bringing together such an impressive team.

Claire (who modestly calls herself "just Claire") at Eddie Brandt's Saturday Matinee Video for spending days and nights researching and printing pictures for this book, pictures that were hidden in an archive of rare photographs catalogued not just in filing cabinets, but in Claire's incredible mental storehouse. Her intense devotion to the project will long be remembered, as will her turquoise specs.

Lou Valentino for honoring Lana Turner, as his collection of rare photographs proves. We thank him for sharing, time and again, both pictures and knowledge.

Liz Roberson, whose love of the movies enhanced this project, and Melinda Nickas, Alison Acken, and Juliana Walters who made research and consultation more fun than work.

Sid Avery and his staff at Motion Picture Television Archive who have, in a relatively short time, created one of the most prestigious collections of photographs in the country. We are proud to include several pictures from the archive and to salute the photographers whose work has preserved the heritage of Hollywood.

Writers Heidi Dvorak, Phillip Dye, Betty Goodwin, Laurie Jacobson, and Sheila Perkins, who delved into topics that added to the scope of this book, and Joseph Carter of the Will Rogers Memorial in Oklahoma, who shared tales and photos of Will Rogers that will keep the memory of this renowned humorist alive for years to come. Jim Heimann and his classic book *Out with the Stars* have already established their esteemed places in the annals of Hollywood, but we are extremely grateful for his willingness to share his rich research in these pages.

We are especially indebted to the film studios who have made their properties available. We thank especially Margaret Adamic at Walt Disney for delving into the archives to find the rare Donald Duck (and clan) drawings included in these pages. They are one of the great treasures of Hollywood. On a personal note, Mr. Duck was Ron Haver's favorite Disney character.

So many other people have lent their time and support to this project that we hesitate to name more, for fear of forgetting even one. But we must attempt a list and ask forgiveness from anyone whose name is not included. Thanks go to: the unbeatable Toms: Krentzen, Wittmer, and Zimmerman; Yen Graney, Steve Banks, Jerry Anker, Marguerite Campbell, Dr.

Richard L. Schatz, the staff of Larry Edmunds Bookshop, Greg Shreiner, Ed Baker, Janelle Grigsby, Stephanie Mork, Robert Redford, and Lorenzo and Luis of Printland.

Our four editors, Jonathon Fairhead, Katie King, Margaret Braver, and Abigail Wilentz, brought this book to fruition and we thank them. Jonathon's imprimatur surfaces throughout this book; it is his and ours. His dedication to the project went far beyond the call of duty. We are also especially thankful to Katie who withstood remarkable pressure to make certain this book was an honorable contribution to Hollywood history. We appreciate Bonnie Eldon for her efforts to keep everyone on track. We are grateful to Antonio Polito, the vice chairman of Rizzoli/Universe International Publications, for the initial idea for *The Hollywood Archive* and his faith in Angel City Press. Charles Miers of Universe Publishing recognized the importance of this book and constantly demanded quality.

Angel City Press is a small but determined bunch, with a support system that never quits. We thank David McAuley, Genevieve McAuley and their friend Mojo for their contributions. Patricia Fox, Antonio Durando, and Nann Durando provide the constancy upon which Angel City Press is built; they know how important they are. Jacqueline Green, Chuck Morrell, Carla Ruff, and Tom Woll have long been friends of the Press—appreciation for their advice and support cannot be expressed fully in words. Charles Phoenix continually offered suggestions and reassurance in times of stress.

In addition to contributing her skills as a writer, Sheila Perkins attended to every detail of this book with a contagious positive attitude. We send to her our respect, love, and thanks.

Finally, to Ann Calistro, who lived the years of Hollywood's Golden Age, we thank you for two things. First, for your wonderful memory of stars and their films. Second, and most importantly, for bringing Ronald Duck Calistro Haver into this world, instilling him with intelligence, humor, and the love of films and film history, and for allowing him the freedom to become one of the world's finest film historians and preservationists. His contributions to so many people's lives is your greatest gift to all of us. You have made all the difference.

Paddy Calistro, Scott McAuley,
and Fred E. Basten
Angel City Press, Santa Monica,
California 2000

CONTRIBUTORS

Angel City Press publishes books that respect the history and nostalgia of Hollywood's popular culture. Each Hollywood book that bears its logo is dedicated to the memory of Ronald D. Haver, world-renowned film historian and curator.

Billy Barty is one of Hollywood's finest actors. He founded Little People of America in 1957. The essay that appears in this book is an excerpt from his forthcoming autobiography.

Roger Corman is a legendary producer, writer, and director whose prolific work was the subject of a 1978 documentary, *Roger Corman—Hollywood's Wild Angel*. In the 1960s, when he produced movies based on the works of Poe, he was known as the master of the macabre.

Richard de Mille, son of Cecil B. DeMille, directed television shows in the 1940s and taught psychology in the 1960s. He is the author of several books, including *My Secret Mother: Lorna Moon*, about his famous family.

Heidi Dvorak is an editor and writer based in Los Angeles.

Phillip Dye has written several television documentaries "The Many Faces of Dracula," "The Many Faces of Zorro," and "Hollywood Animal Stars." He is currently researching and reconstructing the lost film *Cleopatra*, which starred Theda Bara.

Betty Goodwin is a journalist and author who specializes in the entertainment industry. She is the author of *Hollywood Du Jour: Lost Recipes of Legendary Hollywood Haunts* and *Chasen's: Where Hollywood Dined; Recipes and Memories;* and co-author of *Marry Me! Courtships and Proposals of Legendary Couples.*

Robert A. Harris and James C. Katz are film-restoration specialists who have restored some of the world's most important films.

Jim Heimann is the author of the best-selling non-fiction work, *Sins of the City: The Real Los Angeles Noir*. He is a popular-culture specialist and graphic designer who grew up savoring old Hollywood.

Tom Kelley earned his place in Hollywood's history for far more than the fact that he took the renowned nude photo of Marilyn Monroe that helped lead her to stardom. His photographs of numerous Hollywood legends have been shown throughout the world.

Betty Lasky, daughter of Jesse L. Lasky, one of the founders of the movie industry, is a former movie editor and author of *RKO: The Biggest Little Major of Them All*. She is currently associated with the Hollywood History Museum in Hollywood, California.

Harold Michelsen has worked in Hollywood since 1947 as production designer, art director, and illustrator. His many credits include *Dick Tracy* (1990); *Catch-22* (1970); *The Birds* (1963); *West Side Story* (1961); and *Ben-Hur* (1959). He was an Oscar nominee for *Terms of Endearment* (1983) and *Star Trek: The Motion Picture* (1979).

Ann Miller is one of Hollywood's most famous dancers. She is renowned for her wild cavewoman dance in *On the Town* (1949). Her autobiography, *Miller's High Life* was published in 1972.

Clayton Moore (1914–1999) was inducted into the National Cowboy Hall of Fame in 1990 and received his star on the Hollywood Walk of Fame in 1987, the only star to list both the actor and the character he portrayed. He appeared in 169 Lone Ranger episodes, two Lone Ranger films, and dozens of other films and serials. His famed mask was added to the permanent collection of the Smithsonian Institution.

Robert Osborne is a columnist and critic for the *Hollywood Reporter,* a television host on Turner Classic Movies, and the respected author of over eleven books including *70 Years of the Oscar.*

Sheila Perkins has long been fascinated with Hollywood, and at age twelve began researching the life of Judy Garland. She became a devoted fan of Golden Age films and is a noted specialist in the field.

Jon Provost, child actor in numerous films and television shows, is best remembered as Timmy on television's *Lassie* (1957–1964). His original costume hangs in the Smithsonian Institution. Provost has received the Lifetime Achievement Award from the Youth in Film Association and, in 1991, a Genesis Award for Outstanding Television in a Family Series for a story he wrote on inhumane treatment of animals. In 1994, he received his star on the Hollywood Walk of Fame.

Robert Stack is well known as the host of television's *Unsolved Mysteries* and the star of *The Untouchables*. He starred in numerous films after his debut in *First Love* (1939), and was nominated for an Academy Award for his supporting role in *Written on the Wind* (1957).

Marc Wanamaker is one of the world's foremost authorities on motion-picture industry history. A sought-after consultant as well as the owner of Bison Archives, the largest privately owned photo archive of Hollywood historical photos in the world, he co-authored *Hollywood Haunted: A Ghostly Tour of Filmland.*

Barbara Whiting, the daughter of songwriter Richard Whiting and sister of pop singer Margaret Whiting, grew up in a show business family. She has appeared frequently in movies, on radio, and on television.

Fay Wray was born in Los Angeles and starred in Erich von Stroheim's *The Wedding March* in 1928. It was after playing the girl who won King Kong's heart that her name was etched into Hollywood history books.

ABOUT RONALD HAVER

In 1968, Ronald Haver took a job as projectionist at the American Film Institute. Too talented to be confined to the booth, however, he was named oral historian to Merian C. Cooper, producer of *King Kong*. In 1972, Ron left the AFI to join the Los Angeles County Museum of Art where he was soon named director of film programs. For more than twenty years his innovative film series attracted international audiences and established the museum's film department and programs as the finest in the world.

Reviewers unanimously called his first book, *David O. Selznick's Hollywood* (Knopf 1980), one of the most beautiful and thorough volumes on film ever published.

Ron masterminded the restoration of *A Star Is Born* (1954), directed by George Cukor and starring Judy Garland and James Mason. To Cukor's dismay, the film had been mercilessly pruned by Warner Bros. after its initial release, and its missing footage became legendary over the years. Sponsored by the Academy of Motion Picture Arts and Sciences and Warner Bros., Ron was given access to the studio's film vaults and ultimately came up with the goods: twenty of the missing thirty minutes of Cukor's original cut. Ron's greatest disappointment was that his friend Cukor died the night before he was to view the restored film. On June 30, 1983, Ron's restored version of *A Star Is Born* opened to wide acclaim and turn-away crowds at Radio City Music Hall. Sold-out houses followed in Los Angeles and Washington, D.C., as well as at the Venice, Deauville, San Sebastian, and London film festivals.

In 1988, Ron's *A Star Is Born: The Making of the 1954 Movie and Its Restoration* chronicled his work. Film reviewer Kevin Thomas of the *Los Angeles Times* wrote that it was "quite simply one of the best books ever written about Hollywood." The publication inspired additional screenings of the film, which eventually was released on video cassette and laser disc.

At the close of his Selznick tome, Ron expressed what the movies had meant to Selznick, to himself, and to everyone else who had ever stared in hopeful anticipation at a blank movie screen by quoting from a speech made by the producer in May 1940:

To you who feel the burning urge to influence the modes and manners, the social and political ideologies of the future through the medium of the motion picture, I say, 'Here is a challenge, here is a frontier that is and always will be crying for the courage and the energy and the genius of American youth. Here is the Southwest Passage to fame and fortune and influence! Here is the El Dorado of the heart, the soul and the mind.'

Ron Haver died in 1993 of complications from AIDS.

The editors and publisher extend their appreciation to the following institutions, archives, and individuals who provided images that appear in *The Hollywood Archive*. Every effort has been made to determine the origins of the vintage photographs on these pages and give credit where it is due. Any oversights will be corrected in future editions.

Academy of Motion Pictures Arts and Sciences Center for Motion Picture Study Margaret Herrick Library: Front cover (Grace Kelly, Cary Grant), back cover (*Footlight Parade)*, and pages 2 (top left, courtesy the MGM Collection; MGM/Turner Entertainment), 18, 30, 32, 33 (courtesy the MGM Collection; MGM/Turner Entertainment), 34, 49, 50, 64, 66 (bottom), 67, 70 (top), 72 (right), 74, 76 (right), 77, 86, 89 (bottom right), 98, 104, 112, 124, 125 (bottom right), 138, 145, 146, 148, 174, 176, 196, 200, 206, 266, 269, 270 (bottom), 275 (bottom), 289 (top and center), 314, 318, 319, 320, 322 (top left), 323, 328, 330 (right), 331, 332, 334, 340 (top right), 352 (center left).

Personal collection of Jerry Anker and Marguerite Campbell: page 118 (right).

Personal collection of Ed Baker: pages 276, 282 (top).

Personal collection of Billy Barty: pages 116, 118 (left).

Personal collection of Fred E. Basten: Front cover (Jane Russell), back cover (Lana Turner), and pages 15 (bottom), 56, 57, 66 (top), 68, 69, 70 (bottom), 71, 109 (center and bottom), 110, 120 (top), 126, 137, 161, 178, 180 (left), 198 (bottom), 201, 202, 203, 244 (top), 245 (top left and right), 248 (top), 249 (top right), 258 (bottom), 262 (top left), 268 (top), 279, 285, 292 (bottom), 296 (top left), 330 (bottom left), 349.

Eddie Brandt's Saturday Matinee: Back cover (Mae West) and pages 4 (top), 13 (bottom), 52, 89 (bottom left), 125 (bottom left), 128 (bottom), 130 (right), 134, 135, 136, 140, 141, 167, 175, 180 (right), 182 (top), 198 (top left and right), 199 (top), 208 (left), 210, 211, 212, 218, 219, 254, 255, 256, 268 (bottom), 270 (top), 271, 282 (bottom), 283, 284 (top), 294, 295 (top left and right), 296 (bottom left), 298 (right), 299, 301 (left), 322 (bottom right), 326, 339 (top left), 340 (bottom right), 348 (top), 352 (right).

Christie's Images 2000: page 204.

Walt Disney Archive: pages 52, 226, 228, 229, 230 all, © Disney Enterprises, Inc.

Personal collection of Phillip Dye: pages 36, 37, 38, 39, 310, 311, 312, 313.

Larry Edmunds Bookshop, Inc.: Back cover (Jack Lemmon) and pages 182 (bottom), 246 (Day), 247 (bottom left).

Personal collection Patty Fox: pages 2 (bottom left), 246 (top), 128 (top).

Collection of the estate of Ronald D. Haver: pages 94, 96, 97, 184, 306 (right). 348 (top right).

Personal collection of Laurie Jacobson: pages 156, 162, 164.

Tom Kelley Studios, Inc.: pages 72 (left), 120 (bottom), 121, 166, 182 (center), 187, 189, 191, 192, 193, 298 (top).

The Harold Lloyd Estate and Film Trust: pages 214, 216, 217.

Personal collection of Harold Michelson: page 59.

Personal collection of Dawn Moore: pages 157, 158, 159.

Motion Picture & Television Photo Archive: pages 2 (top left), 11 (top, bottom), 13 (top), 15 (top), 16, 35, 87 (bottom), 88, 89 (top), 92, 100 (top), 102, 103, 106, 108 (top), 111, 113, 122, 125 (top), 143, 150, 152, 154, 272, 274, 275 (top left and top right), 280, 295 (bottom), 296 (right), 300, 301 (right), 329 336, 338, 339 (all except top left) 340 (left), 341, 352 (top left).

Personal collection of Liz Roberson: page 172.

Will Rogers Memorial: pages 222, 223, 224, 225.

Personal collection of Lou Valentino: pages 199 (bottom), 324 (right).

Bison Archives/Marc Wanamaker: pages 2 (right), 11, 22, 23, 24, 26, 28, 29, 40, 42, 43, 44, 46, 51, 54, 58, 60, 62, 73 (top), 76 (left), 78, 80, 82, 83, 84, 85, 90, 95, 100 (bottom), 101, 109 (top), 130 (left), 132, 144, 160, 165, 168, 169, 170, 183, 194, 208 (right), 213, 220, 232, 234, 236, 238, 239, 240, 242, 243, 244 (bottom), 245 (bottom left and right), 246 (Hepburn and bottom), 247 (top left and top right; bottom right), 248 (bottom), 249 (top left; bottom left and right), 250, 252, 253, 257, 258 (top left and right), 260, 261, 262 (bottom left and right, top right), 263, 264, 284 (bottom), 286, 288, 289 (bottom), 290, 292 (top three images), 302, 304, 305, 306 (left), 317 (top), 324 (bottom left).

The White House: page 142.

Personal collection of Barbara Whiting: page 114.

Personal collection of Tom Zimmerman: pages 10, 48, 129, 308, 309, 316, 352 (top, bottom left).

The following photographers and artists created the images that appear in the pages of *The Hollywood Archive* and the editors and publisher honor them here. Any oversights will be corrected in future editions.

Bernie Abramson/MPTV: pages 152, 154, 295 (bottom), 338 (top left). Jack Albin/MPTV: page 88. Sid Avery/MPTV: pages 11 (top), 13 (top), 92, 102, 103, 111, 113, 130 (left), 296 (right), 336. Steve Banks: pages 20, 342, 344, 345. Pat Clark/MPTV: page page 11 (bottom). Bud Fraker: page 211, 348 (bottom). Roy George & Assoc.: page 219 (top). Bud Gray/MPTV: pages 150, 272. Grimes/MPTV: page 274. Gunther/MPTV: pages 89 (top), 275 (top left). Fred Hendrickson: page 210. Paul Hesse/MPTV: page 339 (center left). George Hurrell: pages 35 (MPTV), 199 (top right), 314, 329 (MPTV). Tom Kelley: pages 72 (left), 120 (bottom), 121, 166, 182 (center), 187, 189, 191, 192, 193, 298 (top). Charles E. Lynch: page 128 (bottom). Harold Michelson: page 59. Richard Miller/MPTV: page 280. Frank Powolny: page 330 (left). Gabi Rona/MPTV: pages 143, 301 (right). Sanford Roth/A.M.P.A.S./MPTV: pages 300, 339 (bottom left and right). A.L. Schafer: page 255 (bottom). Tazio Secchiaroli: page 108 (bottom). Wallace Seawell/MPTV: pages 122, 341. Eric Skipsey/MPTV: page 87 (bottom). David Sutton/MPTV: pages 108 (top), 152, 154 (bottom). John Swope/MPTV: page 102. Gene Trindl/MPTV: page 338 (center), 352 (top left). Van Pelt: page 289 (bottom). Ken Veeder/Capitol Records/MPTV: page 339 (top right). Ken Whitmore/MPTV: page 100 (top). Bob Willoughby/MPTV: page 275 (top right). Jack Woods/MPTV: page 338 (bottom).